Leading Ca

the Law of Negligence

for 'A' Level

2nd Edition

Butterworths · London · 1986

United Kingdom	Butterworth & Co (Publishers) Ltd
	88 Kingsway, WC2B 6AB
	61A North Castle Street, EH2 3LJ
Australia	Butterworths Pty Ltd
	Sydney, Melbourne, Brisbane, Adelaide, Perth, Canberra
	and Hobart
Canada	Butterworths, Toronto and Vancouver
New Zealand	Butterworths of New Zealand Ltd
	Wellington and Auckland
Singapore	Butterworth & Co (Asia) Pte Ltd, Singapore
South Africa	Butterworth Publishers (Pty) Ltd
	Durban and Pretoria
USA	Butterworth Legal Publishers
	St Paul, Minnesota, Seattle
	Washington, Boston, Massachusetts, Austin, Texas and
	D & S Publishers, Clearwater, Florida

©Butterworth & Co (Publishers) Ltd 1980, 1986

ISBN 0 406 01680 1

Printed by The Whitefriars Press Ltd, Tonbridge, Kent

Contents

Donoghue (or McAlister) v Stevenson

[1932] All ER Rep 1

Estublished neighbour principle

E [HOUSE OF LORDS (Lord Buckmaster, Lord Atkin, Lord Tomlin, Lord Thankerton and Lord Macmillan), December 10, 11, 1931, May 26, 1932]

[Reported [1932] A.C. 562; 101 L.J.P.C. 119; 147 L.T. 281; 48 T.L.R. 494; 76 Sol. Jo. 396; 37 Com. Cas. 350]

Negligence—Duty of manufacturer to consumer—No contractual relation—No possibility **F** *of examination of product before use—Knowledge that absence of reasonable care in preparation of product will result in injury to consumer—Bottle of ginger-beer purchased from retailer—Dead snail in bottle—Purchaser poisoned by drinking contents—Liability of manufacturer.*

A manufacturer of products which he sells in such a form as to show that he intends them to reach the ultimate consumer in the form in which they left him, **G** with no reasonable possibility of intermediate examination, and with the knowledge that the absence of reasonable care in the preparation or putting up of the products will result in injury to the consumer, owes a duty to the consumer to take reasonable care, although the manufacturer does not know the product to be dangerous and no contractual relation exists between him and the consumer.

Per LORD ATKIN: The rule that you are to love your neighbour becomes in law: **H** You must not injure your neighbour; and the lawyer's question: Who is my neighbour? receives a restricted reply. You must take reasonable care to avoid acts or omissions which you can reasonably foresee would be likely to injure your neighbour. Who, then, in law is my neighbour? The answer seems to be persons who are so closely and directly affected by my act that I ought reasonably to have them in contemplation as being so affected when I am directing my mind to the acts or **I** omissions which are called in question.

Per LORD MACMILLAN: A person who for gain engages in the business of manufacturing articles of food and drink intended for consumption by members of the public in the form in which he issues them is under a duty to take care in the manufacture of those articles. That duty he owes to those whom he intends to consume his products. He manufactures his commodities for human consumption; he intends and contemplates that they shall be consumed. By reason of that very fact he places himself in a relationship with all the potential consumers of his

1

commodities, and that relationship, which he assumes and desires for his own ends,   **A**
imposes on him a duty to take care to avoid injuring them. He owes them a duty
not to convert by his own carelessness an article which he issues to them as wholesome and innocent into an article which is dangerous to life and health.

The appellant and a friend visited a café where the friend ordered for her a bottle
of ginger-beer. The proprietor of the café opened the ginger-beer bottle, which was
of opaque glass so that it was impossible to see the contents, and poured some of   **B**
the ginger-beer into a tumbler. The appellant drank some of the ginger-beer. Then
her friend poured the remaining contents of the bottle into the tumbler and with it
a decomposed snail came from the bottle. As a result of her having drunk part of
the impure ginger-beer the appellant suffered from shock and gastric illness. In
an action by her for negligence against the manufacturer of the ginger-beer,

Held by LORD ATKIN, LORD THANKERTON, and LORD MACMILLAN (LORD BUCK-   **C**
MASTER and LORD TOMLIN dissenting), on proof of these facts the appellant would
be entitled to recover.

Notes. Distinguished: *Farr* v. *Butters Bros. & Co.*, p. 339, post. Considered:
Pattendon v. *Beney* (1933), 50 T.L.R. 10. Applied: *Brown* v. *Cotterill* (1934),
51 T.L.R. 21; *Malfroot* v. *Noxal, Ltd.* (1935), 51 T.L.R. 551; *Grant* v. *Australian*   **D**
Knitting Mills, Ltd., [1935] All E.R.Rep. 209. Distinguished: *Evans* v. *Triplex Safety
Glass Co.*, [1936] 1 All E.R. 283. Considered: *Otto* v. *Bolton and Norris*, [1936]
1 All E.R. 960; *Kubach* v. *Hollands*, [1937] 3 All E.R. 907; *Dransfield* v. *British Insulated
Cables, Ltd.*, [1937] 4 All E.R. 382; *Barnes* v. *Irwell Valley Water Board*, [1938] 2
All E.R. 650; *Sharp* v. *Avery and Kerwood*, [1938] 4 All E.R. 85; *Square* v. *Model Farm
Dairies (Bournemouth), Ltd.*, [1938] 2 All E.R. 740; *Daniels and Daniels* v. *White & Sons*,   **E**
Ltd. and Tarbard, [1938] 4 All E.R. 258. Distinguished: *Paine and Colne Valley
Electricity Supply Co.*, [1938] 4 All E.R. 803. Explained and distinguished: *Old Gate
Estates, Ltd.* v. *Toplis and Harding and Russell*, [1939] 3 All E.R. 209. Applied:
Slennett v. *Hancock and Peters*, [1939] 2 All E.R. 578; *Barnes* v. *Irwell Valley Water
Board*, [1939] 1 K.B. 21. Considered: *Burfitt* v. *A. & E. Kille*, [1939] 2 All E.R. 372;
Hanson v. *Wearmouth Coal Co.*, [1939] 3 All E.R. 47. Distinguished: *Davis* v. *Foots*,   **F**
[1939] 4 All E.R. 4. Applied: *Herschthal* v. *Stewart and Ardern, Ltd.*, [1939] 4 All E.R.
123; *Barnett* v. *Packer & Co.*, [1940] 3 All E.R. 575; *Watson* v. *Buckley Osborne, Garrett
& Co. and Wyrovoys Products, Ltd.*, [1940] 1 All E.R. 174; *Buckner* v. *Ashby and Horner,
Ltd.*, [1941] 1 K.B. 321. Distinguished: *Travers* v. *Gloucester Corpn.*, [1946] 2 All E.R.
506; *Jerred* v. *Roddam Dent & Son*, [1948] 2 All E.R. 104. Considered: *Candler* v.
Crane Christmas & Co., [1951] 1 All E.R. 426; *Merrington* v. *Ironbridge Metal Works*,   **G**
Ltd. and Others, [1952] 2 All E.R. 1101. Applied: *White* v. *John Warwick & Co., Ltd.*,
[1953] 2 All E.R. 1021; *Hartley* v. *Mayoh & Co. and another*, [1953] 2 All E.R. 525;
Davis v. *St. Mary's Demolition, etc., Ltd.*, [1954] 1 All E.R. 578. Not applied: *Sellars*
v. *Best*, [1954] 2 All E.R. 389. Referred to: *Cunard* v. *Antifyre, Ltd.*, p. 558, post;
Bishop v. *Consolidated London Properties, Ltd.*, [1933] All E.R.Rep. 963; *Brown* v.
Cotterill (1934), 51 T.L.R. 21; *Haynes* v. *Harwood*, [1934] All E.R.Rep. 103; *Howard* v.   **H**
Furness Houlder Argentine Lines, Ltd. and Brown, Ltd., [1936] 2 All E.R. 781; *London,
Midland and Scottish Rail. Co.* v. *Ribble Hat Works, Ltd.* (1936), 80 Sol. Jo. 1038; *Read*
v. *Croydon Corpn.*, [1938] 4 All E.R. 631; *Kerry* v. *Keighley Electrical Engineering Co.*,
[1940] 3 All E.R. 399; *East Suffolk Rivers Catchment Board* v. *Kent*, [1940] 4 All E.R.
527; *Thomas and Evans, Ltd.* v. *Mid-Rhondda Co-operative Society, Ltd.*, [1940] 4
All E.R. 357; *Haseldine* v. *Daw & Son, Ltd.*, [1941] 3 All E.R. 156; *Bourhill* v. *Young*,   **I**
[1942] 2 All E.R. 396; *Glasgow Corpn.* v. *Muir*, [1943] 2 All E.R. 44; *Read* v. *J. Lyons &
Co.*, [1944] 2 All E.R. 98; *Deyong* v. *Shenburn*, [1946] 1 All E.R. 226; *Woods* v. *Duncan,
Duncan* v. *Hambrook, Duncan* v. *Cammell Laird & Co.*, [1946] A.C. 401; *Read* v. *J. Lyons
& Co.*, [1946] 2 All E.R. 471; *Dodd and Dodd* v. *Wilson and McWilliam*, [1946] 2 All E.R.
691; *Anglo-Saxon Petroleum Co.* v. *Damant, Anglo-Saxon Petroleum Co.* v. *R.*, [1947]
2 All E.R. 465; *Marshall* v. *Cellactite and British Uralite, Ltd.* (1947), 63 T.L.R. 456;
Stansbie v. *Troman*, [1948] 1 All E.R. 599; *Grant* v. *Sun Shipping Co.*, [1948] 2 All E.R.
238; *Buckland* v. *Guildford Gas, Light and Coke Co.*, [1948] 2 All E.R. 1086; *Davies* v.

A *Swan Motor Co. (Swansea)*, [1949] 1 All E.R. 620; *Ball* v. *L.C.C.*, [1949] 2 K.B. 159; *Horton* v. *London Graving Dock Co.*, [1950] 1 All E.R. 180; *Heskell* v. *Continental Express, Ltd.*, [1950] 1 All E.R. 1033; *Denny* v. *Supplies and Transport Co. and Scruttons Ltd.* (1950), 66 (pt. 1) T.L.R. 1168; *Wright* v. *Callwood* (1950), 66 (pt. 2) T.L.R. 72.

As to a manufacturer's duty to the consumer, see 23 HALSBURY'S LAWS (2nd Edn.)
632, 633, and for cases see 36 DIGEST (Repl.) 85 et seq.

B
Cases referred to:

(1) *Langridge* v. *Levy* (1837), 2 M. & W. 519; affirmed (1838), 4 M. & W. 337; 150 E.R. 1458; sub nom. *Levi* v. *Langridge*, 1 Horn & H. 325; 7 L.J.Ex. 387, Ex.Ch.; 35 Digest 51, *464*.

(2) *Longmeid* v. *Holliday* (1851), 6 Exch. 761; 20 L.J.Ex. 430; 17 L.T.O.S. 243;
C   155 E.R. 752; 39 Digest 458, *854*.

(3) *Winterbottom* v. *Wright* (1842), 10 M. & W. 109; 11 L.J.Ex. 415; 152 E.R. 402; 36 Digest (Repl.) 107, *531*.

(4) *Blacker* v. *Lake and Elliot, Ltd.* (1912), 106 L.T. 533, D.C.; 36 Digest (Repl.) 80, *428*.

(5) *George* v. *Skivington* (1869), L.R. 5 Exch. 1; 39 L.J.Ex. 8; 21 L.T. 495; 18 W.R.
D   118; 39 Digest 441, *705*.

(6) *Dominion Natural Gas Co., Ltd.* v. *Collins and Perkins*, [1909] A.C. 640; 79 L.J.P.C. 13; 101 L.T. 359; 25 T.L.R. 831, P.C.; 36 Digest (Repl.) 36, *176*.

(7) *Francis* v. *Cockrell* (1870), L.R. 5 Q.B. 501; 10 B. & S. 950; 39 L.J.Q.B. 291; 23 L.T. 466; 18 W.R. 1205, Ex.Ch.; 34 Digest 166, *1296*.

(8) *Heaven* v. *Pender* (1883), 11 Q.B.D. 503; 52 L.J.Q.B. 702; 49 L.T. 357; 47 J.P.
E   709; 27 Sol. Jo. 667, C.A.; 36 Digest (Repl.) 7, *10*.

(9) *Blakemore* v. *Bristol and Exeter Rail. Co.* (1858), 8 E. & B. 1035; 31 L.T.O.S. 12; 120 E.R. 385; sub nom. *Blackmore* v. *Bristol and Exeter Rail. Co.*, 27 L.J.Q.B. 167; 4 Jur.N.S. 657; 6 W.R. 336; 3 Digest 69, *107*.

(10) *Collis* v. *Selden* (1868). L.R. 3 C.P. 495; 37 L.J.C.P. 233; 16 W.R. 1170; 29 Digest 10, *125*.

F (11) *Le Lievre and another* v. *Gould*, [1893] 1 Q.B. 491; 62 L.J.Q.B. 353; 68 L.T. 626; 57 J.P. 484; 41 W.R. 468; 37 Sol. Jo. 267; 4 R. 274; sub nom. *Dennes* v. *Gould*, 9 T.L.R. 243, C.A.; 36 Digest (Repl.) 9, *27*.

(12) *Earl* v. *Lubbock*, [1905] 1 K.B. 253; 74 L.J.K.B. 121; 91 L.T. 830; 53 W.R. 145; 21 T.L.R. 71; 49 Sol. Jo. 83, C.A.; 36 Digest (Repl.) 107, *532*.

(13) *Bates and another* v. *Batey & Co., Ltd.*, [1913] 3 K.B. 351; 82 L.J.K.B. 963; 108
G   L.T. 1036; 29 T.L.R. 616; 36 Digest (Repl.) 85, *457*.

(14) *Thomas* v. *Winchester* (1852), 6 N.Y. 397.

(15) *McPherson* v. *Buick Motor Co.* (1916), 217 N.Y. 382.

(16) *Mullen* v. *Barr & Co.*; *McGowan* v. *Barr & Co.*, 1929 S.C. 461; 36 Digest (Repl.) 19, **69*.

(17) *Cunnington* v. *Great Northern Rail. Co.* (1883), 49 L.T. 392; 48 J.P. 134, C.A.;
H   36 Digest (Repl.) 5, *2*.

(18) *Hawkins* v. *Smith* (1896), 12 T.L.R. 532, D.C.; 36 Digest (Repl.) 63, *343*.

(19) *Elliott* v. *Hall* (1885), 15 Q.B.D. 315; 54 L.J.Q.B. 518; sub nom. *Elliott* v. *Nailstone Colliery Co.*, 34 W.R. 16; 1 T.L.R. 628, D.C.; 36 Digest (Repl.) 62, *337*.

(20) *Chapman (or Oliver)* v. *Saddler & Co.*, [1929] A.C. 584; 98 L.J.P.C. 87; 141 L.T. 305; 45 T.L.R. 456; 34 Com. Cas. 277, H.L.; 36 Digest (Repl.) 160, *846*.

I (21) *Grote* v. *Chester and Holyhead Rail. Co.* (1848), 2 Exch. 251; 5 Ry. & Can. Cas. 649; 154 E.R. 485; 34 Digest 161, *1262*.

(22) *Dixon* v. *Bell* (1816), 5 M. & S. 198; 1 Stark. 287; 105 E.R. 1023; 36 Digest (Repl.) 80, *431*.

(23) *Hope & Son* v. *Anglo-American Oil Co.* (1922), 12 Ll.L.Rep. 183.

(24) *Brass* v. *Maitland* (1856), 6 E. & B. 470; 26 L.J.Q.B. 49; 27 L.T.O.S. 249; 2 Jur.N.S. 710; 4 W.R. 647; 119 E.R. 940; 8 Digest (Repl.) 148, *938*.

(25) *Farrant* v. *Barnes* (1862), 11 C.B.N.S. 553; 31 L.J.C.P. 137; 8 Jur.N.S. 868; 142 E.R. 912; 8 Digest (Repl.) 148, *937*.

(26) *Caledonian Rail. Co.* v. *Mulholland*, [1898] A.C. 216; 67 L.J.P.C. 1; 46 W.R. 236; 14 T.L.R. 41; sub nom. *Caledonian Rail. Co.* v. *Warwick*, 77 L.T. 570, H.L.; 36 Digest (Repl.) 14, *54*.

(27) *Cavalier* v. *Pope*, [1906] A.C. 428; 75 L.J.K.B. 609; 95 L.T. 65; 22 T.L.R. 648; 50 Sol. Jo. 575, H.L.; 12 Digest (Repl.) 52, *283*.

(28) *Bottomley and another* v. *Bannister and another*, [1932] 1 K.B. 458; 101 L.J.K.B. 46; 146 L.T. 68; 48 T.L.R. 39, C.A.; 36 Digest (Repl.) 80, *429*.

(29) *Kemp and Dougall* v. *Darngavil Coal Co.*, 1909 S.C. 1314.

(30) *Clelland* v. *Robb*, 1911 S.C. 253; 36 Digest (Repl.) 19, **67*.

(31) *Gordon* v. *M'Hardy* 1903, 6 F. (Ct. of Sess.) 210; 41 Sc.L.R. 129; 11 S.L.T. 490; 36 Digest (Repl.) 169, **1403*.

(32) *Emmens* v. *Pottle* (1885), 16 Q.B.D. 354; 55 L.J.Q.B. 51; 53 L.T. 808; 50 J.P. 228; 34 W.R. 116; 2 T.L.R. 115, C.A.; 32 Digest 81, *1120*.

(33) *Cameron and others* v. *Young*, [1908] A.C. 176; 77 L.J.P.C. 68; 98 L.T. 592, H.L.; 12 Digest (Repl.) 52, *285*.

(34) *White and wife* v. *Steadman*, [1913] 3 K.B. 340; 82 L.J.K.B. 846; 109 L.T. 249; 29 T.L.R. 563; 8 Digest (Repl.) 75, *497*.

Appeal from an interlocutor of the Second Division of the Court of Session in Scotland. On Aug. 26, 1928, the appellant, a shop assistant, drank a bottle of ginger-beer manufactured by the respondent, which a friend had ordered on her behalf from a retailer in a shop at Paisley and given to her. She stated that the shopkeeper, who supplied the ginger-beer, opened the bottle, which she said was sealed with a metal cap and was made of dark opaque glass, and poured some of its contents into a tumbler which contained some ice cream, and that she drank some of the contents of the tumbler, that her friend then lifted the bottle and was pouring the remainder of the contents into the tumbler, when a snail which had been in the bottle floated out in a state of decomposition. As a result, the appellant alleged, she had contracted a serious illness, and she claimed from the respondents damages for negligence. She alleged that the respondent, as the manufacturer of an article intended for consumption and contained in a receptacle which prevented inspection, owed a duty to her as consumer of the article to take care that there was no noxious element in the article, that he neglected such duty, and that he was, consequently, liable for any damage caused by such neglect. The case then came before the Lord Ordinary, who rejected the plea in law of the respondent and allowed the parties a proof of their averments, but on a reclaiming note the Second Division (the Lord Justice Clerk, LORD ORMIDALE and LORD ANDERSON; LORD HUNTER dissenting) recalled the interlocutor of the Lord Ordinary and dismissed the action. The plaintiff appealed.

George Morton, K.C., and *W. R. Milligan* (both of the Scottish Bar) for the appellant.
The Attorney-General for Scotland (*Normand*, K.C.), *J. L. Clyde* (of the Scottish Bar) and *T. Elder Jones* for the respondent.

The House took time for consideration.

May 26.   **LORD BUCKMASTER** (read by LORD TOMLIN).—The facts of this case are simple. On Aug. 26, 1928, the appellant drank a bottle of ginger-beer, manufactured by the respondent, which a friend had bought from a retailer and given to her. The bottle contained the decomposed remains of a snail which were not and could not be detected until the greater part of the contents of the bottle had been consumed. As a result she alleged, and at this stage her allegations must be accepted as true, that she suffered from shock and severe gastro-enteritis. She, accordingly, instituted the proceedings against the manufacturer which have given rise to this appeal. The foundation o΄ her case is that the respondent, as the manufacturer of an article intended for consumption and contained in a receptacle which prevented inspection, owed a duty to her as consumer of the article to take care that there was no noxious element in the goods, that he neglected such duty, and that he is, consequently, liable for any damage caused by such neglect. After certain amendments which are now immaterial, the case came before the Lord Ordinary, who rejected the respondent's plea in law and allowed

A   a proof. His interlocutor was revoked by the Second Division of the Court of Session, from whose judgment this appeal has been brought.

Before examining the merits two comments are desirable : (1) that the appellant's case rests solely on the ground of a tort based, not on fraud, but on negligence ; and (ii) that throughout the appeal the case has been argued on the basis, undisputed by the Second Division and never questioned by counsel for the appellant or by any of your Lordships,

B   that the English law and the Scots law on the subject are identical. It is, therefore, upon the English law alone that I have considered the matter, and, in my opinion, it is on the English law alone that in the circumstances we ought to proceed.

The law applicable is the common law, and, though its principles are capable of application to meet new conditions not contemplated when the law was laid down, yet themselves they cannot be changed nor can additions be made to them because any

C   particular meritorious case seems outside their ambit.

The common law must be sought in law books by writers of authority and in the judgments of judges entrusted with its administration. The law books give no assistance because the works of living authors, however deservedly eminent, cannot be used as authorities, though the opinions they express may demand attention, and the ancient books do not assist. I turn, therefore, to the decided cases to see if they can be construed

D   so as to support the appellant's case. One of the earliest is *Langridge* v. *Levy* (1). It is a case often quoted and variously explained. There a man sold a gun, which he knew was dangerous, for the use of the purchaser's son. The gun exploded in the son's hands and he was held to have a right of action in tort against the gunmaker. How far it is from the present case can be seen from the judgment of Baron Parke, who, in delivering the judgment of the court, used these words :

E
   "We should pause before we make a precedent by our decision which would be an authority for an action against the vendors, even of such instruments and articles as are dangerous in themselves, at the suit of any person whomsoever into whose hands they might happen to pass, and who should be injured thereby" ;

and in *Longmeid* v. *Holliday* (2) the same eminent judge points out that the earlier case

F   was based on a fraudulent mis-statement, and he expressly repudiates the view that it has any wider application. *Langridge* v. *Levy* (1), therefore, can be dismissed from consideration with the comment that it is rather surprising that it has so often been cited for a proposition which it cannot support.

Winterbottom v. *Wright* (3) is, on the other hand, an authority that is closely applicable. Owing to negligence in the construction of a carriage it broke down, and a stranger to

G   the manufacture and sale sought to recover damages for injuries which he alleged were due to negligence in the work, and it was held that he had no cause of action. This case seems to me to show that the manufacturer of any article is not liable to a third party injured by negligent construction, for there can be nothing in the character of a coach to place it in a special category. It may be noted also that in this case ALDERSON, B., said :

H
   "The only safe rule is to confine the right to recover to those who enter into the contract ; if we go one step beyond that, there is no reason why we should not go fifty."

Longmeid v. *Holliday* (2) was the case of a defective lamp sold to a man whose wife was injured by its explosion. The vendor of the lamp, against whom the action was brought, was not the manufacturer, so that the case is not parallel to the present, but

I   the statement of PARKE, B., in his judgment covers the case of the manufacturer, for he said :

   "It would be going much too far to say that so much care is required in the ordinary intercourse of life between one individual and another that, if a machine not in its nature dangerous ... but which might become so by a latent defect entirely unknown, although discoverable by the exercise of ordinary care, should be lent or given by one person, even by the person who manufactured it, to another, the former should be answerable to the latter for a subsequent damage accruing by the use of it."

It is true that he uses the words "lent or given" and omits the word "sold," but, if **A** the duty be entirely independent of contract and is a duty owed to a third person, it seems to me the same whether the article be originally given or sold. The fact in the present case that the ginger-beer originally left the premises of the manufacturer on a purchase, as was probably the case, cannot add to his duty, if such existed, to take care in its preparation. It has been suggested that the statement of PARKE, B., does not cover the case of negligent construction. But the omission to exercise reasonable care **B** in the discovery of the defect in the manufacture of an article where the duty of examination exists is just as negligent as the negligent construction itself.

The general principle of these cases is stated by LORD SUMNER (then HAMILTON, J.) in *Blacker* v. *Lake and Elliot, Ltd.* (4) (in these terms 106 L.T. at p. 536):

"The breach of the defendant's contract with A. to use care and skill in and about the manufacture or repair of an article does not of itself give any cause of action **C** to B. when he is injured by reason of the article proving to be defective."

From this general rule there are two well-known exceptions:
(i) in the case of an article dangerous in itself, and (ii) where the article, not in itself dangerous, is in fact dangerous on account of some defect or for any other reason, and this is known to the manufacturer. Until *George* v. *Skivington* (5) I know of no further **D** modification of the general rule.

As to (i), in the case of things dangerous in themselves, there is, in the words of LORD DUNEDIN,

"a peculiar duty to take precaution imposed upon those who send forth or install such articles when it is necessarily the case that other parties will come within their proximity": **E**

Dominion Natural Gas Co., Ltd. v. *Collins* (6) ([1909] A.C. at p. 646). And as to (ii), this depends on the fact that the knowledge of the danger creates the obligation to warn, and its concealment is in the nature of fraud.

In the present case no one can suggest that the ginger-beer was an article dangerous in itself, and the words of LORD DUNEDIN show that the duty attaches only to such **F** articles, for I read the words "a peculiar duty" as meaning a duty peculiar to the special class of subject mentioned.

Of the remaining cases *George* v. *Skivington* (5) is the one nearest to the present, and without that case and the statement of CLEASBY, B., in *Francis* v. *Cockrell* (7) (L.R. 5 Q.B. at p. 515), and the dicta of BRETT, M.R., in *Heaven* v. *Pender* (8) (11 Q.B.D. at pp. 509 et seq.), the appellant would be destitute of authority. *George* v. *Skivington* (5) **G** related to the sale of a noxious hairwash, and a claim made by a person who had suffered from its use, based on its having been negligently compounded, was allowed. It is remarkable that *Langridge* v. *Levy* (1) was used in support of the claim and influenced the judgment of all the parties to the decision. Both KELLY, C.B., and PIGOTT, B., stressed the fact that the article had been purchased to the knowledge of the defendant for the use of the plaintiff, as in *Langridge* v. *Levy* (1), and CLEASBY, B., who, realising **H** that *Langridge* v. *Levy* (1) was decided on the ground of fraud, said:

"Substitute the word 'negligence' for 'fraud,'" and the analogy between *Langridge* v. *Levy* (1) and this case is complete."

It is unnecessary to point out too emphatically that such a substitution cannot possibly be made. No action based on fraud can be supported by mere proof of negligence. I do not propose to follow the fortunes of *George* v. *Skivington* (5); few cases can have **I** lived so dangerously and lived so long. LORD SUMNER, in *Blacker* v. *Lake and Elliot, Ltd.* (4), closely examines its history, and I agree with his analysis. He said that he could not presume to say that it was wrong, but he declined to follow it on the ground, which is I think firm, that it was in conflict with *Winterbottom* v. *Wright* (3).

In *Francis* v. *Cockrell* (7) the plaintiff had been injured by the fall of a racecourse stand, on a seat for which he had paid. The defendant was part proprietor of the stand and acted as receiver of the money. The stand had been negligently erected by a contractor, though the defendant was not aware of the defect. The plaintiff succeeded.

A The case has no bearing upon the present, but in the course of his judgment CLEASBY, B., made the following observations (L.R. 5 Q B at p 515):

B "The point that Mr. Matthews referred to last was raised in the case of *George* v. *Skivington* (5), where there was an injury to one person, the wife, and a contract of sale with another person, the husband. The wife was considered to have a good cause of action, and I would adopt the view which the Lord Chief Baron took in that case. He said there was a duty in the vendor to use ordinary care in compounding the article sold, and that this extended to the person for whose use he knew it was purchased, and, this duty having been violated, and he having failed to use reasonable care, was liable in an action at the suit of the third person."

C It is difficult to appreciate what is the importance of the fact that the vendor knew who was the person for whom the article was purchased unless it be that the case was treated as one of fraud, and that without this element of knowledge it could not be brought within the principle of *Langridge* v. *Levy* (1). Indeed, this is the only view of the matter which adequately explains the references in the judgments in *George* v. *Skivington* (5) to *Langridge* v. *Levy* (1) and the observations of CLEASBY, B., upon *George* v. *Skivington* (5).

D The dicta of BRETT, M.R., in *Heaven* v. *Pender* (8) are rightly relied on by the appellant. The material passage is as follows (11 Q.B.D. at p. 509):

E "The proposition which these recognised cases suggest, and which is, therefore, to be deduced from them, is that wherever one person is by circumstances placed in such a position with regard to another that everyone of ordinary sense who did think would at once recognise that if he did not use ordinary care and skill in his own conduct with regard to those circumstances he would cause danger of injury to the person or property of the other, a duty arises to use ordinary care and skill to avoid such danger. . . . Let us apply this proposition to the case of one person supplying goods or machinery, or instruments or utensils, or the like, for the purpose of their being used by another person, but with whom there is no contract as to the supply. The proposition will stand thus: whenever one person supplies goods

F or machinery, or the like, for the purpose of their being used by another person under such circumstances that everyone of ordinary sense would, if he thought, recognise at once that unless he used ordinary care and skill with regard to the condition of the thing supplied or the mode of supplying it, there will be danger of injury to the person or property of him for whose use the thing is supplied, and who is to use it, a duty arises to use ordinary care and skill as to the condition or manner

G of supplying such thing. And for a neglect of such ordinary care or skill whereby injury happens a legal liability arises, to be enforced by an action for negligence. This includes the case of goods, &c., supplied to be used immediately by a particular person or persons or one of a class of persons, where it would be obvious to the person supplying, if he thought, that the goods would in all probability be used at once by such persons before a reasonable opportunity for discovering any defect

H which might exist, and where the thing supplied would be of such a nature that a neglect of ordinary care or skill as to its condition or the manner of supplying it would probably cause danger to the person or property of the person for whose use it was supplied, and who was about to use it. It would exclude a case in which the goods are supplied under circumstances in which it would be a chance by whom they would be used or whether they would be used or not, or whether they would be used

I before there would probably be means of observing any defect, or where the goods would be of such a nature that a want of care or skill as to their condition or the manner of supplying them would not probably produce danger of injury to person or property. The cases of vendor and purchaser and lender and hirer under contract need not be considered, as the liability arises under the contract, and not merely as a duty imposed by law, though it may not be useless to observe that it seems difficult to import the implied obligation into the contract except in cases in which, if there were no contract between the parties, the law would, according to the rule above stated, imply the duty."

"The recognised cases" to which the Master of the Rolls refers are not definitely **A**
quoted, but they appear to refer to cases of collision and carriage, and the cases of
visitation to premises on which there is some hidden danger, cases far removed from
the doctrine he enunciates.   None the less, this passage has been used as a tabula in
naufragio for many litigants, struggling in the seas of adverse authority.   It cannot,
however, be divorced from the fact that the case had nothing whatever to do with the
question of manufacture and sale.   An unsound staging had been erected on premises **B**
to which there had been an invitation to the plaintiffs to enter, and the case really
depended on the duty of the owner of the premises to persons so invited.   None the
less, it is clear that BRETT, M.R., considered the cases of manufactured articles, for he
examined *Langridge* v. *Levy* (1), and he says that it does not negative the proposition
that the case might have been supported on the ground of negligence.

In the same case, however, COTTON, L.J., in whose judgment BOWEN, L.J., concurred, **C**
said that he was unwilling to concur with the Master of the Rolls in laying down un-
necessarily the larger principle which he entertained, inasmuch as there were many
cases in which the principle was impliedly negatived.   He then referred to *Langridge* v.
Levy (1), and stated that it was based upon fraudulent misrepresentation and had been
so treated by COLERIDGE, J., in *Blakemore* v. *Bristol and Exeter Rail. Co.* (9), and that
in *Collis* v. *Selden* (10) WILLES, J., had said that the judgment in *Langridge* v. *Levy* (1) **D**
was based on the fraud of the defendant.   The lord justice then proceeded as follows:

"This impliedly negatives the existence of the larger general principle which is
relied on, and the decisions in *Collis* v. *Selden* (10) and in *Longmeid* v. *Holliday* (2)
(in each of which the plaintiff failed) are in my opinion at variance with the principle
contended for.   The case of *George* v. *Skivington* (5), and especially what is said by
CLEASBY, B., in giving judgment in that case, seems to support the existence of the **E**
general principle.   But it is not in terms laid down that any such principle exists,
and that case was decided by CLEASBY, B., on the ground that the negligence of the
defendant, which was his own personal negligence, was equivalent, for the purposes
of that action, to fraud, on which (as he said) the decision in *Langridge* v. *Levy* (1)
was based.   In declining to concur in laying down the principle enunciated by the
Master of the Rolls I in no way intimate any doubt as to the principle that anyone **F**
who leaves a dangerous instrument, as a gun, in such a way as to cause danger, or
who without due warning supplies to others for use an instrument or thing which
to his knowledge, from its construction or otherwise, is in such a condition as to
cause danger, not necessarily incident to the use of such an instrument or thing,
is liable for injury caused to others by reason of his negligent act."

G

With the views expressed by COTTON, L.J., I agree.

In *Le Lievre and another* v. *Gould* (11) the mortgagees of the interest of a builder
under a building agreement advanced money to him from time to time on the faith of
certificates given by a surveyor that certain specified stages in the progress of the
buildings had been reached.   The surveyor was not appointed by the mortgagees and
there was no contractual relationship between him and them.   In consequence of the **H**
negligence of the surveyor the certificates contained untrue statements as to the progress of the buildings, but there was no fraud on his part.   It was held that the surveyor
owed no duty to the mortgagees to exercise care in giving his certificates and they could
not maintain an action against him by reason of his negligence.   In this case LORD
ESHER, M.R., seems to have qualified to some extent what he said in *Heaven* v.
Pender (8) for he says this ([1893] 1 Q.B. at p. 497):

I

"But can the plaintiffs rely upon negligence in the absence of fraud?   The question
of liability for negligence cannot arise at all until it is established that the man who
has been negligent owed some duty to the person who seeks to make him liable for
his negligence.   What duty is there when there is no relation between the parties
by contract?   A man is entitled to be as negligent as he pleases towards the whole
world if he owes no duty to them.   The case of *Heaven* v. *Pender* (8) has no bearing
upon the present question.   That case established that, under certain circumstances, one man may owe a duty to another, even though there is no contract

A   between them. If one man is near to another, or is near to the property of another,
a duty lies upon him not to do that which may cause a personal injury to that other,
or may injure his property."

In the same case, at p. 504, A. L. SMITH, L.J., said:

B   "The decision of *Heaven* v. *Pender* (8) was founded upon the principle that a duty
to take due care did arise when the person or property of one was in such proximity
to the person or property of another that, if due care was not taken, damage might
be done by the one to the other. *Heaven* v. *Pender* (8) goes no further than this,
though it is often cited to support all kinds of untenable propositions."

In *Earl* v. *Lubbock* (12) the plaintiff had been injured by a wheel coming off a van
which he was driving for his employer and which it was the duty of the defendant under
C   contract with such employer to keep in repair. The county court judge and the Divisional Court both held that even if negligence was proved the action would not lie.
It was held by the Court of Appeal that the defendant was under no duty to the plaintiff
and that there was no cause of action. In his judgment COLLINS, M.R., said that the case
was concluded by the authority of *Winterbottom* v. *Wright* (3), and he pointed out that
the dictum of LORD ESHER, M.R., in *Heaven* v. *Pender* (8) was not a decision of the
D   court and that it was subsequently qualified and explained by LORD ESHER himself in
Le Lievre and another v. *Gould* (11). STIRLING, L.J., said that in order to succeed in the
action the plaintiff must bring his case within the proposition enunciated by COTTON,
L.J., and agreed to by BOWEN, L.J., in *Heaven* v. *Pender* (8), while MATHEW, L.J., made
the following observation ([1905] 1 K.B. at p. 259):

E   "The argument of counsel for the plaintiff was that the defendant's servants had
been negligent in the performance of the contract with the owners of the van, and
that it followed as a matter of law that anyone in their employment, or, indeed,
anyone else who sustained an injury traceable to that negligence, had a cause of
action against the defendant. It is impossible to accept such a wide proposition,
and, indeed, it is difficult to see how, if it were the law, trade could be carried on.
F   No prudent man would contract to make or repair what the employer intended to
permit others to use in the way of his trade."

In *Bates and another* v. *Batey & Co.* (13) the defendants, ginger-beer manufacturers,
were held not liable to a consumer (who had purchased from a retailer one of their
bottles) for injury occasioned by the bottle bursting as the result of a defect of which the
defendants did not know, but which by the exercise of reasonable care they could have
G   discovered. In reaching this conclusion HORRIDGE, J., stated that he thought the
judgments of PARKE, B., in *Longmeid* v. *Holliday* (2), of COTTON and BOWEN, L.JJ., in
Heaven v. *Pender* (8), of STIRLING, L.J., in *Earl* v. *Lubbock* (12), and of HAMILTON, J., in
Blacker v. *Lake and Elliot* (4), made it clear that the plaintiff was not entitled to recover,
and that he had not felt himself bound by *George* v. *Skivington* (5).

So far, therefore, as *George* v. *Skivington* (5) and the dicta in *Heaven* v. *Pender* (8) are
H   concerned, it is, in my opinion, better that they should be buried so securely that their
perturbed spirits shall no longer vex the law.

One further case mentioned in argument may be referred to, certainly not by way of
authority, but to gain assistance by considering how similar cases are dealt with by
eminent judges of the United States. That such cases can have no close application
and no authority is clear, for, though the source of the law in the two countries may be
I   the same, its current may well flow in different channels. The case referred to is that of
Thomas v. *Winchester* (14). There a chemist issued poison in answer to a request for a
harmless drug, and he was held responsible to a third party injured by his neglect. It
appears to me that the decision might well rest on the principle that he in fact sold a
drug dangerous in itself, none the less so because he was asked to sell something else,
and on this view the case does not advance the matter.

In another case, *McPherson* v. *Buick Motor Co.* (15), where a manufacturer of a defective motor car was held liable for damages at the instance of a third party, the learned
judge appears to base his judgment on the view that a motor car might reasonably be

regarded as a dangerous article. In my view, therefore, the authorities are against **A**
the appellant's contention, and apart from authority it is difficult to see how any common law proposition can be formulated to support her claim.

The principle contended for must be this—that the manufacturer, or, indeed, the
repairer, of any article, apart entirely from contract, owes a duty to any person by
whom the article is lawfully used to see that it has been carefully constructed. All
rights in contract must be excluded from consideration of this principle, for such rights **B**
undoubtedly exist in successive steps from the original manufacturer down to the
ultimate purchaser, embraced in the general rule that an article is warranted as reasonably fit for the purpose for which it is sold. Nor can the doctrine be confined to cases
where inspection is difficult or impossible to introduce. This conception is simply to
misapply to tort doctrines applicable to sale and purchase.

The principle of tort lies completely outside the region where such considerations **C**
apply, and the duty, if it exists, must extend to every person who, in lawful circumstances, uses the article made. There can be no special duty attaching to the manufacture of food, apart from those implied by contract or imposed by statute. If such
a duty exists it seems to me it must cover the construction of every article, and I cannot
see any reason why it should not apply to the construction of a house. If one step, why
not fifty? Yet if a house be, as it sometimes is, negligently built, and in consequence of **D**
that negligence the ceiling falls and injures the occupier or anyone else, no action against
the builder exists according to the English law, although I believe such a right did exist
according to the laws of Babylon. Were such a principle known and recognised, it
seems to me impossible, having regard to the numerous cases that must have arisen to
persons injured by its disregard, that with the exception of *George* v. *Skivington* (5) no
case directly involving the principle has ever succeeded in the courts, and were it well **E**
known and accepted much of the discussion of the earlier cases would have been waste
of time.

In *Mullen* v. *Barr & Co., McGowan* v. *Barr & Co.* (16), a case indistinguishable from
the present, except upon the ground that a mouse is not a snail, and necessarily adopted
by the Second Division in their judgment, LORD ANDERSON says this (1929 S.C. at
p. 479):   **F**

> "In a case like the present, where the goods of the defenders are widely distributed
> throughout Scotland, it would seem little short of outrageous to make them
> responsible to members of the public for the condition of the contents of every
> bottle which issues from their works. It is obvious that, if such responsibility
> attached to the defenders, they might be called on to meet claims of damages   **G**
> which they could not possibly investigate or answer."

In agreeing, as I do, with the judgment of LORD ANDERSON, I desire to add that I
find it hard to dissent from the emphatic nature of the language with which his judgment is clothed. I am of opinion that this appeal should be dismissed, and I beg to
move your Lordships accordingly.

H

LORD ATKIN.—The sole question for determination in this case is legal: Do the
averments made by the pursuer in her pleading, if true, disclose a cause of action? I
need not re-state the particular facts. The question is whether the manufacturer of an
article of drink sold by him to a distributor in circumstances which prevent the distributor or the ultimate purchaser or consumer from discovering by inspection any
defect is under any legal duty to the ultimate purchaser or consumer to take reasonable **I**
care that the article is free from defect likely to cause injury to health. I do not think
a more important problem has occupied your Lordships in your judicial capacity,
important both because of its bearing on public health and because of the practical test
which it applies to the system of law under which it arises. The case has to be determined in accordance with Scots law, but it has been a matter of agreement between the
experienced counsel who argued this case, and it appears to be the basis of the
judgments of the learned judges of the Court of Session, that for the purposes of
determining this problem the law of Scotland and the law of England are the same. I

A   speak with little authority on this point, but my own research, such as it is, satisfies me that the principles of the law of Scotland on such a question as the present are identical with those of English law, and I discuss the issue on that footing. The law of both countries appears to be that in order to support an action for damages for negligence the complainant has to show that he has been injured by the breach of a duty owed to him in the circumstances by the defendant to take reasonable care to avoid such injury.

B   In the present case we are not concerned with the breach of the duty; if a duty exists, that would be a question of fact which is sufficiently averred and for the present purposes must be assumed. We are solely concerned with the question whether as a matter of law in the circumstances alleged the defender owed any duty to the pursuer to take care.

  It is remarkable how difficult it is to find in the English authorities statements of

C general application defining the relations between parties that give rise to the duty. The courts are concerned with the particular relations which come before them in actual litigation, and it is sufficient to say whether the duty exists in those circumstances. The result is that the courts have been engaged upon an elaborate classification of duties as they exist in respect of property, whether real or personal, with further divisions as to ownership, occupation or control, and distinctions based on the particular relations of

D the one side or the other, whether manufacturer, salesman or landlord, customer, tenant, stranger, and so on. In this way it can be ascertained at any time whether the law recognises a duty, but only where the case can be referred to some particular species which has been examined and classified. And yet the duty which is common to all the cases where liability is established must logically be based upon some element common to the cases where it is found to exist. To exist a complete logical definition of the

E general principle is probably to go beyond the function of the judge, for, the more general the definition, the more likely it is to omit essentials or introduce non-essentials. The attempt was made by Lord Esher in *Heaven* v. *Pender* (8) in a definition to which I will later refer. As framed it was demonstrably too wide, though it appears to me, if properly limited, to be capable of affording a valuable practical guide.

  At present I content myself with pointing out that in English law there must be and

F is some general conception of relations giving rise to a duty of care, of which the particular cases found in the books are but instances. The liability for negligence, whether you style it such or treat it as in other systems as a species of "culpa," is no doubt based upon a general public sentiment of moral wrongdoing for which the offender must pay. But acts or omissions which any moral code would censure cannot in a practical world be treated so as to give a right to every person injured by them to demand

G relief. In this way rules of law arise which limit the range of complainants and the extent of their remedy. The rule that you are to love your neighbour becomes in law: You must not injure your neighbour, and the lawyers' question: Who is my neighbour? receives a restricted reply. You must take reasonable care to avoid acts or omissions which you can reasonably foresee would be likely to injure your neighbour. Who then, in law, is my neighbour? The answer seems to be persons who are so closely and directly

H affected by my act that I ought reasonably to have them in contemplation as being so affected when I am directing my mind to the acts or omissions which are called in question. This appears to me to be the doctrine of *Heaven* v. *Pender* (8) as laid down by Lord Esher when it is limited by the notion of proximity introduced by Lord Esher himself and A. L. Smith, L.J., in *Le Lievre and another* v. *Gould* (11). Lord Esher, M.R., says ([1893] 1 Q.B. at p. 497):

I

    "That case established that, under certain circumstances, one man may owe a duty to another, even though there is no contract between them. If one man is near to another, or is near to the property of another, a duty lies upon him not to do that which may cause a personal injury to that other, or may injure his property."

So A. L. Smith, L.J., says ([1893] 1 Q.B. at p. 504):

    "The decision of *Heaven* v. *Pender* (8) was founded upon the principle that a duty to take due care did arise when the person or property of one was in such proximity

A

to the person or property of another that, if due care was not taken damage might
be done by the one to the other."

I think that this sufficiently states the truth if proximity be not confined to mere
physical proximity, but be used, as I think it was intended, to extend to such close and
direct relations that the act complained of directly affects a person whom the person
alleged to be bound to take care would know would be directly affected by his careless
act.   That this is the sense in which nearness or "proximity" was intended by LORD
ESHER is obvious from his own illustration in *Heaven* v. *Pender* (8) (11 Q.B.D. at p. 510)
of the application of his doctrine to the sale of goods.

B

"This [i.e., the rule he has just formulated] includes the case of goods, &c., supplied to be used immediately by a particular person or persons, or one of a class of
persons, where it would be obvious to the person supplying, if he thought, that the
goods would in all probability be used at once by such persons before a reasonable
opportunity for discovering any defect which might exist, and where the thing
supplied would be of such a nature that a neglect of ordinary care or skill as to its
condition or the manner of supplying it would probably cause danger to the person
or property of the person for whose use it was supplied, and who was about to use it.
It would exclude a case in which the goods are supplied under circumstances in
which it would be a chance by whom they would be used, or whether they would
be used or not, or whether they would be used before there would probably be means
of observing any defect, or where the goods would be of such a nature that a want
of care or skill as to their condition or the manner of supplying them would not
probably produce danger of injury to person or property."

C

D

I draw particular attention to the fact that LORD ESHER emphasises the necessity of
goods having to be "used immediately" and "used at once before a reasonable opportunity of inspection."   This is obviously to exclude the possibility of goods having their
condition altered by lapse of time, and to call attention to the proximate relationship,
which may be too remote where inspection even by the person using, certainly by an
intermediate person, may reasonably be interposed.   With this necessary qualification
of proximate relationship, as explained in *Le Lievre and another* v. *Gould* (11), I think
the judgment of LORD ESHER expresses the law of England.   Without the qualification, I think that the majority of the court in *Heaven* v. *Pender* (8) was justified in
thinking that the principle was expressed in too general terms.   There will, no doubt,
arise cases where it will be difficult to determine whether the contemplated relationship
is so close that the duty arises.   But in the class of case now before the court I cannot
conceive any difficulty to arise.   A manufacturer puts up an article of food in a container which he knows will be opened by the actual consumer.   There can be no inspection by any purchaser and no reasonable preliminary inspection by the consumer.
Negligently in the course of preparation he allows the contents to be mixed with poison.
It is said that the law of England and Scotland is that the poisoned consumer has no
remedy against the negligent manufacturer.   If this were the result of the authorities,
I should consider the result a grave defect in the law and so contrary to principle that
I should hesitate long before following any decision to that effect which had not the
authority of this House.   I would point out that in the assumed state of the authorities
not only would the consumer have no remedy against the manufacturer, he would have
none against anyone else, for in the circumstances alleged there would be no evidence
of negligence against anyone other than the manufacturer, and except in the case of a
consumer who was also a purchaser no contract and no warranty of fitness, and in the
case of the purchase of a specific article under its patent or trade name, which might
well be the case in the purchase of some articles of food or drink, no warranty protecting
even the purchaser-consumer.   There are other instances than of articles of food and
drink where goods are sold intended to be used immediately by the consumer, such as
many forms of goods sold for cleaning purposes, when the same liability must exist.
The doctrine supported by the decision below would not only deny a remedy to the
consumer who was injured by consuming bottled beer or chocolates poisoned by the
negligence of the manufacturer, but also to the user of what should be a harmless

E

F

G

H

I

A proprietary medicine, an ointment, a soap, a cleaning fluid or cleaning powder. I confine myself to articles of common household use, where everyone, including the manufacturer, knows that the articles will be used by persons other than the actual ultimate purchaser—namely, by members of his family and his servants, and, in some cases, his guests. I do not think so ill of our jurisprudence as to suppose that its principles are so remote from the ordinary needs of civilised society and the ordinary claims which it

B makes upon its members as to deny a legal remedy where there is so obviously a social wrong.

It will be found, I think, on examination, that there is no case in which the circumstances have been such as I have just suggested where the liability has been negatived. There are numerous cases where the relations were much more remote where the duty has been held not to exist. There are also dicta in such cases which go further than was

C necessary for the determination of the particular issues, which have caused the difficulty experienced by the courts below. I venture to say that in the branch of the law which deals with civil wrongs, dependent in England, at any rate, entirely upon the application by judges of general principles also formulated by judges, it is of particular importance to guard against the danger of stating propositions of law in wider terms than is necessary, lest essential factors be omitted in the wider survey and the inherent adaptability

D of English law be unduly restricted. For this reason it is very necessary, in considering reported cases in the law of torts, that the actual decision alone should carry authority, proper weight, of course, being given to the dicta of the judges.

In my opinion, several decided cases support the view that in such a case as the present the manufacturer owes a duty to the consumer to be careful. A direct authority is *George v. Skivington (5).* That was a decision on a demurrer to a declaration which

E averred that the defendant professed to sell a hairwash made by himself and that the plaintiff, Joseph George, bought a bottle to be used by his wife, the plaintiff Emma George, as the defendant then knew, and that the defendant had so negligently conducted himself in preparing and selling the hairwash that it was unfit for use, whereby the female plaintiff was injured. KELLY, C.B., said that there was no question of warranty, but whether the chemist was liable in an action on the case for unskilfulness and

F negligence in the manufacture of it:

> "Unquestionably there was such a duty towards the purchaser, and it extends, in my judgment, to the person for whose use the vendor knew the compound was purchased."

PIGOTT and CLEASBY, BB., put their judgments on the same ground.

G I venture to think that COTTON, L.J., in *Heaven v. Pender* (8) (11 Q.B.D. at p. 517), misinterprets CLEASBY, B.'s judgment in the reference to *Langridge v. Levy* (1). CLEASBY, B., appears to me to make it plain that, in his opinion, the duty to take reasonable care can be substituted for the duty which existed in *Langridge v. Levy* (1) not to defraud. It is worth noticing that *George v. Skivington* (5) was referred to by CLEASBY, B., himself sitting as a member of the Court of Exchequer Chamber in *Francis v. Cock-*

H *rell* (7) (L.R. 5 Q.B. at p. 515) and was recognised by him as based on an ordinary duty to take care. It was also affirmed by BRETT, M.R., in *Cunnington v. Great Northern Rail. Co.* (17), decided on July 2, 1883, at a date between the argument and the judgment in *Heaven v. Pender* (8), though as in that case the court negatived any breach of duty the expression of opinion is not authoritative.

The existence of the duty contended for is also supported by *Hawkins v. Smith* (18),

I where a dock labourer in the employ of the dock company was injured by a defective sack which had been hired by the consignees from the defendant, who knew the use to which it was to be put, and which had been provided by the consignees for the use of the dock company which had been employed by them to unload the ship on the dock company's premises. The Divisional Court (DAY, J., and LAWRANCE, J.) held the defendant liable for negligence. Similarly, in *Elliott v. Hall or Nailstone Colliery Co.* (19) the defendants, colliery owners, consigned coal to the plaintiff's employers, coal merchants, in a truck hired by the defendants from a wagon company. The plaintiff was injured in the course of unloading the coal by reason of the defective condition of the

truck, and was held by a Divisional Court (GROVE, J., and A. L. SMITH, J.) entitled to **A**
recover on the ground of the defendants' breach of duty to see that the truck was not in
a dangerous condition.   It is to be noticed that in neither case was the defective chattel
in the defendants' occupation, possession or control, or on their premises, while in the
latter case it was not even their property.   It is sometimes said that the liability in
these cases depends upon an invitation by the defendant to the plaintiff to use his chattel.
I do not find the decisions expressed to be based upon this ground, but rather upon the **B**
knowledge that the plaintiff, in the course of the contemplated use of the chattel, would
use it, and the supposed invitation appears to me to be in many cases a fiction and
merely a form of expressing the direct relation between supplier and user which gives rise
to the duty to take care.

A very recent case, which has the authority of this House, is *Chapman (or Oliver)* v.
Saddler & Co. (20).   In that case a firm of stevedores employed to unload a cargo of **C**
maize in bags provided the rope slings by which the cargo was raised to the ship's deck
by their own men using the ship's tackle and was then transported to the dock side by
the shore porters, of whom the plaintiff was one.   The porters relied on examination
by the stevedores and had themselves no opportunity of examination.   In these circumstances this House, reversing the decision of the First Division, held that there was a
duty owed by the stevedore company to the porters to see that the slings were fit for use, **D**
and restored the judgment of the Lord Ordinary, LORD MORISON, in favour of the
pursuer.   I find no trace of the doctrine of invitation in the opinions expressed in this
House, of which mine was one: the decision was based upon the fact that the direct
relations established, especially the circumstance that the injured porter had no opportunity of independent examination, gave rise to a duty to be careful.

I should not omit in this review of cases the decision in *Grote* v. *Chester and Holyhead* **E**
Rail. Co. (21).   That was an action on the case in which it was alleged that the
defendants had constructed a bridge over the Dee on their railway and had licensed the
use of the bridge to the Shrewsbury and Chester Rail. Co. to carry passengers over it,
and had so negligently constructed the bridge that the plaintiff, a passenger on the last-
named railway, had been injured by the falling of the bridge.   At the trial before
VAUGHAN WILLIAMS, J., the judge had directed the jury that the plaintiff was entitled **F**
to recover if the bridge was not constructed with reasonable care and skill.   On a
motion for a new trial the Attorney-General, Sir John Jervis, contended that there was
misdirection, for the defendants were liable only for negligence, and the jury might have
understood that there was an absolute liability.   The Court of Exchequer, after con-
sulting the trial judge as to his direction, refused the rule.   This case is said by KELLY,
C.B., in *Francis* v. *Cockrell* (7), in the Exchequer Chamber (L.R. 5 Q.B. at p. 505), to **G**
have been decided upon an implied contract with every person lawfully using the bridge
that it was reasonably fit for the purpose.   I can find no trace of such a ground in the
pleadings or in the argument or judgment.   It is true that the defendants were the
owners and occupiers of the bridge.   The law as to the liability to invitees and licensees
had not then been developed.   The case is interesting because it is a simple action on
the case for negligence, and the court upheld the duty to persons using the bridge to **H**
take reasonable care that the bridge was safe.

It now becomes necessary to consider the cases which have been referred to in the
courts below as laying down the proposition that no duty to take care is owed to the
consumer in such a case as this.

In *Dixon* v. *Bell* (22) the defendant had left a loaded gun at his lodgings and sent his
servant, a mulatto girl aged about thirteen or fourteen, for the gun, asking the landlord **I**
to remove the priming and give it her.   The landlord did remove the priming and gave
the gun to the girl, who later levelled it at the plaintiff's small son, drew the trigger, and
injured the boy.   The action was in case for negligently entrusting the young servant
with the gun.   The jury at the trial before LORD ELLENBOROUGH had returned a verdict
for the plaintiff.   A motion by the Attorney-General, Sir William Garrow, for a new
trial was dismissed by the court, LORD ELLENBOROUGH and BAYLEY, J., the former
remarking that it was incumbent on the defendant, who by charging the gun had made
it capable of doing mischief, to render it safe and innoxious.

A   In *Langridge* v. *Levy* (1) the action was in case and the declaration alleged that the defendant, by falsely and fraudulently warranting a gun to have been made by Nock and to be a good, safe, and secure gun, sold the gun to the plaintiff's father for the use of himself and his son, and that one of his sons, confiding in the warranty, used the gun, which burst and injured him. Plea: Not Guilty and no warranty as alleged. The report is not very satisfactory. No evidence is reported of any warranty or statement

B   except that the gun was an elegant twist gun by Nock. The judge left to the jury whether the defendant had warranted the gun to be by Nock and to be safe, whether it was in fact unsafe, and whether the defendant warranted it to be safe knowing that it was not so. The jury returned a general verdict for the plaintiff. It appears to have been argued that the plaintiff could recover wherever there is a breach of duty imposed on the defendant by contract or otherwise and the plaintiff is injured by reason of its

C   breach; by this is meant, apparently, that the duty need not be owed to the plaintiff, but that he can take advantage of the breach of a duty owed to a third party. This contention was negatived by the court, who held, however, that the plaintiff could recover if a representation known to be false was made to a third person with the intention that a chattel should be used by the plaintiff, even though it does not appear that the defendant intended the false representation to be communicated to him: see

D   per Parke, B. (2 M. & W. at p. 531). The same view was adopted by the Exchequer Chamber, the user by the plaintiff being treated by the court as one of the acts contemplated by the fraudulent defendant. It is unnecessary to consider whether the proposition can be supported in its widest form. It is sufficient to say that the case was based, as I think, in the pleading, and certainly in the judgment, on the ground of fraud, and it appears to add nothing of value positively or negatively to the present dis-

E   cussion.

    Winterbottom v. *Wright* (3) was a case decided on a demurrer. The plaintiff had demurred to two of the pleas as to which there was no decision by the court, but on the hearing of the plaintiff's demurrer the court, in accordance with the practice of the day, were entitled to consider the whole record, including the declaration, and, owing to the conclusion that this declaration disclosed no cause of action, gave judgment for the

F   defendant: see Sutton's Personal Actions at Common Law, p. 113. The advantage of the procedure is that we are in a position to know the precise issue at law which arose for determination. The declaration was in case and alleged that the defendant had contracted with the Postmaster-General to provide the mail coach to convey mails from Hartford to Holyhead and to keep the mails in safe condition, that Atkinson and others, with notice of the said contract, had contracted with the Postmaster-General to

G   convey the road mail coach from Hartford to Holyhead, and that the plaintiff, relying on the said first contract, hired himself to Atkinson to drive the mail coach, but that the defendant so negligently conducted himself and so utterly disregarded his aforesaid contract that, the defendant having the means of knowing and well knowing all the aforesaid premises, the mail coach, being in a dangerous condition owing to certain latent defects and to no other cause, gave way, whereby the plaintiff was thrown from

H   his seat and injured. It is to be observed that no negligence apart from breach of contract was alleged—in other words, no duty was alleged other than the duty arising out of the contract. It is not stated that the defendant knew or ought to have known of the latent defect. The argument of the defendant was that on the fact of the declaration the wrong arose merely out of the breach of a contract, and that only a party to the contract could sue. The Court of Exchequer adopted that view, as clearly appears

I   from the judgments of Alderson and Rolfe, BB. There are dicta by Lord Abinger which are too wide as to an action of negligence being confined to cases of breach of a public duty. The actual decision appears to have been manifestly right, no duty to the plaintiff arose out of the contract, and the duty of the defendant under the contract with the Postmaster-General to put the coach in good repair would not have involved such direct relations with the servant of the person whom the Postmaster-General employed to drive the coach as would give rise to a duty of care owed to such servant.

    We now come to *Longmeid* v. *Holliday* (2), the dicta in which have had considerable effect in subsequent decisions. In that case the declaration in case alleged that the

plaintiff, Frederick Longmeid, had bought from the defendant, the maker and seller of **A**
"the Holliday lamp," a lamp to be used by himself and his wife Eliza in the plaintiffs'
shop; that the defendant induced the sale by the false and fraudulent warranty that the
lamp was reasonably fit for the purpose; and that the plaintiff Eliza, confiding in the
said warranty, lighted the lamp, which exploded, whereby she was injured. It is,
perhaps, not an extravagant guess to suppose that the plaintiffs' pleader had read
Langridge v. *Levy* (1). The jury found all the facts for the plaintiffs except the allega- **B**
tion of fraud; they were not satisfied that the defendant knew of the defects. The
plaintiff Frederick had already recovered damages on the contract of sale for breach of
the implied warranty of fitness. The declaration made no averment of negligence.
Verdict was entered at the trial by MARTIN, B., for the plaintiff, but with liberty to the
defendant to move to enter the verdict for him. A rule having been obtained, plaintiff's
counsel sought to support the verdict on the ground that this was an action, not for a **C**
breach of duty arising solely from contract, but for an injury resulting from conduct
amounting to fraud.

PARKE, B., who delivered the judgment of the court, held that, fraud having been
negatived, the action could not be maintained on that ground. He then went on to
discuss cases in which a third person not a party to a contract may sue for damages
sustained if it is broken. After dealing with the negligence of a surgeon or of a carrier, **D**
or of a firm in breach of contract committing a nuisance on a highway, he deals with the
case where anyone delivers to another without notice an instrument in its nature dangerous or under particular circumstances, as a loaded gun, and refers to *Dixon* v. *Bell* (22),
though what this case has to do with contract it is difficult to see. He then goes on:

> "But it would be going much too far to say that so much care is required in the **E**
> ordinary intercourse of life between one individual and another that, if a machine
> not in its nature dangerous—a carriage, for instance—but which might become so
> by a latent defect entirely unknown, although discoverable by the exercise of ordi-
> nary care, should be lent or given by one person, even by the person who manu-
> factured it, to another, the former should be answerable to the latter for a sub-
> sequent damage accruing by the use of it."
> **F**

It is worth noticing how guarded this dictum is. The case put is a machine, such as a
carriage, not in its nature dangerous, which might become dangerous by a latent defect
entirely unknown. Then there is the saving "although discoverable by the exercise of
ordinary care," discoverable by whom it is not said; it may include the person to whom
the innocent machine is "lent or given." Then the dictum is confined to machines "lent
or given" (a later sentence makes it clear that a distinction is intended between these **G**
words and "delivered to the purchaser under the contract of sale"), and the manufacturer is introduced for the first time—"even by the person who manufactured it."
I do not for a moment believe that PARKE, B., had in his mind such a case as a loaf
negligently mixed by the baker with poison which poisoned a purchaser's family. He
is, in my opinion, confining his remarks primarily to cases where a person is seeking to
rely upon a duty of care which arises out of a contract with a third party, and has **H**
never even discussed the case of a manufacturer negligently causing an article to be
dangerous and selling it in that condition whether with immediate or mediate effect upon
the consumer. It is noteworthy that he refers only to "letting or giving" chattels,
operations known to the law, where the special relations thereby created have a
particular bearing on the existence or non-existence of a duty to take care.

Next in his chain of authority come *George* v. *Skivington* (5) and *Heaven* v. *Pender* (8), **I**
which I have already discussed. The next case is *Earl* v. *Lubbock* (12). The plaintiff
sued in the county court for personal injuries due to the negligence of the defendant.
The plaintiff was a driver in the employ of a firm who owned vans. The defendant, a
master wheelwright, had contracted with the firm to keep their vans in good and substantial repair. The allegation of negligence was that the defendant's servant had
negligently failed to inspect and repair a defective wheel, and had negligently repaired
the wheel. The learned county court judge had held that the defendant owed no
duty to the plaintiff, and the Divisional Court (LORD ALVERSTONE, C.J., WILLS and

A KENNEDY, JJ.) and the Court of Appeal agreed with him. COLLINS, M.R., said that the case was concluded by *Winterbottom* v. *Wright* (3). In other words, he must have treated the duty as alleged to arise only from a breach of contract, for, as has been pointed out, that was the only allegation in *Winterbottom* v. *Wright* (3), negligence, apart from contract, being neither averred nor proved.   It is true that he cites with approval the dicta of LORD ABINGER in the case, but obviously I think his approval

B must be limited to those dicta so far as they related to the particular facts before the Court of Appeal, and to cases where, as LORD ABINGER says, the law permits a contract to be turned into a tort. STIRLING, L.J., it is true, said that to succeed the plaintiff must bring his case within the proposition of the majority in *Heaven* v. *Pender* (8), that any one who, without due warning, supplies to others for use an instrument which to his knowledge is in such a condition as to cause danger is liable for injury.   I venture

C to think that the lord justice was mistakenly treating a proposition which applies one test of a duty as though it afforded the only criterion. MATHEW, L.J., appears to me to put the case on its proper footing when he says:

> "The argument of counsel for the plaintiff was that the defendant's servants had
> been negligent in the performance of the contract with the owners of the van, and
D > that it followed as a matter of law that anyone in their employment . . . had a cause
> of action against the defendant.   It is impossible to accept such a wide proposition,
> and, indeed, it is difficult to see how, if it were the law, trade could be carried on."

I entirely agree.   I have no doubt that in that case the plaintiff failed to show that the repairer owed any duty to him.   The question of law in that case seems very different from that raised in the present case. *Blacker* v. *Lake and Elliot, Ltd.* (4)

E approaches more nearly the facts of this case.   I have read and re-read it, having unfeigned respect for the authority of the two learned judges, HAMILTON and LUSH, JJ., who decided it, and I am bound to say I have found difficulty in formulating the precise grounds upon which the judgment was given.   The plaintiff had been injured by the bursting of a brazing lamp which he had bought from a shopkeeper, who had bought it from the manufacturer, the defendant.   The plaintiff had used the lamp for twelve

F months before the accident.   The case was tried in the county court before that excellent lawyer, the late JUDGE SIR HOWLAND ROBERTS.   That learned judge had directed the jury that the plaintiff could succeed if the defendants had put upon the market a lamp not fit for use in the sense that a person working it with reasonable care would incur a risk which a properly constructed lamp would not impose upon him.   The jury found that the lamp was defective by reason of an improper system of making an

G essential joint between the container and the vaporiser; that the defendants did not know that it was dangerous, but ought, as reasonable men, to have known it. HAMILTON, J., seems to have thought that there was no evidence of negligence in this respect. LUSH, J., expressly says so, and implies by the words "I also think" that HAMILTON, J., so thought.   If so, the case resolves itself into a series of important dicta. HAMILTON, J., says (106 L.T. at p. 536) that it has been decided in authorities from

H *Winterbottom* v. *Wright* (3) to *Earl* v. *Lubbock* (12) that the breach of the defendant's contract with A. to use care and skill in and about the manufacture or repair of an article does not itself give any cause of action to B. when injured by the article proving to be defective in breach of that contract.   He then goes on to say: How is the case of the plaintiff any better when there is no contract proved of which there could be breach?   I think, with respect, that this saying does not give sufficient weight to the

I actual issues raised by the pleadings, on which alone the older cases are an authority. If the issue raised was an alleged duty created by contract, it would have been irrelevant to consider duties created without reference to contract, and contract cases cease to be authorities for duties alleged to exist beyond or without contract.   Moreover, it is a mistake to describe the authorities as dealing with the breach of care or skill in the manufacture of goods, as contrasted with repair.

The only manufacturing case was *Longmeid* v. *Holliday* (2), where negligence was not alleged.   HAMILTON, J., recognises that *George* v. *Skivington* (5) was a decision which, if it remained an authority, bound him.   He says that, without presuming to say it

was wrong, he cannot follow it because it is in conflict with *Winterbottom* v. *Wright* (3). **A**
I find this very difficult to understand, for *George* v. *Skivington* (5) was based upon a duty
in the manufacturer to take care independently of contract, while *Winterbottom* v.
Wright (3) was decided on a demurrer in a case where the alleged duty was based solely
on breach of a contractual duty to keep in repair and no negligence was alleged.
LUSH, J., says in terms that there are only three classes of cases in which a stranger to a
contract can sue for injury by a defective chattel: one is fraud, the second is the case of **B**
articles dangerous or noxious in themselves where the duty is only to warn, the third
is public nuisance. He does not bring the cases represented by *Elliott* v. *Hall* (19) (the
defective coal wagon) within his classes at all. He says (106 L.T. at p. 541) that they
belong to a totally different class

> "where the control of premises or the management of a dangerous thing upon **C**
> premises creates a duty."

I have already pointed out that this distinction is unfounded in fact, for in *Elliott* v.
Hall (19), as in *Hawkins* v. *Smith* (18) (the defective sack), the defendant exercised no
control over the article and the accident did not occur on his premises. With all respect
I think that the judgments in the case err by seeking to confine the law to rigid and
exclusive categories, and by not giving sufficient attention to the general principle **D**
which governs the whole law of negligence in the duty owed to those who will be immediately injured by lack of care.

The last case I need refer to is *Bates and another* v. *Batey & Co.* (13), where manufacturers of ginger-beer were sued by a plaintiff who had been injured by the bursting
of a bottle of ginger-beer bought from a shopkeeper who had obtained it from the manufacturers. The manufacturers had bought the actual bottle from its maker, but were **E**
found by the jury to have been negligent in not taking proper means to discover whether
the bottle was defective or not. HORRIDGE, J., found that a bottle of ginger-beer was
not dangerous in itself, but that this defective bottle was in fact dangerous, but, as the
defendants did not know it was dangerous, they were not liable, though by the exercise
of reasonable care they could have discovered the defect. This case differs from the present only by reason of the fact that it was not the manufacturers of the ginger-beer **F**
who caused the defect in the bottle, but, on the assumption that the jury were right in
finding a lack of reasonable care in not examining the bottle, I should have come to the
conclusion that, as the manufacturers must have contemplated the bottle being handled
immediately by the consumer, they owed a duty to him to take care that he should not
be injured externally by explosion, just as I think they owed a duty to him to take
care that he should not be injured internally by poison or other noxious thing. **G**

I do not find it necessary to discuss at length the cases dealing with duties where a
thing is dangerous, or, in the narrower category, belongs to a class of things which are
dangerous in themselves. I regard the distinction as an unnatural one so far as it is
used to serve as a logical differentiation by which to distinguish the existence or non-
existence of a legal right. In this respect I agree with what was said by SCRUTTON, L.J.,
in *Hope & Son* v. *Anglo-American Oil Co.* (23) (12 Ll.L.R. at p. 187), a case which was **H**
ultimately decided on a question of fact:

> "Personally, I do not understand the difference between a thing dangerous in itself
> as poison and a thing not dangerous as a class, but by negligent construction
> dangerous as a particular thing. The latter, if anything, seems the more dangerous
> of the two; it is a wolf in sheep's clothing instead of an obvious wolf."

The nature of the thing may very well call for different degrees of care, and the person **I**
dealing with it may well contemplate persons as being within the sphere of his duty
to take care who would not be sufficiently proximate with less dangerous goods, so that
not only the degree of care but the range of persons to whom a duty is owed may be
extended. But they all illustrate the general principle. In *Dominion Natural Gas Co.,
Ltd.* v. *Collins* (6) the appellants had installed a gas apparatus and were supplying natural
gas on the premises of a railway company. They had installed a regulator to control the
pressure and their men negligently made an escape valve discharge into the building
instead of into the open air. The railway workmen—the plaintiffs—were injured by an

A   explosion in the premises. The defendants were held liable. LORD DUNEDIN, in giving
the judgment of the Judicial Committee, consisting of himself, LORD MACNAGHTEN,
LORD COLLINS, and SIR ARTHUR WILSON, after stating that there was no relation of
contract between the plaintiffs and the defendants, proceeded ([1909] A.C. at p. 646):

B
> "There may be, however, in the case of anyone performing an operation, or setting
> up and installing a machine, a relationship of duty. What that duty is will vary
> according to the subject-matter of the things involved. It has, however, again
> and again been held that in the case of articles dangerous in themselves, such as
> loaded firearms, poisons, explosives, and other things ejusdem generis, there is a
> peculiar duty to take precaution imposed upon those who send forth or install such
> articles when it is necessarily the case that other parties will come within their
C   proximity."

This, with respect, exactly sums up the position. The duty may exist independently
of contract. Whether it exists or not depends upon the subject-matter involved, but
clearly in the class of things enumerated there is a special duty to take precautions.
This is the very opposite of creating a special category in which alone the duty exists.
I may add, though it obviously would make no difference in the creation of a duty,
D   that the installation of an apparatus to be used for gas perhaps more closely resembles
the manufacture of a gun than a dealing with a loaded gun. In both cases the actual
work is innocuous; it is only when the gun is loaded or the apparatus charged with gas
that the danger arises. I do not think it necessary to consider the obligation of a
person who entrusts to a carrier goods which are dangerous or which he ought to know
are dangerous. As far as the direct obligation of the consignor to the carrier is concerned,
E   it has been put upon an implied warranty, *Brass* v. *Maitland* (24), but it is also a duty
owed independently of contract—e.g., to the carrier's servant, *Farrant* v. *Barnes* (25).
So far as the cases afford an analogy they seem to support the proposition now
asserted. I need only mention, to distinguish them, two cases in this House which are
referred to in some of the cases which I have reviewed. The first is *Caledonian Rail.
Co.* v. *Warwick* (26), in which the appellant company were held not liable for injuries
F   caused by a defective brake on a coal wagon conveyed by the railway company to a
point in the transit where their contract ended and where the wagons were taken over
for haulage for the last part of the journey by a second railway company, on which
part the accident happened. It was held that the first railway company were under no
duty to the injured workman to examine the wagon for defects at the end of their
contractual haulage. There was ample opportunity for inspection by the second
G   railway company. The relations were not proximate. In the second, *Cavalier* v.
Pope (27), the wife of the tenant of a house let unfurnished sought to recover from the
landlord damages for personal injuries arising from the non-repair of the house, on the
ground that the landlord had contracted with her husband to repair the house. It was
held that the wife was not a party to the contract, and that the well-known absence of
any duty in respect of the letting an unfurnished house prevented her from relying on
H   any cause of action for negligence.
In the most recent case, *Bottomley and another* v. *Bannister and another* (28), an action
under Lord Campbell's Act, the deceased man, the father of the plaintiff, had taken an
unfurnished house from the defendants, who had installed a gas boiler with a special
gas burner which, if properly regulated, required no flue. The father and his wife were
killed by fumes from the apparatus. The case was determined on the ground that the
I   apparatus was part of the realty and that the landlord did not know of the danger, but
there is a discussion of the case on the supposition that it was a chattel. GREER, L.J.,
states with truth that it is not easy to reconcile all the authorities, and that there is no
authority binding on the Court of Appeal that a person selling an article which he did
not know to be dangerous can be held liable to a person with whom he has made no
contract, by reason of the fact that reasonable inquiries might have enabled him to
discover that the article was in fact dangerous. When the danger is in fact occasioned
by his own lack of care then in cases of proximate relationship, this case will, I trust,
supply the deficiency.

It is always satisfaction to an English lawyer to be able to test his application of A
fundamental principles of the common law by the development of the same doctrines
by the lawyers of the courts of the United States.   In that country I find that the law
appears to be well established in the sense which I have indicated.   The mouse had
emerged from the ginger-beer bottle in the United States before it appeared in Scotland,
but there it brought a liability upon the manufacturer.   I must not in this long judgment
do more than refer to the illuminating judgment of CARDOZO, J., in *McPherson* v. B
Buick Motor Co. (15), in the New York Court of Appeals, in which he states the principles
of the law as I should desire to state them and reviews the authorities in States other than
his own.   Whether the principle which he affirms would apply to the particular facts of
that case in this country would be a question for consideration if the case arose.   It
might be that the course of business, by giving opportunities of examination to the
immediate purchaser or otherwise, prevented the relation between manufacturer and C
the user of the car from being so close as to create a duty.   But the American decision
would undoubtedly lead to a decision in favour of the pursuer in the present case.

If your Lordships accept the view that the appellant's pleading discloses a relevant
cause of action, you will be affirming the proposition that by Scots and English law alike
a manufacturer of products which he sells in such a form as to show that he intends
them to reach the ultimate consumer in the form in which they left him, with no reason- D
able possibility of intermediate examination, and with the knowledge that the absence
of reasonable care in the preparation or putting up of the products will result in injury
to the consumer's life or property, owes a duty to the consumer to take that reasonable
care.

It is a proposition that I venture to say no one in Scotland or England who was
not a lawyer would for one moment doubt.   It will be an advantage to make it clear E
that the law in this matter, as in most others, is in accordance with sound common sense.
I think that this appeal should be allowed.

LORD TOMLIN.—I have had an opportunity of considering the opinion prepared by
my noble and learned friend LORD BUCKMASTER, which I have already read.   As the
reasoning of that opinion and the conclusions reached therein accord in every respect F
with my own views, I propose to say only a few words.

First, I think that if the appellant is to succeed it must be upon the proposition that
every manufacturer or repairer of any article is under a duty to everyone who may
thereafter legitimately use the article to exercise due care in the manufacture or repair.
It is logically impossible to stop short of this point.   There can be no distinction between
food and any other article.   Moreover, the fact that an article of food is sent out in a G
sealed container can have no relevancy on the question of duty.   It is only a factor
which may render it easier to bring negligence home to the manufacturer.

Secondly, I desire to say that, in my opinion, the decision in *Winterbottom* v. *Wright* (3)
is directly in point against the appellant.   The examination of the report makes it, I
think, plain (i) that negligence was alleged and was the basis of the claim, and (ii) that
the wide proposition which I have indicated was that for which the plaintiff was con- H
tending.   The declaration averred (inter alia) that the defendant "so improperly and
negligently conducted himself" that the accident complained of happened.   The
plaintiff's counsel said: "Here the declaration alleges the accident to have happened
through the defendant's negligence and want of care."   The alarming consequences of
accepting the validity of this proposition were pointed out by the defendant's counsel,
who said: "For example, every one of the sufferers by such an accident as that which I
recently happened on the Versailles Railway might have his action against the manufacturer of the defective axle."

That the action, which was in case, embraced a cause of action in tort is I think
implicit in its form and appears from the concluding sentence of LORD ABINGER'S
judgment, which was in these terms:

"By permitting this action, we should be working this injustice, that after the
defendant had done everything to the satisfaction of his employer, and after all
matters between them had been adjusted, and all accounts settled on the footing of

A   their contract, we should subject them to be ripped open by this action of tort being brought against him.''

I will only add to what has been already said by my noble and learned LORD BUCK-MASTER with regard to the decisions and dicta relied upon by the appellant, and the other relevant reported cases, that I am unable to explain how the cases of dangerous
B   articles can have been treated as "exceptions" if the appellant's contention is well founded. Upon the view which I take of the matter the reported cases, some directly, others impliedly, negative the existence as part of the common law of England of any principle affording support to the appellant's claim, and therefore there is, in my opinion, no material from which it is legitimate for your Lordships' House to deduce such a principle.

C

LORD THANKERTON.—In this action the appellant claims reparation from the respondent in respect of illness and other injurious effects resulting from the presence of a decomposed snail in a bottle of ginger-beer, which is alleged to have been manu-factured by the respondent, and which was partially consumed by her, it having been ordered by a friend on her behalf in a café in Paisley.
D   The action is based on negligence, and the only question in this appeal is whether, taking the appellant's averments pro veritate, they disclose a case relevant in law, so as to entitle her to have them remitted for proof. The Lord Ordinary allowed a proof, but, on a reclaiming note for the respondent, the Second Division of the Court of Session recalled the Lord Ordinary's interlocutor and dismissed the action, following their decision in the recent cases of *Mullen* v. *Burr & Co.* and *McGowan* v. *Barr & Co.* (16).
E   The appellant's case is that the bottle was sealed with a metal cap, and was made of dark opaque glass, which not only excluded access to the contents before consumption if the contents were to retain their aerated condition, but also excluded the possibility of visual examination of the contents from outside; and that on the side of the bottle there was pasted a label containing the name and address of the respondent, who was the manufacturer. She states that the shopkeeper who supplied the ginger-beer opened
F   it and poured some of its contents into a tumbler, which contained some ice cream, and that she drank some of the contents of the tumbler; that her friend then lifted the bottle and was pouring the remainder of the contents into the tumbler when a snail, which had been, unknown to her, her friend, or the shopkeeper, in the bottle, and was in a state of decomposition, floated out of the bottle.

The duties which the appellant accuses the respondent of having neglected may be
G   summarised as follows: (a) that the ginger-beer was manufactured by the respondent or his servants to be sold as an article of drink to members of the public (including the appellant), and that, accordingly, it was his duty to exercise the greatest care in order that snails should not get into the bottles, render the ginger-beer dangerous and harm-ful, and be sold with the ginger-beer; (b) a duty to provide a system of working his business which would not allow snails to get into the sealed bottles, and, in particular,
H   would not allow the bottles when washed to stand in places to which snails had access; (c) a duty to provide an efficient system of inspection, which would prevent snails from getting into the sealed bottles; and (d) a duty to provide clear bottles, so as to facilitate the said system of inspection.

There can be no doubt, in my opinion, that equally in the law of Scotland and of England it lies upon the party claiming redress in such a case to show that there was
I   some relation of duty between her and the defender which required the defender to exercise due and reasonable care for her safety. It is not at all necessary that there should be any direct contract between them, because the action is not based upon contract but upon negligence; but it is necessary for the pursuer in such an action to show there was a duty owed to her by the defender, because a man cannot be charged with negligence if he has no obligation to exercise diligence: *Kemp and Dougall* v. *Darngavil Coal Co.* (29), per LORD KINNEAR (1909 S.C. at p. 1319); see also *Clelland* v. *Robb* (30), per LORD PRESIDENT DUNEDIN and LORD KINNEAR (1911 S.C. at p. 256). The question in each case is whether the pursuer has established, or, in the stage of the

present appeal, has relevantly averred, such facts as involve the existence of such a **A** relation of duty.

We are not dealing here with a case of what is called an article per se dangerous or one which was known by the defender to be dangerous, in which cases a special duty of protection or adequate warning is placed upon the person who uses or distributes it. The present case is that of a manufacturer and a consumer, with whom he has no con- **B** tractual relation, of an article which the manufacturer did not know to be dangerous, and, unless the consumer can establish a special relationship with the manufacturer, it is clear, in my opinion, that neither the law of Scotland nor the law of England will hold that the manufacturer has any duty towards the consumer to exercise diligence. In such a case the remedy of the consumer, if any, will lie against the intervening party from whom he has procured the article. I am aware that the American courts, in the decisions referred to by my noble and learned friend LORD MACMILLAN, have taken a **C** view more favourable to the consumer.

The special circumstances, from which the appellant claims that such a relationship of duty should be inferred, may, I think, be stated thus, namely, that the respondent, in placing his manufactured article of drink upon the market, has intentionally so excluded interference with, or examination of, the article by any intermediate handler of the goods between himself and the consumer that he has, of his own accord, brought **D** himself into direct relationship with the consumer, with the result that the consumer is entitled to rely upon the exercise of diligence by the manufacturer to secure that the article shall not be harmful to the consumer. If that contention be sound, the con- sumer, on her showing that the article has reached her intact, and that she has been injured by the harmful nature of the article owing to the failure of the manufacturer to take reasonable care in its preparation before its enclosure in the sealed vessel, will be **E** entitled to reparation from the manufacturer.

In my opinion, the existence of a legal duty in such circumstances is in conformity with the principles of both the law of Scotland and the law of England. The English cases demonstrate how impossible it is finally to catalogue, amid the ever-varying types of human relationships, those relationships in which a duty to exercise care arises apart from contract, and each of these cases relates to its own set of circumstances, out **F** of which it was claimed that the duty had arisen. In none of these cases were the cir- cumstances identical with the present case as regards that which I regard as the essential element in this case, namely, the manufacturer's own action in bringing himself into direct relationship with the party injured. I have had the privilege of considering the discussion of these authorities by my noble and learned friend LORD ATKIN in the judgment which he has just delivered, and I so entirely agree with it that I cannot **G** usefully add anything to it.

An interesting illustration of similar circumstances is to be found in *Gordon* v. *M'Hardy* (31), in which the pursuer sought to recover damages from a retail grocer on account of the death of his son by ptomaine poisoning, caused by eating tinned salmon purchased from the defender. The pursuer averred that the tin, when sold, was dented, but he did not suggest that the grocer had cut through the metal and allowed air to get **H** in, or had otherwise caused injury to the contents. The action was held irrelevant, the LORD JUSTICE CLERK remarking,

"I do not see how the defender could have examined the tin of salmon which he is alleged to have sold without destroying the very condition which the manufacturer had established in order to preserve the contents, the tin not being intended to be **I** opened until immediately before use."

Apparently in that case the manufacturers' label was off the tin when sold, and they had not been identified. I should be sorry to think that the meticulous care of the manufacturer to exclude interference or inspection by the grocer in that case should relieve the grocer of any responsibility to the consumer without any corresponding assumption of duty by the manufacturer.

I am of opinion that the contention of the appellant is sound and that she has

A   relevantly averred a relationship of duty as between the respondent and herself, as also
that her averments of the respondent's neglect of that duty are relevant.
The cases of *Mullen* and *McGowan* (16), which the learned judges of the Second
Division followed in the present case, related to facts similar in every respect except
that the foreign matter was a decomposed mouse.   In these cases the same court—
LORD HUNTER dissenting—held that the manufacturer owed no duty to the consumer.
B   The view of the majority was that the English authorities excluded the existence of such
a duty, but LORD ORMIDALE (1929 S.C. at p. 471) would otherwise have been prepared to
come to a contrary conclusion.   LORD HUNTER'S opinion seems to be in conformity with
the view which I have expressed above.   My conclusion rests upon the facts averred in this
case, and would apparently also have applied in the cases of *Mullen* and *McGowan* (16),
in which, however, there had been a proof before answer, and there was also a question
C   as to whether the pursuers had proved their averments.   I am, therefore, of opinion that
the appeal should be allowed and the case should be remitted for proof, as the pursuer
did not ask for an issue.

LORD MACMILLAN.—The incident which in its legal bearings your Lordships are
called upon to consider in this appeal was in itself of a trivial character, though the
D   consequences to the appellant, as she describes them, were serious enough.   It appears
from the appellant's allegation that on an evening in August, 1928 she and a friend
visited a café in Paisley, where her friend ordered for her some ice cream and a bottle
of ginger-beer.   These were supplied by the shopkeeper, who opened the ginger-beer
bottle and poured some of the contents over the ice cream which was contained in a
tumbler.   The appellant drank part of the mixture and her friend then proceeded to
E   pour the remaining contents of the bottle into the tumbler.   As she was doing so a
decomposed snail floated out with the ginger-beer.   In consequence of her having
drunk part of the contaminated contents of the bottle the appellant alleges that she
contracted a serious illness.   The bottle is stated to have been of dark opaque glass, so
that the condition of the contents could not be ascertained by inspection, and to have
been closed with a metal cap, while on the side was a label bearing the name of the
F   respondent, who was the manufacturer of the ginger-beer, of which the shopkeeper was
merely the retailer.
The allegations of negligence on which the appellant founds her action against the
respondent may be shortly summarised.   She says that the ginger-beer was manufactured by the respondent for sale as an article of drink to members of the public
including herself: that the presence of a decomposing snail in ginger-beer renders
G   the ginger-beer harmful and dangerous to those consuming it; and that it was
the duty of the respondent to exercise his process of manufacture with sufficient
care to prevent snails from getting into or remaining in the bottles which he filled
with ginger-beer.   The appellant attacks the respondent's system of conducting his
business, alleging that he kept his bottles in premises to which snails had access,
and that he failed to have his bottles properly inspected for the presence of foreign
H   matter before he filled them.   The respondent challenged the relevancy of the
appellant's averments and, taking them pro veritate, as for this purpose he was bound to
do, pleaded that they disclosed no ground of legal liability on his part to the appellant.
The Lord Ordinary repelled the respondent's plea to the relevancy and allowed the
parties a proof of their averments, but on a reclaiming note their Lordships of the
Second Division (LORD HUNTER dissenting, or, perhaps more accurately, protesting)
I   dismissed the action, and in doing so followed their decision in the previous cases of
Mullen v. *Barr & Co.* and *McGowan* v. *Barr & Co.* (16).   The only difference in fact
between those cases and the present case is that it was a mouse and not a snail which
was found in the ginger-beer.   The present appeal is, consequently, in effect against the
decision in these previous cases, which I now proceed to examine.
The two cases, being to all intents and purposes identical, were heard and decided
together.   In *Mullen* v. *Barr & Co.* (16) the sheriff-substitute allowed a proof, but the
sheriff on appeal dismissed the action as irrelevant.   In *McGowan* v. *Barr & Co.* (16) the
sheriff-substitute allowed a proof and the sheriff altered his interlocutor by allowing

a proof before answer—that is to say, a proof under reservation of all objections to the **A**
relevancy of the action.   On the cases coming before the Second Division on the appeals
of the pursuer and the defenders respectively their Lordships ordered a proof before
answer in each case and the evidence was taken before LORD HUNTER.   It will be
sufficient to refer to *Mullen's Case* (16), in which their Lordships gave their reasons for
assoilzieing the defenders in both cases.   The LORD JUSTICE CLERK held that negligence
had not been proved, and, therefore, he did not pronounce upon the question of **B**
relevancy.   LORD ORMIDALE held that there was no relevant case against the defenders,
but would have been prepared if necessary to hold that in any case negligence had not
been established by the evidence.   LORD HUNTER held that the case was relevant and
that negligence had been proved.   LORD ANDERSON held that the pursuer had no case
in law against the defenders, but that, if this view was erroneous, negligence had not
been proved.   **C**
    I desire to draw special attention to certain passages in the opinions of their Lordships.
At 1929 S.C., p. 470, the learned LORD JUSTICE CLERK states that he prefers

> "to base my judgment on the proposition that the pursuer has failed to prove fault
> on the part of the defenders" [and feels] "absolved from expressing a concluded
> opinion on the thorny and difficult question of law whether, assuming fault to be
> proved on the part of the defenders, the pursuer has in law a right to sue them."   **D**

In the present case his Lordship, after pointing out that he had formally reserved his
opinion on the point in *Mullen v. Barr & Co.* (16), proceeds:

> "I think I indicated not obscurely the view which I entertained on a perusal of the
> English cases,"

and to that view, in deference to the English cases which his Lordship has re-considered,   **E**
he has given effect adversely to the present appellant.   That the opinions of the majority
of the judges of the Second Division in *Mullen's Case* (16) on the question of relevancy
are founded entirely on their reading of the series of English cases cited to them is made
clear by LORD ORMIDALE.   After stating the questions in the case, the first being

> "whether in the absence of any contractual relation between the pursuers and the   **F**
> defenders, the latter owed a duty to the pursuers, as the consumers of the beer, of
> taking precautions to see that nothing of a poisonous or deleterious nature was
> allowed to enter and remain in the bottles,"

his Lordship proceeds:

> "I recognise the difficulty of determining the first of these questions with either con-   **G**
> fidence or satisfaction; and were it not for the unbroken and consistent current of
> decisions beginning with *Winterbottom* v. *Wright* (3) to which we were referred I
> should have been disposed to answer it in the affirmative.   The evidence shows that
> the greatest care is taken by the manufacturers to ensure by tab and label that the
> ginger-beer should pass, as it were, from the hand of the maker to the hand of the
> ultimate user uninterfered with by the retail dealer—who has little interest in, and   **H**
> no opportunity of, examining the contents of the containers.   Accordingly, it would
> appear to be reasonable and equitable to hold that, in the circumstances and apart
> altogether from contract, there exists a relationship of duty as between the maker
> and the consumer of the beer.   Such considerations, however, as I read the autho-
> rities, have been held to be irrelevant in analogous circumstances."

LORD ORMIDALE thus finds himself constrained to reach a conclusion which appears to **I**
him to be contrary to reason and equity by his reading of what he describes as an
"unbroken and consistent current of decisions beginning with *Winterbottom* v. *Wright* (3)."
In view of the defence thus paid to English precedents, it is a singular fact that the
case of *Winterbottom* v. *Wright* (3) is one in which no negligence in the sense of breach
of a duty owed by the defendant to the plaintiff was alleged on the part of the plaintiff.
The truth, as I hope to show, is that there is in the English reports no such "unbroken
and consistent current of decisions" as would justify the aspersion that the law of
England has committed itself irrevocably to what is neither reasonable nor equitable,

A   or require a Scottish judge in following them to do violence to his conscience. "In my opinion," said Lord Esher in *Emmens* v. *Pottle* (32) (16 Q.B.D. at pp. 357–358),

"any proposition the result of which would be to show that the common law of England is wholly unreasonable and unjust cannot be part of the common law of England."

B   At your Lordships' Bar counsel for both parties to the present appeal, accepting, as I do also, the view that there is no distinction between the law of Scotland and the law of England in the legal principles applicable to the case, confined their arguments to the English authorities. The appellant endeavoured to establish that according to the law of England the pleadings disclose a good cause of action; the respondent endeavoured to show that on the English decisions the appellant had stated no admissible case. I C propose, therefore, to address myself at once to an examination of the relevant English precedents.

I observe in the first place that there is no decision of this House upon the point at issue, for I agree with Lord Hunter that such cases as *Cavalier* v. *Pope* (27) and *Cameron and others* v. *Young* (33) which decided that

D   "a stranger to a lease cannot found upon a landlord's failure to fulfil obligations undertaken by him under contract with his lessee,"

are in a different chapter of the law. Nor can it by any means be said that the cases present "an unbroken and consistent current" of authority, for some flow one way and some the other.

It humbly appears to me that the diversity of view which is exhibited in such cases E   as *George* v. *Skivington* (5) on the one hand, and *Blacker* v. *Lake and Elliot* (4) on the other hand—to take two extreme instances—is explained by the fact that in the discussion of the topic which now engages your Lordships' attention two rival principles of the law find a meeting place where each has contended for supremacy. On the one hand, there is the well-established principle that no one other than a party to a contract can complain of a breach of that contract. On the other hand, there is the equally F   well-established doctrine that negligence, apart from contract, gives a right of action to the party injured by that negligence—and here I use the term negligence, of course, in its technical legal sense, implying a duty owed and neglected. The fact that there is a contractual relationship between the parties which may give rise to an action for breach of contract does not exclude the co-existence of a right of action founded on negligence as between the same parties independently of the contract though arising G   out of the relationship in fact brought about by the contract. Of this the best illustration is the right of the injured railway passenger to sue the railway company either for breach of the contract of safe carriage or for negligence in carrying him. And there is no reason why the same set of facts should not give one person a right of action in contract and another person a right of action in tort. I may be permitted to adopt as my own the language of a very distinguished English writer on this subject.

H   "It appears, [says Sir Frederick Pollock (Law of Torts (13th Edn.) 570)] that there has been (though, perhaps, there is no longer) a certain tendency to hold that facts which constitute a contract cannot have any other legal effect. The authorities formerly relied on for this proposition really proved something different and much more rational, namely, that if A. breaks his contract with B. (which may happen without any personal default in A. or A.'s servants), that is not I   of itself sufficient to make A. liable to C., a stranger to the contract, for consequential damage. This, and only this, is the substance of the perfectly correct decisions of the Court of Exchequer in *Winterbottom* v. *Wright* (3) and *Longmeid* v. *Holliday* (2). In each case the defendant delivered, under a contract of sale or hiring, a chattel which was in fact unsafe to use, but in the one case it was not alleged, in the other was alleged but not proved, to have been so to his knowledge. In each case a stranger to the contract, using the chattel—a coach in the one case, a lamp in the other—in the ordinary way, came to harm through its dangerous condition, and was held not to have any cause of action against the

A

purveyor. Not in contract, for there was no contract between these parties; not in tort, for no bad faith or negligence on the defendant's part was proved.''

Where, as in cases like the present, so much depends upon the avenue of approach to the question it is very easy to take the wrong turning. If you begin with the sale by the manufacturer to the retail dealer, then the consumer who purchases from the retailer is at once seen to be a stranger to the contract between the retailer and the manufacturer and so disentitled to sue upon it. There is no contractual relation between the manufacturer and the consumer, and thus the plaintiff if he is to succeed is driven to try to bring himself within one or other of the exceptional cases where the strictness of the rule that none but a party to a contract can found on a breach of that contract has been mitigated in the public interest, as it has been in the case of a person who issues a chattel which is inherently dangerous or which he knows to be in a dangerous condition. If, on the other hand, you disregard the fact that the circumstances of the case at one stage include the existence of a contract of sale between the manufacturer and the retailer and approach the question by asking whether there is evidence of carelessness on the part of the manufacturer and whether he owed a duty to be careful in a question with the party who has been injured in consequence of his want of care, the circumstance that the injured party was not a party to the incidental contract of sale becomes irrelevant and his title to sue the manufacturer is unaffected by that circumstance. The appellant in the present instance asks that her case be approached as a case of delict, not as a case of breach of contract. She does not require to invoke the exceptional cases in which a person not a party to a contract has been held to be entitled to complain of some defect in the subject-matter of the contract which has caused him harm. The exceptional case of things dangerous in themselves or known to be in a dangerous condition has been regarded as constituting a peculiar category outside the ordinary law both of contract and of tort. I may observe that it seems to me inaccurate to describe the case of dangerous things as an exception to the principle that no one but a party to a contract can sue on that contract. I rather regard this type of case as a special instance of negligence where the law exacts a degree of diligence so stringent as to amount practically to a guarantee of safety.

With these preliminary observations I turn to the series of English cases which is said to compose the consistent body of authority on which we are asked to non-suit the appellant. It will be found that in most of them the facts were very different from the facts of the present case and did not give rise to the special relationship and consequent duty which, in my opinion, is the deciding factor here. *Dixon* v. *Bell* (22) is the starting point. There a maidservant was sent to fetch a gun from a neighbour's house; on the way back she pointed it at a child and the gun went off and injured the child. The owner of the gun was held liable for the injury to the child on the ground that he should have seen that the charge was drawn before he entrusted the gun to the maidservant.

"It was incumbent on him who, by charging the gun, had made it capable of doing mischief to render it safe and innoxious.''

This case, in my opinion, merely illustrates the high degree of care, amounting in effect to insurance against risk, which the law exacts from those who take the responsibility of giving out such dangerous things as loaded firearms. The decision, if it has any relevance, is favourable to the appellant, who submits that human drink, rendered poisonous by careless preparation, may be as dangerous to life as any loaded firearm.

Langridge v. *Levy* (1) is another case of a gun, this time of defective make and known to the vendor to be defective. The purchaser's son was held entitled to sue for damages in consequence of injuries sustained by him through the defective condition of the gun causing it to explode. The ground of the decision seems to have been that there was a false representation by the vendor that the gun was safe, and the representation appears to have been held to extend to the purchaser's son. The case is treated by commentators as turning on its special circumstances and as not deciding any principle of general application. As for *Winterbottom* v. *Wright* (3) and *Longmeid* v. *Holliday* (2) neither of these cases is really in point for the reason indicated in the passage from Sir FREDERICK POLLOCK's treatise which I have quoted above.

A   Then comes *George* v. *Skivington* (5), which is entirely in favour of the appellant's contention.   There was a sale in that case by a chemist of some hairwash to a purchaser for the use of his wife, who suffered injury from using it by reason of its having been negligently compounded.   As Kelly, C.B., points out, the action was not founded on any warranty implied in the contract of sale between the vendor and the purchaser, and the plaintiff, the purchaser's wife, was not seeking to sue on the contract, to which she
B   was not a party.   The question, as the Chief Baron stated it, was

> "whether the defendant, a chemist, compounding the article sold for a particular purpose, and knowing of the purpose for which it was bought, is liable in an action on the case for unskilfulness and negligence in the manufacture of it whereby the person who used it was injured."

C   And this question the court unanimously answered in the affirmative.   I may mention in passing that Lord Atkinson in this House, speaking of that case and *Langridge* v. *Levy* (1), observed in *Cavalier* v. *Pope* (27) ([1906] A.C. at p. 433) that

> "in both these latter cases the defendant represented that the article sold was fit and proper for the purposes for which it was contemplated that it should be used, and the party injured was ignorant of its unfitness for these purposes."

D   It is true that *George* v. *Skivington* (5) has been the subject of some criticism and was said by Hamilton, J., as he then was, in *Blacker* v. *Lake and Elliot, Ltd.* (4), to have been in later cases as nearly disaffirmed as is possible without being expressly overruled. I am not sure that it has been so severely handled as that.   At any rate, I do not think that it deserved to be, and, certainly, so far as I am aware, it has never been, disapproved in this House.
E   *Heaven* v. *Pender* (8) has probably been more quoted and discussed in this branch of the law than any other authority, because of the dicta of Brett, M.R., as he then was, on the general principles regulating liability to third parties.   In his opinion,

> "it may safely be affirmed to be a true proposition [that] wherever one person is by circumstances placed in such a position with regard to another that everyone of
F   ordinary sense who did think would at once recognise that if he did not use ordinary care and skill in his own conduct with regard to those circumstances he would cause danger of injury to the person or property of the other, a duty arises to use ordinary care and skill to avoid such danger."

The passage specially applicable to the present case is as follows:

> "Whenever one person supplies goods . . . for the purpose of their being used by
G   another person under such circumstances that everyone of ordinary sense would, if he thought, recognise at once that, unless he used ordinary care and skill with regard to the condition of the thing supplied or the mode of supplying it, there will be danger of injury to the person or property of him for whose use the thing is supplied, and who is to use it, a duty arises to use ordinary care and skill as to the condition or manner of supplying such thing.   And for a neglect of such ordinary
H   care or skill whereby injury happens a legal liability arises, to be enforced by an action for negligence."

Cotton, L.J., with whom Bowen, L.J., agreed, expressed himself as

> "unwilling to concur with the Master of the Rolls in laying down unnecessarily the larger principle which he entertains, inasmuch as there are many cases in which
I   the principle was impliedly negatived,"

but the decision of the Court of Appeal was unanimously in the plaintiff's favour.   The passages I have quoted, like all attempts to formulate principles of law compendiously and exhaustively, may be open to some criticism, and their universality may require some qualification, but as enunciations of general legal doctrine, I am prepared, like Lord Hunter, to accept them as sound guides.
I now pass to the three modern cases of *Earl* v. *Lubbock* (12), *Blacker* v. *Lake and Elliot, Ltd.* (4), and *Bates and another* v. *Batey & Co., Ltd.* (13).   The first of these cases related to a van which had recently been repaired by the defendant under contract

with the owner of the van.   A driver in the employment of the owner was injured in   **A**
consequence of a defect in the van which was said to be due to the careless manner in
which the repairer had done his work.   It was held that the driver had no right of action
against the repairer.   The case turns upon the rule that a stranger to a contract cannot
found an action of tort on a breach of that contract.   It was pointed out that there was
no evidence that the plaintiff had been invited by the defendant to use the van and the
van owner was not complaining of the way in which the van had been repaired.   The   **B**
negligence, if negligence there was, was too remote, and the practical consequences of
affirming liability in such a case were considered to be such as would render it difficult
to carry on a trade at all.

"No prudent man [says MATHEW, L.J.] would contract to make or repair what the
employer intended to permit others to use in the way of his trade."   **C**

The special facts in that case seem to me to differ widely from the circumstances of the
present case, where the manufacturer has specifically in view the use and consumption
of his products by the consumer and where the retailer is merely the vehicle of trans-
mission of the products to the consumer and by the nature of the products is precluded
from inspecting or interfering with them in any way.

Blacker v. *Lake and Elliot* (4) is of importance because of the survey of previous   **D**
decisions which it contains.   It related to a brazing lamp which, by exploding owing to
a latent defect, injured a person other than the purchaser of it, and the vendor was held
not liable to the party injured.   There appears to have been some difference of opinion
between HAMILTON, J., and LUSH, J., who heard the case in the Divisional Court,
whether the lamp was an inherently dangerous thing.   The case seems to have turned
largely on the question whether, there being a contract for sale of the lamp between the   **E**
vendor and the purchaser, the article was of such a dangerous character as to impose
upon the vendor in a question with a third party any responsibility for its condition.
This question was answered in the negative.   So far as negligence was concerned, it may
well have been regarded as too remote, for I find that HAMILTON, J., used these words
(106 L.T. at p. 537):
   F
"In the present case all that can be said is that the defendants did not know that
their lamp was not perfectly safe and had no reason to believe that it was not so in
the sense that no one had drawn their attention to the fact, but that had they been
wiser men or more experienced engineers they would then have known what the
plaintiff's experts say that they ought to have known."

I should doubt indeed if that is really a finding of negligence at all.   The case on its   **G**
facts is very far from the present one, and if any principle of general application can be
derived from it adverse to the appellant's contention I should not be disposed to approve
of such principle.   I may add that in *White and wife* v. *Steadman* (34) ([1913] 3 K.B.
at p. 348) I find that LUSH, J., who was a party to the decision in *Blacker* v. *Lake and
Elliot, Ltd.* (4), expressed the view that
   H
"a person who has the means of knowledge and only does not know that the
animal or chattel which he supplies is dangerous because he does not take ordinary
care to avail himself of his opportunity of knowledge is in precisely the same position as the person who knows."

As for *Bates* v. *Batey & Co., Ltd.* (13), where a ginger-beer bottle burst owing to a defect
in it which, though unknown to the manufacturer of the ginger-beer, could have been   **I**
discovered by him by the exercise of reasonable care, HORRIDGE, J., there held that the
plaintiff who bought the bottle of ginger-beer from a retailer to whom the manufacturer
had sold it and who was injured by its explosion had no right to action against the
manufacturer.   The case does not advance matters, for it really turns upon the fact
that the manufacturer did not know that the bottle was defective, and this, in the view
of HORRIDGE, J., as he read the authorities, was enough to absolve the manufacturer.
I would observe that in a true case of negligence knowledge of the existence of the defect
causing damage is not an essential element at all.

A   This summary survey is sufficient to show what more detailed study confirms, that the current of authority has by no means always set in the same direction. In addition to *George* v. *Skivington* (5) there is the American case of *Thomas* v. *Winchester* (14), which has met with considerable acceptance in this country and which is distinctly on the side of the appellant. There a chemist carelessly issued, in response to an order for extract of dandelion, a bottle containing belladonna which he labelled "extract of

B   dandelion," with the consequence that a third party who took a dose from the bottle suffered severely. The chemist was held responsible. This case is quoted by Lord Dunedin in giving the judgment of the Privy Council in *Dominion Natural Gas Co.* v. *Collins* (6) as an instance of liability to third parties, and I think it was a sound decision.

In the American courts the law has advanced considerably in the development of the principle exemplified in *Thomas* v. *Winchester* (14). In one of the latest cases in

C   the United States, *McPherson* v. *Buick Motor Co.* (15), the plaintiff, who had purchased from a retailer a motor car, manufactured by the defendant company, was injured in consequence of a defect in the construction of the car and was held entitled to recover damages from the manufacturer. Cardozo, J., the very eminent Chief Judge of the New York Court of Appeals, and now an associate justice of the United States Supreme Court, thus stated the law:

D
"There is no claim that the defendant knew of the defect and wilfully concealed it. . . . The charge is one not of fraud but of negligence. The question to be determined is whether the defendant owed a duty of care and vigilance to anyone but the immediate purchaser. . . . The principle of *Thomas* v. *Winchester* (14) is not limited to poisons, explosives, and things of like nature, to things which in their normal operation are implements of destruction. If the nature of a thing

E   is such that it is reasonably certain to place life and limb in peril when negligently made, it is then a thing of danger. Its nature gives warning of the consequences to be expected. If to the element of danger there is added knowledge that the thing will be used by persons other than the purchaser, and used without new tests, then, irrespective of contract, the manufacturer of this thing of danger is under a duty to make it carefully. That is as far as we are required to go for the

F   decision of this case. There must be knowledge of a danger, not merely possible, but probable. . . . There must also be knowledge that in the usual course of events the danger will be shared by others than the buyer. Such knowledge may often be inferred from the nature of the transaction. . . . The dealer was indeed the one person of whom it might be said with some approach to certainty that by him the car would not be used. Yet the defendant would have us say that he

G   was the one person whom it [the defendant company] was under a legal duty to protect. The law does not lead us to so inconsequent a conclusion."

The prolonged discussion of English and American cases into which I have been led might well dispose your Lordships to think that I have forgotten that the present is a Scottish appeal, which must be decided according to Scots law. But this discussion

H   has been rendered inevitable by the course of the argument at your Lordships' Bar, which, as I have said, proceeded on the footing that the law applicable to the case was the same in England and Scotland. Having regard to the inconclusive state of the authorities in the courts below, and to the fact that the important question involved is now before your Lordships for the first time, I think it desirable to consider the matter from the point of view of the principles applicable to this branch of law which are

I   admittedly common to both English and Scottish jurisprudence.

The law takes no cognizance of carelessness in the abstract. It concerns itself with carelessness only where there is a duty to take care and where failure in that duty has caused damage. In such circumstances carelessness assumes the legal quality of negligence and entails the consequences in law of negligence. What then are the circumstances which give rise to this duty to take care? In the daily contacts of social and business life human beings are thrown into or place themselves in an infinite variety of relationships with their fellows, and the law can refer only to the standards of the reasonable man in order to determine whether any particular relationship gives rise to a duty to take care as between those who stand in that relationship to each other. The **A** grounds of action may be as various and manifold as human errancy, and the conception of legal responsibility may develop in adaptation to altering social conditions and standards. The criterion of judgment must adjust and adapt itself to the changing circumstances of life. The categories of negligence are never closed. The cardinal principle of liability is that the party complained of should owe to the party complaining a duty to take care and that the party complaining should be able to prove **B** that he has suffered damage in consequence of a breach of that duty. Where there is room for diversity of view is in determining what circumstances will establish such a relationship between the parties as to give rise on the one side to a duty to take care and on the other side to a right to have care taken.

To descend from these generalities to the circumstances of the present case I do not think that any reasonable man or any twelve reasonable men would hesitate to hold **C** that if the appellant establishes her allegations the respondent has exhibited carelessness in the conduct of his business. For a manufacturer of aerated water to store his empty bottles in a place where snails can get access to them and to fill his bottles without taking any adequate precautions by inspection or otherwise to ensure that they contain no deleterious foreign matter may reasonably be characterised as carelessness without applying too exacting a standard. But, as I have pointed out, it is **D** not enough to prove the respondent to be careless in his process of manufacture. The question is: Does he owe a duty to take care, and to whom does he owe that duty? I have no hesitation in affirming that a person who for gain engages in the business of manufacturing articles of food and drink intended for consumption by members of the public in the form in which he issues them is under a duty to take care in the manufacture of these articles. That duty, in my opinion, he owes to those whom he **E** intends to consume his products. He manufactures his commodities for human consumption; he intends and contemplates that they shall be consumed. By reason of that very fact he places himself in a relationship with all the potential consumers of his commodities, and that relationship, which he assumes and desires for his own ends, imposes upon him a duty to take care to avoid injuring them. He owes them a duty not to convert by his own carelessness an article which he issues to them as wholesome and **F** innocent into an article which is dangerous to life and health.

It is sometimes said that liability can arise only where a reasonable man would have foreseen and could have avoided the consequences of his act or omission. In the present case the respondent, when he manufactured his ginger-beer, had directly in contemplation that it would be consumed by members of the public. Can it be said that he could not be expected as a reasonable man to foresee that if he conducted his **G** process of manufacture carelessly he might injure those whom he expected and desired to consume his ginger-beer? The possibility of injury so arising seems to me in no sense so remote as to excuse him from foreseeing it. Suppose that a baker through carelessness allows a large quantity of arsenic to be mixed with a batch of his bread, with the result that those who subsequently eat it are poisoned, could he be heard to say that he owed no duty to the consumers of his bread to take care that it was free from poison, **H** and that, as he did not know that any poison had got into it, his only liability was for breach of warranty under his contract of sale to those who actually bought the poisoned bread from him? Observe that I have said "through carelessness" and thus excluded the case of a pure accident such as may happen where every care is taken. I cannot believe, and I do not believe, that neither in the law of England nor in the law of Scotland is there redress for such a case. The state of facts I have figured might well **I** give rise to a criminal charge, and the civil consequences of such carelessness can scarcely be less wide than its criminal consequences. Yet the principle of the decision appealed from is that the manufacturer of food products intended by him for human consumption does not owe to the consumers whom he has in view any duty of care, not even the duty to take care that he does not poison them.

The recognition by counsel that the law of Scotland applicable to the case was the same as the law of England implied that there was no special doctrine of Scots law which either the appellant or the respondent could invoke to support her or his case, and

A your Lordships have thus been relieved of the necessity of a separate consideration of the law of Scotland.   For myself I am satisfied that there is no speciality of Scots law involved, and that the case may safely be decided on principles common to both systems. I am happy to think that in their relation to the practical problem of everyday life which this appeal presents the legal systems of the two countries are in no way at variance and that the principles of both alike are sufficiently consonant with justice and

B common sense to admit of the claim which appellant seeks to establish.

I am anxious to emphasise that the principle of judgment which commends itself to me does not give rise to the sort of objection stated by PARKE, B., in *Longmeid v. Holliday* (2), where he said (6 Exch. at p. 768):

C "But it would be going much too far to say that so much care is required in the ordinary intercourse of life between one individual and another, that if a machine not in its nature dangerous—a carriage for instance—but which might become so by a latent defect entirely unknown, although discoverable by the exercise of ordinary care, should be lent or given by one person, even by the person who manufactured it, to another, the former should be answerable to the latter for a subsequent damage accruing by the use of it."

D I read this passage rather as a note of warning that the standard of care exacted in the dealings of human beings with one another must not be pitched too high than as giving any countenance to the view that negligence may be exhibited with impunity.   It must always be a question of circumstances whether the carelessness amounts to negligence and whether the injury is not too remote from the carelessness.   I can readily conceive that where a manufacturer has parted with his product and it has passed into

E other hands it may well be exposed to vicissitudes which may render it defective or noxious and for which the manufacturer could not in any view be held to be to blame. It may be a good general rule to regard responsibility as ceasing when control ceases. So also where between the manufacturer and the user there is interposed a party who has the means and opportunity of examining the manufacturer's product before he re-issues it to the actual user.   But where, as in the present case, the article of consumption

F is so prepared as to be intended to reach the consumer in the condition in which it leaves the manufacturer and the manufacturer takes steps to ensure this by sealing or otherwise closing the container, so that the contents cannot be tampered with, I regard his control as remaining effective until the article reaches the consumer and the container is opened by him.   The intervention of any exterior agency is intended to be excluded, and was in fact in the present case excluded.   It is doubtful whether in such

G a case there is any redress against the retailer: *Gordon v. M'Hardy* (31).

The burden of proof must always be upon the injured party to establish that the defect which caused the injury was present in the article when it left the hands of the party whom he sues, that the defect was occasioned by the carelessness of that party, and that the circumstances are such as to cast upon the defender a duty to take care not to injure the pursuer.   There is no presumption of negligence in such a case as the

H present, nor is there any justification for applying the maxim res ipsa loquitur.   Negligence must be both averred and proved.   The appellant accepts this burden of proof and, in my opinion, she is entitled to have an opportunity of discharging it if she can. I am, accordingly, of opinion that this appeal should be allowed, the judgment of the Second Division of the Court of Session reversed, and the judgment of the Lord Ordinary restored.

I *Appeal allowed.*

Solicitors: *Horner & Horner*, for *W. G. Leechman & Co.*, Glasgow and Edinburgh; *Lawrence Jones & Co.*, for *Niven, Macniven & Co.*, Glasgow, and *Macpherson & Mackay*, W.S., Edinburgh.

[*Reported by* E. J. M. CHAPLIN, ESQ., *Barrister-at-Law.*]

Hedley Byrne & Co Ltd v Heller & Partners Ltd

[1963] 2 All ER 575

Established liability for negligent advice.

HEDLEY BYRNE & CO., LTD. *v.* HELLER & PARTNERS, LTD.

D [HOUSE OF LORDS (Lord Reid, Lord Morris of Borth-y-Gest, Lord Hodson, Lord Devlin and Lord Pearce), February 25, 26, 27, 28, March 4, 5, 6, 7, May 28, 1963.]

Negligence—Duty to take care—Statements—Information or advice—Knowledge of informant or advisor that he was being trusted or that reliance was placed on his skill or judgment—Whether duty to exercise care imposed on person
E *giving information or advice.*

Bank—Statement in answer to inquiry—Financial references given honestly but without due care—Bank giving references to other bank—Use by second bank's customer expected—First bank financing customer whose reference given—Whether first bank liable to second bank's customer.

F If, in the ordinary course of business or professional affairs, a person seeks information or advice from another, who is not under contractual or fiduciary obligation to give the information or advice, in circumstances in which a reasonable man so asked would know that he was being trusted, or that his skill or judgment was being relied on, and the person asked chooses to give the information or advice without clearly so qualifying his answer as to show that he does not accept responsibility, then the person replying accepts a legal duty to exercise such care as the circumstances
G require in making his reply; and for a failure to exercise that care an action for negligence will lie if damage results (see p. 583, letter D, p. 588, letter I, to p. 589, letter A, p. 590, letter B, p. 594, letter C, p. 598, letter A, p. 601, letter B, p. 606, letter H, p. 610, letters E to H, and p. 617, letter G, *post*).

Cann v. *Willson* ((1888), 39 Ch.D. 39), *Fish* v. *Kelly* ((1864), 17 C.B.N.S.
H 194), approved.

Nocton v. *Lord Ashburton* ([1914-15] All E.R. Rep. 45), *Robinson* v. *National Bank of Scotland* (1916 S.C. (H.L.) 154), and view of DENNING, L.J., dissenting in *Candler* v. *Crane, Christmas & Co.* ([1951] 1 All E.R., see, e.g., at p. 432, letter A) applied.

Candler v. *Crane, Christmas & Co.* ([1951] 1 All E.R. 426) and *Le Lievre*
I v. *Gould*, ([1893] 1 Q.B. 491) disapproved.

A bank inquired by telephone of the respondent merchant bankers concerning the financial position of a customer for whom the respondents were bankers. The bank said that they wanted to know in confidence and without responsibility on the part of the respondents, the respectability and standing of E. Ltd., and whether E. Ltd. would be good for an advertising contract for £8,000 to £9,000. Some months later the bank wrote to the respondents asking in confidence the respondents' opinion of the respectability and standing of E. Ltd. by stating whether the respondents

32

considered E. Ltd. trustworthy, in the way of business, to the extent of A
£100,000 per annum. The respondents' replies to the effect that E. Ltd.
was respectably constituted and considered good for its normal business
engagements were communicated to the bank's customers, the appellants.
Relying on these replies the appellants, who were advertising agents, placed
orders for advertising time and space for E. Ltd., on which orders the
appellants assumed personal responsibility for payment to the television and B
newspaper companies concerned. E. Ltd. went into liquidation and the
appellants lost over £17,000 on the advertising contracts. The appellants
sued the respondents for the amount of the loss, alleging that the respondents' replies to the bank's inquiries were given negligently, in the sense
of misjudgment, by making a statement which gave a false impression as
to E. Ltd.'s credit. Negligence was found at the trial and contested on C
appeal; the appeal was determined, however, on the assumption that there
had been negligence, but without deciding whether there had or had not
been negligence.

Held: although in the present case, but for the respondents' disclaimer,
the circumstances might have given rise to a duty of care on their part,
yet their disclaimer of responsibility for their replies on the occasion of the D
first inquiry was adequate to exclude the assumption by them of a legal
duty of care, with the consequence that they were not liable in negligence
(see p. 586, letter H, p. 595, letter A, p. 599, letter D, p. 613, letter D, and
p. 618, letter C, post).

Robinson v. *National Bank of Scotland* (1916 S.C. (H.L.) 154) applied.

SEMBLE (per LORD REID, LORD MORRIS OF BORTH-Y-GEST and LORD E
HODSON) in the absence of special circumstances requiring particular search
and consideration on the part of a bank giving to another bank a reference
concerning a customer's credit-worthiness there is no legal duty on the
replying bank beyond that of giving an honest answer (see p. 594, letter I,
to p. 595, letter A, p. 586, letter G, and p. 600, letter B, post; cf. p. 613,
letter B, and p. 618, letter D, post). F

Decision of the COURT OF APPEAL ([1961] 3 All E.R. 891) affirmed, but
not on the same ground.

[**Editorial Note.** The statement of principle at p. 575, letter F, ante represents
an endeavour to combine the reasons of all the opinions delivered, but is based
principally on the formulation made by LORD REID; attention is drawn in this
connexion to LORD DEVLIN'S words regarding the circumstances which give G
rise to a relation where a legal duty to exercise care in giving information exists—
" I am prepared ", he said, " to adopt any one of your lordships' statements as
showing the general rule; and I pay the same respect to the statement by
DENNING, L.J., in his dissenting judgment in *Candler* v. *Crane, Christmas & Co.*
([1951] 1 All E.R. 426, see e.g., at p. 433) about circumstances in which he says
a duty to use care in making a statement exists " (see p. 611, letter C, post). H

It may be convenient to summarise here the characteristics principally distinguishing this case from other actions for negligence, namely, that it was an
action for negligence in word, not deed, causing financial loss, not physical
damage, and to mention, by way of distinction, some other causes of action (apart
from defamation) on which liability in damages for misstatement may be founded,
viz., breach of contract or fiduciary relation and fraud. The present decision shows I
that a duty to exercise proper care may arise either out of special relationship of a
general character, e.g., the relation of solicitor and client or of banker and customer, or out of a particular relationship created ad hoc (see, e.g., p. 611, letter G,
post).

As to the arising of a duty to take reasonable care, see 28 HALSBURY'S LAWS
(3rd Edn.) 7, para. 4, p. 20, para. 17; and for cases on the subject, see 36 DIGEST
(Repl.) 12-18, *34-79.*

A   As to bankers answering inquiries as to a customer's financial position, see 2 HALSBURY'S LAWS (3rd Edn.) 241, para. 455; and for cases on the subject, see 3 DIGEST (Repl.) 344, 1115-1117.]

Cases referred to:

B   *Banbury* v. *Bank of Montreal*, [1918-19] All E.R. Rep. 1; [1918] A.C. 626; 87 L.J.K.B. 1158; 119 L.T. 446; 36 Digest (Repl.) 14, *59*.

Candler v. *Crane, Christmas & Co.*, [1951] 1 All E.R. 426; [1951] 2 K.B. 164; 36 Digest (Repl.) 17, *75*.

Cann v. *Willson*, (1888), 39 Ch.D. 39; 57 L.J.Ch. 1034; 59 L.T. 723; 35 Digest 33, *242*.

C   *Coggs* v. *Bernard*, (1703), 1 Sm. L.C. (13th Edn.) 175; 1 Salk. 26; 1 Com. 133; Holt, K.B. 13; 2 Ld. Raym. 909; 3 Salk. 11; 92 E.R. 107; 36 Digest (Repl.) 32, *144*.

Dartnall v. *Howard*, (1825), 4 B. & C. 345; 6 Dow. & Ry. K.B. 438; 3 L.J.O.S.K.B. 246; 107 E.R. 1088; 12 Digest (Repl.) 251, *1947*.

De la Bere v. *Pearson, Ltd.*, [1904-7] All E.R. Rep. 755; [1908] 1 K.B. 280; 77 L.J.K.B. 380; 98 L.T. 71; 36 Digest (Repl.) 44, *235*.

D   *Derry* v. *Peek*, (1889), 14 App. Cas. 337; 58 L.J.Ch. 864; 61 L.T. 265; 54 J.P. 148; *revsg. Peek* v. *Derry*, (1887), 37 Ch.D. 541; 57 L.J.Ch. 347; 59 L.T. 78; 9 Digest (Repl.) 127, *685*.

Donoghue (*or McAlister*) v. *Stevenson*, [1932] All E.R. Rep. 1; [1932] A.C. 562; 1932 S.C. (H.L.) 31; 101 L.J.P.C. 119; 147 L.T. 281; 36 Digest (Repl.) 85, *458*.

E   *Everett* v. *Griffiths*, [1920] 3 K.B. 163; 89 L.J.K.B. 929; 123 L.T. 280; 84 J.P. 161; *affd.* H.L., [1921] 1 A.C. 631; 90 L.J.K.B. 737; 125 L.T. 230; 85 J.P. 149; 33 Digest 267, *1862*.

Fish v. *Kelly*, (1864), 17 C.B.N.S. 194; 144 E.R. 78; 42 Digest 108, *1032*.

George v. *Skivington*, (1869), L.R. 5 Exch. 1; 39 L.J.Ex. 8; 21 L.T. 495; 39 Digest 441, *705*.

F   *Gladwell* v. *Steggall*, (1839), 5 Bing. N.C. 733; 8 Scott 60; 8 L.J.C.P. 361; 132 E.R. 1283; 34 Digest 549, *80*.

Glanzer v. *Shepard*, (1922), 233 N.Y. 236;

Grant v. *Australian Knitting Mills*, [1935] All E.R. Rep. 209; [1936] A.C. 85; 105 L.J.P.C. 6; 154 L.T. 18; 36 Digest (Repl.) 86, *461*.

G   *Haseldine* v. *Daw & Son, Ltd.*, [1941] 3 All E.R. 156; [1941] 2 K.B. 343; 111 L.J.K.B. 45; 165 L.T. 185; 36 Digest (Repl.) 29, *125*.

Heaven v. *Pender*, (1883), 11 Q.B.D. 503; 52 L.J.Q.B. 702; 49 L.T. 357; 47 J.P. 709; 36 Digest (Repl.) 7, *10*.

Heilbut, Symons & Co. v. *Buckleton*, [1911-13] All E.R. Rep. 83; [1913] A.C. 30; 82 L.J.K.B. 245; 107 L.T. 769; 9 Digest (Repl.) 259, *1643*.

Herschel v. *Mrupe*, 1954 (3) S.A. 464 (South African Law Reports).

H   *Heskell* v. *Continental Express, Ltd.*, [1950] 1 All E.R. 1033; 17 Digest (Repl.) 131, *380*.

Le Lievre v. *Gould*, [1893] 1 Q.B. 491; 62 L.J.Q.B. 353; 68 L.T. 626; 57 J.P. 484; 36 Digest (Repl.) 9, *27*.

Low v. *Bouverie*, [1891] 3 Ch. 82; 60 L.J.Ch. 594; 65 L.J. 533; 43 Digest 852, *3002*.

I   *Morrison Steamship Co., Ltd.* v. *Greystoke Castle (Cargo Owners)*, [1946] 2 All E.R. 696; [1947] A.C. 268; [1947] L.J.R. 297; 176 L.T. 66; 2nd Digest Supp.

Nocton v. *Lord Ashburton*, [1914-15] All E.R. Rep. 45; [1914] A.C. 932; 83 L.J.Ch. 784; 111 L.T. 641; 42 Digest 107, *1017*.

Old Gate Estates, Ltd. v. *Toplis and Harding and Russell*, [1939] 3 All E.R. 209; 161 L.T. 227; 1 Digest (Repl.) 790, *3180*.

Parsons v. *Barclay & Co., Ltd.*, [1908-10] All E.R. Rep. 429; 103 L.T. 196; 3 Digest (Repl.) 344, *1115*.

Pasley v. *Freeman*, (1789), 3 Term Rep. 51; 2 Smith L.C. (12th Edn.) 71; 100   A
      E. R. 450; 1 Digest (Repl.) 27, 205.
Perlman v. *Zoutendyk*, 1934 C.P.D. 151 (South Africa; Cape of Good Hope
      Provincial Division).
Plowright v. *Lambert*, (1885), 52 L.T. 646; 43 Digest 978, *4180*.
Robinson v. *National Bank of Scotland*, 1916 S.C. 46; *affd.* H.L., 1916 S.C.
      (H.L.) 154; 26 Digest (Repl.) 33, *63*.   B
Rutter v. *Palmer*, [1922] All E.R. Rep. 367; [1922] 2 K.B. 87; 91 L.J.K.B. 657;
      127 L.T. 419; 3 Digest (Repl.) 78, *159*.
Scholes v. *Brook*, (1891), 63 L.T. 837; *affd.* C.A., 64 L.T. 674; 35 Digest 53, *477*.
Shiells v. *Blackburne*, (1789), 1 Hy. Bl. 158; 126 E.R. 94; 3 Digest (Repl.) 71,
      111.
Skelton v. *London and North Western Ry. Co.*, (1867), L.R. 2 C.P. 631; 36   C
      L.J.C.P. 249; 16 L.T. 563; 36 Digest (Repl.) 28, *121*.
Tournier v. *National Provincial and Union Bank of England*, [1923] All E.R.
      Rep. 550; [1924] 1 K.B. 461; 93 L.J.K.B. 449; 130 L.T. 682; 32 Digest
      70, *985*.
Ultramares Corpn. v. *Touche*, (1931), 255 N.Y. 170.
Wilkinson v. *Coverdale*, (1793), 1 Esp. 74; 12 Digest (Repl.) 251, *1945*.   D
Woods v. *Martins Bank, Ltd.*, [1958] 3 All E.R. 166; [1959] 1 Q.B. 55; [1958]
      1 W.L.R. 1018; 3 Digest (Repl.) 182, *324*.

Appeal.

This was an appeal from an order of the Court of Appeal (ORMEROD, HARMAN
and PEARSON, L.JJ.) dated Oct. 18, 1961, and reported [1961] 3 All E.R. 891,
dismissing an appeal by the appellants, Hedley Byrne & Co., Ltd., from the   E
judgment of McNAIR, J., dated Dec. 20, 1960, dismissing the claim of the appellants against the respondents, Heller & Partners, Ltd., who were merchant
bankers, for alleged negligence or breach of duty in the giving of two bankers'
references relating to the credit of a customer of the respondents, called Easipower, Ltd. The facts are summarised in the opinion of LORD REID.
                                                                                 F
Gerald Gardiner, Q.C., D. G. A. Lowe and *B. H. Anns* for the appellants.
J. G. Foster, Q.C., J. M. Shaw and *L. J. Blom-Cooper* for the respondents.

The House took time for consideration.
May 28. The following opinions were read.

   LORD REID: My Lords, this case raises the important question whether   G
and in what circumstances a person can recover damages for loss suffered by reason
of his having relied on an innocent but negligent misrepresentation. I cannot do
better than adopt the following statement of the case from the judgment of
McNAIR, J.:

   " This case raised certain interesting questions of law as to the liability of   H
   bankers giving references as to the credit-worthiness of their customers. The
   [appellants] are a firm of advertising agents. The [respondents] are merchant
   bankers. In outline, the [appellants'] case against the [respondents] is that,
   having placed on behalf of a client, Easipower, Ltd., on credit terms substantial orders for advertising time on television programmes and for advertising space in certain newspapers on terms under which they, the [appellants],   I
   became personally liable to the television and newspaper companies, they
   caused inquiries to be made through their own bank of the [respondents] as
   to the credit-worthiness of Easipower, Ltd. who were customers of the
   [respondents] and were given by the [respondents] satisfactory references.
   These references turned out not to be justified, and the [appellants] claim
   that in reliance on the references, which they had no reason to question, they
   refrained from cancelling the orders so as to relieve themselves of their
   current liabilities."

A The appellants, becoming doubtful about the financial position of Easipower, Ltd., got their bank to communicate with the respondents who were Easipower, Ltd.'s bankers. This was done by telephone and the following is a contemporaneous note of the conversation which both parties agree is accurate:

B " Heller & Partners, Ltd. Minute of telephone conversation. Call from National Provincial Bank, Ltd., 15, Bishopsgate, E.C.2. 18.8.58. Person called: L. Heller. re Easipower, Ltd. They wanted to know in confidence, and without responsibility on our part, the respectability and standing of Easipower, Ltd., and whether they would be good for an advertising contract for £8,000 to £9,000. I replied the company recently opened an account with us. Believed to be respectably constituted and considered good for its normal business engagements. The company is a subsidiary of Pena Industries, Ltd.,

C which is in liquidation, but we understand that the managing director, Mr. Williams, is endeavouring to buy the shares of Easipower, Ltd., from the liquidator. We believe that the company would not undertake any commitments they are unable to fulfil."

Some months later the appellants sought a further reference and on Nov. 7, 1958, the city office of National Provincial Bank, Ltd. wrote to the respondents

D in the following terms:

" Dear Sir, We shall be obliged by your opinion in confidence as to the respectability and standing of Easipower, Ltd., 27, Albemarle Street, London, W.1 and by stating whether you consider them trustworthy, in the way of business, to the extent of £100,000 per annum, advertising contract. Yours

E faithfully, . . ."

On Nov. 11, 1958, the respondents replied as follows:

" CONFIDENTIAL

" For your private use and without responsibility on the part of the bank or its officials.

" Dear Sir, In reply to your inquiry of 7th instant. We beg to advise:—

F Re E...................... Ltd. Respectably constituted company, considered good for its ordinary business engagements. Your figures are larger than we are accustomed to see. Yours faithfully, . . . Per pro. Heller & Partners, Ltd."

National Provincial Bank communicated these replies to their customers, the appellants, and it is not suggested that this was improper or not warranted by

G modern custom. The appellants relied on these statements and as a result they lost over £17,000 when Easipower, Ltd. went into liquidation.

The appellants now seek to recover this loss from the respondents as damages on the ground that these replies were given negligently and in breach of the respondents' duty to exercise care in giving them. In his judgment McNAIR, J., said:

H " On the assumption stated above as to the existence of the duty, I have no hesitation in holding (1) that Mr. Heller was guilty of negligence in giving such a reference without making plain—as he did not—that it was intended to be a very guarded reference, and (2) that properly understood according to its ordinary and natural meaning the reference was not justified by facts known to Mr. Heller."

I Before your lordships the respondents were anxious to contest this finding but your lordships found it unnecessary to hear argument on this matter being of opinion that the appeal must fail even if Mr. Heller was negligent. Accordingly I cannot and do not express any opinion on the question whether Mr. Heller was in fact negligent. But I should make it plain that the appellants' complaint is not that Mr. Heller gave his reply without adequate knowledge of the position, nor that he intended to create a false impression, but that what he said was in fact calculated to create a false impression and that he ought to have realised that. The same applies to the respondents' letter of Nov. 11.

McNair, J., gave judgment for the respondents on the ground that they owed **A** no duty of care to the appellants. He said:

" I am accordingly driven to the conclusion by authority binding upon me that no such action lies in the absence of contract or fiduciary relationship. On the facts before me there is clearly no contract, nor can I find a fiduciary relationship. It was urged on behalf of the [appellants] that the facts that Easi-power, Ltd. were heavily indebted to the [respondents] and that the **B** [respondents] might benefit from the advertising campaign financed by the [appellants], were facts from which a special duty to exercise care might be inferred. In my judgment, however, these facts, though clearly relevant on the question of honesty if this had been in issue, are not sufficient to establish any special relationship involving a duty of care even if it was open to extend the sphere of special relationship beyond that of contract and fiduciary **C** relationship."

This judgment was affirmed by the Court of Appeal (1) both because they were bound by authority and because they were not satisfied that it would be reasonable to impose on a banker the obligation suggested.

Before coming to the main question of law it may be well to dispose of an **D** argument that there was no sufficiently close relationship between these parties to give rise to any duty. It is said that the respondents did not know the precise purpose of the inquiries and did not even know whether National Provincial Bank, Ltd. wanted the information for its own use or for the use of a customer: they know nothing of the appellants. I would reject that argument. They knew that the inquiry was in connexion with an advertising contract, and it was at **E** least probable that the information was wanted by the advertising contractors. It seems to me quite immaterial that they did not know who these contractors were: there is no suggestion of any speciality which could have influenced them in deciding whether to give information or in what form to give it. I shall therefore treat this as if it were a case where a negligent misrepresentation is made directly to the person seeking information, opinion or advice, and I shall not **F** attempt to decide what kind or degree of proximity is necessary before there can be a duty owed by the defendant to the plaintiff.

The appellants' first argument was based on *Donoghue (or McAlister)* v. *Stevenson* (2). That is a very important decision, but I do not think that it has any direct bearing on this case. That decision may encourage us to develop existing lines of authority, but it cannot entitle us to disregard them. Apart **G** altogether from authority I would think that the law must treat negligent words differently from negligent acts. The law ought so far as possible to reflect the standards of the reasonable man, and that is what *Donoghue (or McAlister)* v. *Stevenson* (2) sets out to do. The most obvious difference between negligent words and negligent acts is this. Quite careful people often express definite opinions on social or informal occasions, even when they see that others are likely **H** to be influenced by them; and they often do that without taking that care which they would take if asked for their opinion professionally, or in a business connexion. The appellants agree that there can be no duty of care on such occasions, and we were referred to American and South African authorities where that is recognised, although their law appears to have gone much further than ours has yet done. But it is at least unusual casually to put into circulation negligently-made articles which are dangerous. A man might give a friend a negligently-**I** prepared bottle of home-made wine and his friend's guests might drink it with dire results; but it is by no means clear that those guests would have no action against the negligent manufacturer. Another obvious difference is that a negligently-made article will only cause one accident, and so it is not very difficult to find the necessary degree of proximity or neighbourhood between the

(1) [1961] 3 All E.R. 891; [1962] 1 Q.B. 396.
(2) [1932] All E.R. Rep. 1; [1932] A.C. 562.

A negligent manufacturer and the person injured. But words can be broadcast with or without the consent or the foresight of the speaker or writer. It would be one thing to say that the speaker owes a duty to a limited class, but it would be going very far to say that he owes a duty to every ultimate " consumer " who acts on those words to his detriment. It would be no use to say that a speaker or writer owes a duty, but can disclaim responsibility if he wants to. He, like the manu-

B facturer, could make it part of a contract that he is not to be liable for his negli- gence: but that contract would not protect him in a question with a third party at least if the third party was unaware of it.

So it seems to me that there is good sense behind our present law that in general an innocent but negligent misrepresentation gives no cause of action. There must be something more than the mere misstatement. I therefore turn to the authori-

C ties to see what more is required. The most natural requirement would be that expressly or by implication from the circumstances the speaker or writer has undertaken some responsibility, and that appears to me not to conflict with any authority which is binding on this House. Where there is a contract there is no difficulty as regards the contracting parties: the question is whether there is a warranty. The refusal of English law to recognise any jus quaesitum tertio causes

D some difficulties, but they are not relevant here. Then there are cases where a person does not merely make a statement, but performs a gratuitous service. I do not intend to examine the cases about that, but at least they show that in some cases that person owes a duty of care apart from any contract, and to that extent they pave the way to holding that there can be a duty of care in making a state- ment of fact or opinion which is independent of contract.

E Much of the difficulty in this field has been caused by *Derry* v. *Peek* (3). The action was brought against the directors of a company in respect of false state- ments in a prospectus. It was an action of deceit based on fraud and nothing else. But it was held that the directors had believed that their statements were true although they had no reasonable grounds for their belief. The Court of Appeal held that this amounted to fraud in law, but naturally enough this House held

F that there can be no fraud without dishonesty and that credulity is not dishonesty. The question was never really considered whether the facts had imposed on the directors a duty to exercise care. It must be implied that on the facts of that case there was no such duty. But that was immediately remedied by the Directors Liability Act, 1890, which provided that a director is liable for untrue statements in a prospectus unless he proves that he had reasonable ground to believe and did

G believe that they were true.

It must now be taken that *Derry* v. *Peek* (3) did not establish any universal rule that in the absence of contract an innocent but negligent misrepresentation cannot give rise to an action. It is true that Lord Bramwell said (4): " To found an action for damages there must be a contract and breach, or fraud "; and for the next twenty years it was generally assumed that *Derry* v. *Peek* (3)

H decided that. But it was shown in this House in *Nocton* v. *Lord Ashburton* (5) that that is much too widely stated. We cannot therefore now accept as accurate the numerous statements to that effect in cases between 1889 and 1914, and we must now determine the extent of the exceptions to that rule.

In *Nocton* v. *Lord Ashburton* (5) a solicitor was sued for fraud. Fraud was not proved, but he was held liable for negligence. Viscount Haldane, L.C., dealt

I with *Derry* v. *Peek* (3) and pointed out (6) that while the relationship of the parties in that case was not enough, the case did not decide

" that where a different sort of relationship ought to be inferred from the circumstances, the case is to be concluded by asking whether an action for deceit will lie . . . There are other obligations besides that of honesty the breach of which may give a right to damages. These obligations depend on

(3) (1889), 14 App. Cas. 337.   (4) (1889), 14 App. Cas. at p. 347.
(5) [1914-15] All E.R. Rep. 45; [1914] A.C. 932.
(6) [1914-15] All E.R. Rep. at p. 49; [1914] A.C. at p. 947.

A

principles which the judges have worked out in the fashion that is characteristic of a system where much of the law has always been judge-made and
unwritten."

It hardly needed *Donoghue* v. *Stevenson* (7) to show that that process can still
operate. LORD HALDANE (8) quoted a passage from the speech of LORD HERSCHELL
in *Derry* v. *Peek* (9) where he excluded from the principle of that case

B

"those cases where a person within whose special province it lay to know a
particular fact has given an erroneous answer to an inquiry made with regard
to it by a person desirous of ascertaining the fact for the purpose of determining his course."

Then (10) he explained the expression " constructive fraud " and said (10):

C

"What it really means in this connexion is not moral fraud in the ordinary
sense, but breach of the sort of obligation which is enforced by a court which
from the beginning regarded itself as a court of conscience."

He went on (11) to refer to " breach of special duty " and said (11):

"If such a duty can be inferred in a particular case of a person issuing a
prospectus, as, for instance, in the case of directors issuing to the shareholders
of the company which they direct a prospectus inviting the subscription by
them of further capital, I do not find in *Derry* v. *Peek* (12) an authority for
the suggestion that an action for damages for misrepresentation without an
actual intention to deceive may not lie."

D

I find no dissent from these views by the other noble and learned Lords. LORD
SHAW OF DUNFERMLINE also quoted the passage which I have quoted from the
speech of LORD HERSCHELL, and, dealing with equitable relief, he approved (13)
a passage in an argument of Sir Roundell Palmer (14) which concluded (13):

E

"in order that a person may avail himself of relief founded on it he must
show that there was such approximate relation between himself and the
person making the representation as to bring them virtually into the position
of parties contracting with each other ";

F

an interesting anticipation in 1873 of the test of who is my neighbour.

LORD HALDANE gave a further statement of his view in *Robinson* v. *National
Bank of Scotland* (15) a case to which I shall return. Having said that in that
case there was no duty excepting the duty of common honesty, he went on to say
(16):

G

"In saying that I wish emphatically to repeat what I said in advising this
House in the case of *Nocton* v. *Lord Ashburton* (17), that it is a great mistake
to suppose that, because the principle in *Derry* v. *Peek* (12) clearly covers all
cases of the class to which I have referred, therefore the freedom of action of
the courts in recognising special duties arising out of other kinds of relationship which they find established by the evidence is in any way affected. I
think, as I said in *Nocton's* case (17), that an exaggerated view was taken by a
good many people of the scope of the decision in *Derry* v. *Peek* (12). The whole
of the doctrine as to fiduciary relationships, as to the duty of care arising
from implied as well as express contracts, as to the duty of care arising from
other special relationships which the courts may find to exist in particular

H

(7) [1932] All E.R. Rep. 1; [1932] A.C. 562.
(8) [1914-15] All E.R. Rep. at p. 50; [1914] A.C. at p. 950.
(9) (1889), 14 App. Cas. at p. 360.
(10) [1914-15] All E.R. Rep. at p. 53; [1914] A.C. at p. 954.
(11) [1914-15] All E.R. Rep. at p. 53; [1914] A.C. at p. 955.
(12) (1889), 14 App. Cas. 337.
(13) [1914-15] All E.R. Rep. at p. 62; [1914] A.C. at p. 971.
(14) In *Peek* v. *Gurney* (1873), L.R. 13 Eq. 79, at p. 97.
(15) 1916 S.C. (H.L.) 154.   (16) 1916 S.C. (H.L.) at p. 157.
(17) [1914-15] All E.R. Rep. 45; [1914] A.C. 932.

A   cases, still remains, and I should be very sorry if any word fell from me which should suggest that the courts are in any way hampered in recognising that the duty of care may be established when such cases really occur.''

B   This passage makes it clear that LORD HALDANE did not think that a duty to take care must be limited to cases of fiduciary relationship in the narrow sense of relationships which had been recognised by the Court of Chancery as being of a fiduciary character. He speaks of other special relationships, and I can see no logical stopping place short of all those relationships where it is plain that the party seeking information or advice was trusting the other to exercise such a degree of care as the circumstances required, where it was reasonable for him to do that, and where the other gave the information or advice when he knew or ought

C   to have known that the inquirer was relying on him. I say '' ought to have known '' because in questions of negligence we now apply the objective standard of what the reasonable man would have done.

A reasonable man, knowing that he was being trusted or that his skill and judgment were being relied on, would, I think, have three courses open to him. He could keep silent or decline to give the information or advice sought: or he could

D   give an answer with a clear qualification that he accepted no responsibility for it or that it was given without that reflection or inquiry which a careful answer would require: or he could simply answer without any such qualification. If he chooses to adopt the last course he must, I think, be held to have accepted some responsibility for his answer being given carefully, or to have accepted a relationship with the inquirer which requires him to exercise such care as the circumstances require.

E   If that is right then it must follow that *Candler* v. *Crane, Christmas & Co.* (18) was wrongly decided. There the plaintiff wanted to see the accounts of a company before deciding to invest in it. The defendants were the company's accountants and they were told by the company to complete the company's accounts as soon as possible because they were to be shown to the plaintiff who was a potential

F   investor in the company. At the company's request the defendants showed the completed accounts to the plaintiff, discussed them with him, and allowed him to take a copy. The accounts had been carelessly prepared and gave a wholly misleading picture. It was obvious to the defendants that the plaintiff was relying on their skill and judgment and on their having exercised that care which by contract they owed to the company, and I think that any reasonable man in the

G   plaintiff's shoes would have relied on that. This seems to me to be a typical case of agreeing to assume a responsibility: they knew why the plaintiff wanted to see the accounts and why their employers, the company, wanted them to be shown to him, and agreed to show them to him without even a suggestion that he should not rely on them.

The majority of the Court of Appeal held that they were bound by *Le Lievre* v.

H   *Gould* (19) and that *Donoghue* v. *Stevenson* (20) had no application. In so holding I think that they were right. The Court of Appeal have bound themselves to follow all rationes decidendi of previous Court of Appeal decisions, and, in face of that rule, it would have been very difficult to say that the ratio in *Le Lievre* v. *Gould* (19) did not cover *Candler's* case (18). LORD DENNING, who dissented, distinguished *Le Lievre* v. *Gould* (19) on its facts, but, as I understand the rule which the Court of Appeal have adopted, that is not sufficient if the ratio applies;

I   and this is not an appropriate occasion to consider whether the Court of Appeal's rule is a good one. So the question which we now have to consider is whether the ratio in *Le Lievre* v. *Gould* (19) can be supported. But before leaving *Candler's* case (18) I must note that COHEN, L.J. (as he then was), attached considerable importance to a New York decision *Ultramares Corporation* v. *Touche* (21), a decision of CARDOZO, C.J. But I think that another decision of that great judge,

---

(18) [1951] 1 All E.R. 426; [1951] 2 K.B. 164.   (19) [1893] 1 Q.B. 491.
(20) [1932] All E.R. Rep. 1; [1932] A.C. 562.   (21) (1931), 255 N.Y. 170.

Glanzer v. *Shepard* (22), is more in point because in the latter case there was a **A**
direct relationship between the weigher who gave a certificate and the purchaser
of the goods weighed, who the weigher knew was relying on his certificate: there
the weigher was held to owe a duty to the purchaser with whom he had no contract. The *Ultramares* case (23) can be regarded as nearer to *Le Lievre* v. *Gould*
(24).

In *Le Lievre* v. *Gould* (24) a surveyor, Gould, gave certificates to a builder, who **B**
employed him. The plaintiffs were mortgagees of the builders' interest and Gould
knew nothing about them or the terms of their mortgage; but the builder, without
Gould's authority, chose to show them Gould's report. I have said that I do not
intend to decide anything about the degree of proximity necessary to establish
a relationship giving rise to a duty of care, but it would seem difficult to find such
proximity in this case and the actual decision in *Le Lievre* v. *Gould* (24) may there- **C**
fore be correct. The decision, however, was not put on that ground: if it had been
Cann v. *Willson* (25) would not have been overruled. LORD ESHER, M.R., held
that there was no contract between the plaintiffs and the defendant and that this
House in *Derry* v. *Peek* (26) had (27) " restated the old law that, in the absence of
contract, an action for negligence cannot be maintained when there is no fraud ".
BOWEN, L.J., gave a similar reason: he said (28): **D**

" Then *Derry* v. *Peek* (26) decided this further point—viz. that in cases
like the present (of which *Derry* v. *Peek* (26) was itself an instance) there is no
duty enforceable in law to be careful."

He added that the law of England (29)

" does not consider that what a man writes on paper is like a gun or other **E**
dangerous instrument; and, unless he intended to deceive, the law does not,
in the absence of contract, hold him responsible for drawing his certificate
carelessly."

So both he and LORD ESHER held that *Cann* v. *Willson* (25) was wrong in deciding
that there was a duty to take care. We now know on the authority of *Donoghue*
v. *Stephenson* (30) that BOWEN, L.J., was wrong in limiting duty of care to guns **F**
or other dangerous instruments, and I think that, for reasons which I have already
given, he was also wrong in limiting the duty of care with regard to statements to
cases where there is a contract. On both points BOWEN, L.J., was expressing
what was then generally believed to be the law, but later statements in this House
have gone far to remove those limitations. I would therefore hold that the ratio
in *Le Lievre* v. *Gould* (24) was wrong and that *Cann* v. *Willson* (25) ought not to **G**
have been overruled.

Now I must try to apply these principles to the present case. What the appellants complain of is not negligence in the ordinary sense of carelessness, but rather
misjudgment in that Mr. Heller, while honestly seeking to give a fair assessment,
in fact made a statement which gave a false and misleading impression of his
customer's credit. It appears that bankers now commonly give references with **H**
regard to their customers as part of their business. I do not know how far their
customers generally permit them to disclose their affairs, but even with permission
it cannot always be easy for a banker to reconcile his duty to his customer with
his desire to give a fairly balanced reply to an inquiry; and inquirers can hardly
expect a full and objective statement of opinion or accurate factual information
such as skilled men would be expected to give in reply to other kinds of inquiry. **I**
So it seems to me to be unusually difficult to determine just what duty, beyond a
duty to be honest, a banker would be held to have undertaken if he gave a reply
without an adequate disclaimer of responsibility or other warning. It is in light of

(22) (1922), 233 N.Y. 236.   (23) (1931), 255 N.Y. 170.
(24) [1893] 1 Q.B. 491.   (25) (1888), 39 Ch.D. 39.
(26) (1889), 14 App. Cas. 337.   (27) [1893] 1 Q.B. at p. 498.
(28) [1893] 1 Q.B. at p. 501.   (29) [1893] 1 Q.B. at p. 502.
(30) [1932] All E.R. Rep. 1; [1932] A.C. 562.

A such considerations that I approach an examination of the case of *Robinson* v. *National Bank of Scotland* (31).

It is not easy to extract the facts from the report of the case in the Court of Session (32). Several of the witnesses were held to be unreliable and the principal issue in the case, fraud, is not relevant for present purposes. But the position appears to have been this. Harley and two brothers Inglis wished to raise money.

B They approached an insurance company on the false basis that Harley was to be the borrower and the Inglis brothers were to be guarantors. To satisfy the company as to the financial standing of the Inglis brothers Harley got his London bank to write to McArthur, a branch agent of the National Bank of Scotland, and McArthur on July 28, 1910, sent a reply which was ultimately held to be culpably careless but not fraudulent. Robinson, the pursuer in the action, said that he had

C been approached by Harley to become a guarantor before the inquiry was made by Harley but he was disbelieved by the Lord Ordinary who held that he was not brought into the matter before September. This was accepted by the majority in the Inner House and there is no indication that any of their lordships in this House questioned the finding that the letter of July 28, 1910, was not obtained on behalf of Robinson. Harley and the brothers Inglis did not proceed with their

D scheme in July, but they resumed negotiations in September. The company wanted an additional guarantor and Harley approached Robinson. A further reference was asked and obtained from McArthur on Oct. 1 about the brothers Inglis, but no point was made of this. The whole case turned on McArthur's letter of July 28, 1910. After further negotiation the company made a loan to Harley with the brothers Inglis and Robinson as guarantors. Harley and the

E brothers Inglis all became bankrupt and Robinson had to pay the company under his guarantee. Robinson sued the National Bank of Scotland and McArthur. He alleged that McArthur's letter was fraudulent and that he had been induced by it to guarantee the loan. He also alleged that McArthur had a duty to disclose certain facts about the brothers Inglis which were known to him, but this alternative case played a very minor part in the litigation. Long opinions were given in

F the Court of Session on the question of fraud, but the alternative case of a duty to disclose was dealt with summarily. The Lord Justice Clerk (Lord Scott Dickson) said (33):

" It appears to me that there was no such duty of disclosure imposed upon Mr. McArthur towards the pursuer as would justify us in applying the principle on which *Nocton's* case (34) was decided, . . ."

G
Lord Dundas referred (35) to cases of liability of a solicitor to his client for erroneous advice and of similar liability arising from a fiduciary relationship and said " such decisions seem to me to have no bearing on or application to the facts of the present case." He also drew attention to the last sentence of the letter of July 28, 1910, which he said would become important if fraud were out of the case.

H That sentence is: " The above information is to be considered strictly confidential and is given on the express understanding that we incur no responsibility whatever in furnishing it." Lord Salvesen, who dissented, did not deal with the point and Lord Guthrie merely said (36) that here there was no fiduciary relationship. In this House an unusual course was taken during the argument. I quote from the Session Cases report (37):

I " . . . after counsel for the respondents had been heard for a short time Earl Loreburn informed him that their lordships, as at present advised, thought that there was no special duty on McArthur towards the pursuer; that the respondents were not liable unless McArthur's representations were dishonest; and that their lordships had not been satisfied as yet that the representa-

(31) 1916 S.C. (H.L.) 154.   (32) 1916 S.C. 46.
(33) 1916 S.C. at p. 63.   (34) [1914-15] All E.R. Rep. 45; [1914] A.C. 932.
(35) 1916 S.C. at p. 67.   (36) 1916 S.C. at p. 85.
(37) 1916 S.C. (H.L.) at pp. 154, 155.

tions were dishonest . . . that under the circumstances the House was   A
prepared to dismiss the appeal; but that they considered that the pursuer had
been badly treated, though he had not any cause of action at law, and that,
therefore, their lordships were disposed to direct that there should be no costs
of the action on either side. EARL LOREBURN said that counsel might prefer
to argue the case further and endeavour to alter these views, but of course
he would run the risk of altering their lordships' views as to the legal res-   B
ponsibility as well as upon the subject of costs."

Counsel then—wisely no doubt—said no more, and judgment was given for the
bank but with no costs here or below.

That case is very nearly indistinguishable from the present case. LORD LORE-
BURN regarded the fact that McArthur knew that his letter might be used to
influence others besides the immediate inquirer as entitling Robinson to found on   C
it if fraud had been proved. But it is not clear to me that he intended to decide
that there would have been sufficient proximity between Robinson and McArthur
to enable him to maintain that there was a special relationship involving a duty of
care if the other facts had been sufficient to create such a relationship. I would
not regard this as a binding decision on that question. With regard to the bank's
duty LORD HALDANE said (38):   D

    " There is only one other point about which I wish to say anything, and
    that is the question which was argued by the appellant, as to there being
    a special duty of care under the circumstances here. I think the case of
    Derry v. *Peek* (39) in this House has finally settled in Scotland, as well as in
    England and Ireland, the conclusion that in a case like this no duty to be
    careful is established. There is the general duty of common honesty, and   E
    that duty of course applies in the circumstances of this case as it applies to
    all other circumstances. But when a mere inquiry is made by one banker of
    another, who stands in no special relation to him, then, in the absence of
    special circumstances from which a contract to be careful can be inferred, I
    think there is no duty excepting the duty of common honesty to which I have
    referred."   F

I think that by " a contract to be careful " LORD HALDANE must have meant
an agreement or undertaking to be careful. This was a Scots case and by Scots
law there can be a contract without consideration: LORD HALDANE cannot have
meant that similar cases in Scotland and England would be decided differently
on the matter of special relationship for that reason. I am, I think, entitled
to note that this was an extempore judgment. So LORD HALDANE was con-   G
trasting a " mere inquiry " with a case where there are special circumstances
from which an undertaking to be careful can be inferred. In *Robinson's* case (40)
any such undertaking was excluded by the sentence in McArthur's letter which I
have quoted (41) and in which he said that the information was given " on the
express understanding that we incur no responsibility whatever in furnishing
it ".   H

It appears to me that the only possible distinction in the present case is that
here there was no adequate disclaimer of responsibility. Here, however, the
appellants' bank, who were their agents in making the enquiry, began by saying
that " they wanted to know in confidence and without responsibility on our part ",
i.e. on the part of the respondents. So I cannot see how the appellants can now
be entitled to disregard that and maintain that the respondents did incur a   I
responsibility to them.

The appellants founded on a number of cases in contract where very clear words
were required to exclude the duty of care which would otherwise have flowed from
the contract. To that argument there are, I think, two answers. In the case of a
contract it is necessary to exclude liability for negligence, but in this case the

---

(38) 1916 S.C. (H.L.) at p. 157.   (39) (1889), 14 App. Cas. 337.
(40) 1916 S.C. (H.L.) 154.   (41) Page 585, letter H, ante.

A question is whether an undertaking to assume a duty to take care can be inferred; and that is a very different matter. Secondly, even in cases of contract general words may be sufficient if there was no other kind of liability to be excluded except liability for negligence: the general rule is that a party is not exempted from liability for negligence " unless adequate words are used "—per Scrutton, L.J., in *Rutter* v. *Palmer* (42). It being admitted that there was

B here a duty to give an honest reply, I do not see what further liability there could be to exclude except liability for negligence: there being no contract there was no question of warranty.

I am therefore of opinion that it is clear that the respondents never undertook any duty to exercise care in giving their replies. The appellants cannot succeed unless there was such a duty and therefore in my judgment this appeal must be

C dismissed.

LORD MORRIS OF BORTH-Y-GEST (read by Lord Hodson): My Lords, the important question of law which has concerned your lordships in this appeal is whether in the circumstances of the case there was a duty of care owed by the respondents, whom I will call " the bank ", to the appellants, whom I will

D call " Hedleys ". In order to recover the damages which they claim Hedleys must establish that the bank owed them a duty, that the bank failed to discharge such duty, and that as a consequence Hedleys suffered loss.

An allegation of fraud was originally made but was abandoned. The learned judge held that the bank had been negligent, but that they owed no duty to Hedleys to exercise care. The Court of Appeal agreed with the learned judge that

E no such duty was owed, and it was therefore not necessary for them to consider whether the finding of negligence ought or ought not be upheld. In your lordships' House the legal issues were debated and again it did not become necessary to consider whether the finding of negligence ought or ought not be upheld. It is but fair to the bank to state that they firmly contend that they were not in any way negligent and that they were prepared to make submissions by way of

F challenge of the conclusions of the learned judge.

Hedleys were doing business with a company called Easipower, Ltd. In August, 1958, Hedleys wanted a banker's report concerning that company who then had an account with the bank. [In November, 1957, Hedleys had received a report about the company which had been given by another bank though not by direct communication.] Hedleys banked at a Piccadilly branch of National Provincial

G Bank, Ltd. Hedleys asked that a report concerning Easipower, Ltd. should be obtained. The Piccadilly branch communicated with the City office of their bank, the National Provincial. The National Provincial City office telephoned the bank on Aug. 18, 1958, and it is common ground that the representative of the National Provincial said that " they wanted to know in confidence " and " without responsibility " on the part of the bank as to the respectability and standing of

H Easipower, Ltd. and whether Easipower, Ltd. " would be good for an advertising contract for £8/9,000 ". To that oral inquiry the bank then gave an oral answer. In due course the answer then given was communicated by the Piccadilly branch of the National Provincial to Hedleys. It was communicated orally and a letter of confirmation from that branch (dated Aug. 21, 1958) was sent to Hedleys. The letter had the headings " Confidential " and " For your private use and without

I responsibility on the part of this bank or the manager ". The oral answer which the bank had given to the City office of the National Provincial was passed on with the prefatory words—" In reply to your telephoned inquiry of Aug. 18, bankers say:—". There was a later inquiry. On Nov. 4, 1958, in a letter to the Piccadilly branch of the National Provincial, Hedleys wrote: " I have been requested by the Directors to again ask you to check the financial structure and status of Easipower Limited ": Hedleys made some particular references and concluded their letter with the words: " I would be appreciative if you could make your check as

---

(42) [1922] 2 K.B. 87 at p. 92; cf. [1922] All E.R. Rep. 367 at p. 370.

exhaustive as you reasonably can." In a letter dated Nov. 7 and headed " Private   A
and Confidential " the City office of the National Provincial asked the bank for
their " opinion in confidence as to the respectability and standing of Easipower,
Ltd." and asked the bank to state whether they considered Easipower, Ltd.
" trustworthy, in the way of business, to the extent of £100,000 per annum,
advertising contract". The bank replied in a letter dated Nov. 11, and sent to the
City office of the National Provincial. The letter had the headings " Confidential "   B
and " For your private use and without responsibility on the part of this Bank or
its officials ". On Nov. 14 the Piccadilly branch of the National Provincial wrote
to Hedleys (heading their letter " Confidential. For your private use and without
responsibility on the part of this Bank or the Manager ") and, with the prefatory
words: " In reply to your inquiry letter of Nov. 4, Bankers say ", passed on
what the bank had stated in their letter to the City office of the National Provin-   C
cial.

It is, I think, a reasonable and proper inference that the bank must have known
that the National Provincial were making their inquiry because some customer of
theirs was or might be entering into some advertising contract in respect of which
Easipower, Ltd., might become under a liability to such customer to the extent of
the figures mentioned. The inquiries were from one bank to another. The name   D
of the customer (Hedleys) was not mentioned by the inquiring bank (National
Provincial) to the answering bank (the bank): nor did the inquiring bank
(National Provincial) give to the customer (Hedleys) the name of the answering
bank (the bank). These circumstances do not seem to me to be material. The
bank must have known that the inquiry was being made by someone who was
contemplating doing business with Easipower Ltd. and that their answer or the   E
substance of it would in fact be passed on to such person. The conditions subject
to which the bank gave their answers are important, but the fact that the person
to whom the answers would in all probability be passed on was unnamed and
unknown to the bank is not important for the purposes of a consideration of the
legal issue which now arises. It is inherently unlikely that the bank would have
entertained a direct application from Hedleys asking for a report or would have   F
answered an inquiry made by Hedleys themselves: even if they had they would
certainly have stipulated that their answer was without responsibility. The
present appeal does not raise any question as to the circumstances under which a
banker is entitled (apart from direct authorisation) to answer an inquiry. I leave
that question as it was left by ATKIN, L.J., in *Tournier* v. *National Provincial &*
Union Bank of England when he said (43):   G

" I do not desire to express any final opinion on the practice of bankers to
give one another information as to the affairs of their respective customers
except to say that it appears to me that, if it is justified, it must be upon the
basis of an implied consent of the customer."

The legal issue which arises is therefore whether the bank would have been under
a liability to Hedleys if they had failed to exercise care. This involves the ques-   H
tions whether the circumstances were such that the bank owed a duty of care to
Hedleys, or would have owed such a duty but for the words " without responsibility ", or whether they owed such a duty but were given a defence by the words
" without responsibility ", which would protect them if they had failed to exercise
due care.

My lords, it seems to me that if A assumes a responsibility to B to tender him   I
deliberate advice there could be a liability if the advice is negligently given. I
say " could be " because the ordinary courtesies and exchanges of life would
become impossible if it were sought to attach legal obligation to every kindly and
friendly act. But the principle of the matter would not appear to be in doubt. If
A employs B (who might, for example, be a professional man such as an accountant
or a solicitor or a doctor) for reward to give advice, and if the advice is negligently

(43) [1923] All E.R. Rep. 550 at p. 561; [1924] 1 K.B. 461 at p. 486.

A   given, there could be a liability in B to pay damages. The fact that the advice is given in words would not, in my view, prevent liability from arising. Quite apart, however, from employment or contract there may be circumstances in which a duty to exercise care will arise if a service is voluntarily undertaken. A medical man may unexpectedly come across an unconscious man, who is a complete stranger to him, and who is in urgent need of skilled attention: if the medical

B   man, following the fine traditions of his profession, proceeds to treat the unconscious man he must exercise reasonable skill and care in doing so. In his speech in *Banbury* v. *Bank of Montreal* (44) LORD ATKINSON said (45):

> " It is well established that if a doctor proceeded to treat a patient gratuitously even in a case where the patient was insensible at the time and incapable of employing him to do so, the doctor would be bound to exercise

C   > all the professional skill and knowledge he possessed or professed to possess, and would be guilty of gross negligence if he omitted to do so."

To a similar effect were the words of Lord Loughborough in the much earlier case of *Shiells* v. *Blackburne* when he said (46):

> " If a man gratuitously undertakes to do a thing to the best of his skill, where his situation or profession is such as to imply skill, an omission of that

D   > skill is imputable to him as gross negligence."

Compare also *Wilkinson* v. *Coverdale* (47). I can see no difference of principle in the case of a banker. If someone who was not a customer of a bank made a formal approach to the bank with a definite request that the bank would give him deliberate advice as to certain financial matters of a nature with which the bank ordinarily dealt the bank would be under no obligation to accede to the request:

E   if however they undertook, though gratuitously, to give deliberate advice (I exclude what I might call casual and perfunctory conversations) they would be under a duty to exercise reasonable care in giving it. They would be liable if they were negligent although, there being no consideration, no enforceable contractual relationship was created.

F   In the absence of any direct dealings between one person and another, there are many and varied situations in which a duty is owed by one person to another. A road user owes a duty of care towards other road users. They are his " neighbours ". A duty was owed by the dock owner in *Heaven* v. *Pender* (48). Under a contract with a shipowner he had put up a staging outside a ship in his dock. The plaintiff used the staging because he was employed by a ship painter who had

G   contracted with the shipowner to paint the outside of the ship. The presence of the plaintiff was for business in which the dock owner was interested, and the plaintiff was to be considered as having been invited by the dock owner to use the staging. The dock owner was therefore under an obligation to take reasonable care that at the time when the staging was provided by him for immediate use it was in a fit state to be used. For an injury which the plaintiff suffered, because the

H   staging had been carelessly put up, he was entitled to succeed in a claim against the defendant. The chemist in *George* v. *Skivington* (49) sold the bottle of hair wash to the husband knowing that it was to be used by the wife. It was held on demurrer that the chemist owed a duty towards the wife to use ordinary care in compounding the hair wash. In *Donoghue* (or *McAlister*) v. *Stevenson* (50) it was held that the manufacturer of an article of food, medicine, or the like, was under

I   a duty to the ultimate consumer to take reasonable care that the article was free from defect likely to cause injury to health.

My lords, these are but familiar and well-known illustrations, which could be multiplied, which show that irrespective of any contractual or fiduciary relationship and irrespective of any direct dealing, a duty may be owed by one person to

(44) [1918-19] All E.R. Rep. 1; [1918] A.C. 626.
(45) [1918-19] All E.R. Rep. at p. 18; [1918] A.C. at p. 689.
(46) (1789), 1 Hy. Bl. 158 at p. 162.   (47) (1793), 1 Esp. 74.
(48) (1883), 11 Q.B.D. 503.   (49) (1869), L.R. 5 Exch.1.
(50) [1932] All E.R. Rep. 1; [1932] A.C. 562.

another. It is said, however, that where careless (but not fraudulent) misstate- **A**
ments are in question there can be no liability in the maker of them unless there is
either some contractual or fiduciary relationship with a person adversely affected
by the making of them or unless through the making of them something is created
or circulated or some situation is created which is dangerous to life, limb or
property. In logic I can see no essential reason for distinguishing injury which is
caused by a reliance on words from injury which is caused by a reliance on the **B**
safety of the staging to a ship, or by a reliance on the safety for use of the
contents of a bottle of hair wash or a bottle of some consumable liquid.   It
seems to me, therefore, that if A claims that he has suffered injury or loss as a
result of acting upon some missstatement made by B who is not in any contractual
or fiduciary relationship with him the inquiry that is first raised is whether B
owed any duty to A: if he did the further inquiry is raised as to the nature of **C**
the duty. There may be circumstances under which the only duty owed by B to
A is the duty of being honest: there may be circumstances under which B owes
to A the duty not only of being honest but also a duty of taking reasonable care.
The issue in the present case is whether the bank owed any duty to Hedleys
and if so what the duty was.
     Leaving aside cases where there is some contractual or fiduciary relationship **D**
there may be many situations in which one person voluntarily or gratuitously
undertakes to do something for another person and becomes under a duty to
exercise reasonable care. I have given illustrations. Apart from cases where
there is some direct dealing, there may be cases where one person issues a document
which should be the result of an exercise of the skill and judgment required by
him in his calling and where he knows and intends that its accuracy will be relied **E**
on by another. In this connexion it will be helpful to consider the case of *Cann* v.
Willson (51). The owner of some property wished to obtain an advance of money
on mortgage of the property and applied to a firm of solicitors for the purpose
of finding a mortgagee. Being informed by the solicitors that for the purpose of
finding a mortgagee he should have a valuation made of the property he consulted
the defendants and asked them to make a valuation. They surveyed and inspected **F**
the property and then made a valuation which they sent to the solicitors. The
solicitors then particularly called the defendants' attention to the purpose for
which the valuation was wanted and to the responsibility they were undertaking.
The defendants stated that their valuation was a moderate one and certainly
was not made in favour of the borrower. The valuation and representations so
made by the defendants to the solicitors were communicated to the plaintiff **G**
(and a co-trustee of his) by the solicitors. The plaintiff (and his co-trustee, who
died before the commencement of the action) then advanced money to the
owner on the security of a mortgage of his property. CHITTY, J., held on the
evidence (a) that the defendants were aware of the purpose for which the valuation was made and (b) that the valuation was sent by the defendants direct to
the agents of the plaintiff for the purpose of inducing the plaintiff and his co- **H**
trustee to lay out the trust money on mortgage. The owner made default in
payment and the property proved insufficient to answer the mortgage.   The
plaintiff alleged that the value of the property was not anything like the value
given by the defendants in their valuation. CHITTY, J., held that the valuation as
made was in fact no valuation at all. In those circumstances the claim made
was on the basis that the plaintiff has sustained loss through the negligence, **I**
want of skill, breach of duty and misrepresentation of the defendants. CHITTY, J.,
held the defendants liable. His decision was principally based upon his finding
that the defendants owed a duty of care to the plaintiff. It had been argued
that there was also liability in the defendants in contract (referred to in the
judgment as the first ground) and on the ground of fraud (referred to as the
third ground). At the end of his judgment CHITTY, J., said (52):

---

(51) (1888), 39 Ch.D. 39.   (52) (1888), 39 Ch.D. at p. 44.

A   " I have entirely passed by the question of contract. It is unnecessary to decide that point. I consider on these two last grounds—and if I were to prefer one to the other it would be the second ground—that the defendant is liable for the negligence."

In the course of his judgment he said (53):

B   " It is not necessary, in my opinion, to decide the case with reference to the third point, but even on the third point I think the defendants are liable—and that is what may be termed fraudulent misrepresentation."

CHITTY, J., then (i.e. on June 7, 1888) referred to the judgment in the Court of Appeal in *Peek* v. *Derry* (54). That judgment was reversed in the House of Lords (55) on July 1, 1889. CHITTY, J., compared the situation with that which

C arose in *Heaven* v. *Pender* (56). He pointed out that in that case there was (57)

    " no contractual relation between the plaintiff and the dock owner, and there was no personal direct invitation to the plaintiff to come and do the work on that ship, yet it was held that the dock owner had undertaken an obligation towards the plaintiff, who was one of the persons likely to come and do the work to the vessel, and that he was liable to him and was under

D   an obligation to him to use due diligence in the construction of the staging."

CHITTY, J., went on, therefore, to hold as the defendants had " knowingly placed themselves " in the position of sending their valuation " direct to the agents of the plaintiff for the purpose of inducing the plaintiff " then they " in point of law incurred a duty towards him to use reasonable care in the preparation

E of the document." He likened the case to *George* v. *Skivington* (58) and continued (53):

    " In this case the document supplied appears to me to stand upon a similar footing and not to be distinguished from that case, as if it had been an actual article that had been handed over for the particular purpose of being so used. I think, therefore, that the defendants stood with regard to

F   the plaintiff—quite apart from any question of there being a contract or not in the peculiar circumstances of this case—in the position of being under an obligation or duty towards him."

My lords, I can see no fault or flaw in this reasoning and I am prepared to uphold it. If it is correct, then it is submitted that in the present case the bank knew that some existing (though to them by name unknown) person was going to

G place reliance on what they said and that accordingly they owed a duty of care to such person. I will examine this submission. Before doing so I must, however, further consider *Cann* v. *Willson* (59). It was overruled by the Court of Appeal in *Le Lievre* v. *Gould* (60). The latter case, binding on the Court of Appeal, in turn led to the decision in *Candler* v. *Crane, Christmas & Co.* (61). It is necessary therefore to consider the reasons which governed the Court of Appeal in *Le*

H *Lievre* v. *Gould* (60) in overruling *Cann* v. *Willson* (59). I do not propose to examine the facts in *Le Lievre* v. *Gould* (60): nor need I consider whether the result would have been no different had *Cann* v. *Willson* (59) not been overruled. LORD ESHER, M.R., said (62):

    " But I do not hesitate to say that *Cann* v. *Willson* (59) is not now law.

I CHITTY, J., in deciding that case acted upon an erroneous proposition of law which has been since overruled by the House of Lords in *Derry* v. *Peek* (55) when they restated the old law that, in the absence of contract, an action for negligence cannot be maintained when there is no fraud."

---

(53) (1888), 39 Ch.D. at p. 43.
(55) (1889), 14 App. Cas. 337.
(57) (1888), 39 Ch.D. at p. 42.
(59) (1888), 39 Ch.D. 39.
(61) [1951] 1 All E.R. 426; [1951] 2 K.B. 164.

(54) (1886), 37 Ch.D. 541.
(56) (1883), 11 Q.B.D. 503.
(58) (1869), L.R. 5 Exch. 1.
(60) [1893] 1 Q.B. 491.
(62) [1893] 1 Q.B. at p. 497.

BOWEN, L.J., said (63) that he considered that *Derry* v. *Peek* (64) had over- A
ruled *Cann* v. *Willson* (65). He considered that *Heaven* v. *Pender* (66) gave no
support for that decision, because it was no more than an instance of the class
of case where one who, having the conduct and control of premises which may
injure those whom he knows will have a right to and will use them, owes a duty
to protect them. He said (67):

B
> " Then *Derry* v. *Peek* (64) decided this further point—viz., that in cases
> like the present (of which *Derry* v. *Peek* (64) was itself an instance) there is
> no duty enforceable in law to be careful."

He followed the view expressed by ROMER, J., in *Scholes* v. *Brook* (68) that the
decision of the House of Lords in *Derry* v. *Peek* (64) by implication negatived
the existence of any such general rule as laid down in *Cann* v. *Willson* (65). The C
reasoning of A. L. SMITH, L.J., in overruling *Cann* v. *Willson* (65) was on
similar lines.

The inquiry is thus raised whether it was correct to say that *Derry* v. *Peek* (64)
had either directly or at least by implication overruled that part of the reasoning
in *Cann* v. *Willson* (65) which led CHITTY, J., to say that quite apart from contract and quite apart from fraud there was a duty of care owed by the defendants D
to the plaintiffs. My lords, whatever views may have been held at one time
as to the effect of *Derry* v. *Peek* (64), authoritative guidance as to this matter
was given in your lordships' House in 1914 in the case of *Nocton* v. *Lord Ashburton* (69). In his speech in that case VISCOUNT HALDANE, L.C., said (70):

E
> " The discussion of the case by the noble and learned lords who took part
> in the decision appears to me to exclude the hypothesis that they considered
> any other question to be before them than what was the necessary founda-
> tion of an ordinary action for deceit. They must indeed be taken to have
> thought that the facts proved as to the relationship of the parties in *Derry* v.
> *Peek* (64) were not enough to establish any special duty arising out of that
> relationship other than the general duty of honesty. But they do not say
> that where a different sort of relationship ought to be inferred from the F
> circumstances the case is to be concluded by asking whether an action for
> deceit will lie. I think that the authorities subsequent to the decision of the
> House of Lords shew a tendency to assume that it was intended to mean more
> than it did. In reality the judgment covered only a part of the field in which
> liabilities may arise. There are other obligations besides that of honesty
> the breach of which may give a right to damages. These obligations depend G
> on principles which the judges have worked out in the fashion that is
> characteristic of a system where much of the law has always been judge-
> made and unwritten."

After a review of many authorities LORD HALDANE said (71):

> " But side by side with the enforcement of the duty of universal obligation
> to be honest and the principle which gave the right to rescission, the courts, H
> and especially the Court of Chancery, had to deal with the other cases to
> which I have referred, cases raising claims of an essentially different character,
> which have often been mistaken for actions of deceit. Such claims raise the
> question whether the circumstances and relations of the parties are such
> as to give rise to duties of particular obligation which have not been fulfilled."

I
LORD HALDANE, pointed out that from the circumstances and relations of
the parties a special duty may arise: there may be an implied contract at law
or a fiduciary obligation in equity. What *Derry* v. *Peek* (64) decided was that

---

(63) [1893] 1 Q.B. at p. 499.   (64) (1889), 14 App. Cas. 337.
(65) (1888), 39 Ch.D. 39.   (66) (1883), 11 Q.B.D. 503.
(67) [1893] 1 Q.B. at p. 501.   (68) (1891), 63 L.T. 837.
(69) [1914-15] All E.R. Rep. 45; [1914] A.C. 932.
(70) [1914-15] All E.R. Rep. at p. 49; [1914] A.C. at p. 947.
(71) [1914-15] All E.R. Rep. at p. 53; [1914] A.C. at p. 955.

A the directors were under no fiduciary duty to the public to whom they had addressed the invitation to subscribe. (I need not here refer to statutory enactments since *Derry* v. *Peek* (72)). In his speech in the same case (73) LORD DUNEDIN pointed out that there can be no negligence unless there is a duty, but that a duty may arise in many ways. There may be duties owing to the world at large: alterum non laedere. There may be duties arising from contract. There may be

B duties which arise from a relationship without the intervention of contract in the ordinary sense of the term, such as the duties of a trustee to his cestui que trust or of a guardian to his ward.

Beneficiary

LORD SHAW in his speech pointed out (74) that *Derry* v. *Peek* (72)

C " was an action wholly and solely of deceit, founded wholly and solely on fraud, was treated by this House on that footing alone and that this being so what was decided was that fraud must ex necessitate contain the element of actual moral delinquency. Certain expressions by learned lords may seem to have made incursions into the region of negligence, but *Derry* v. *Peek* (72) as a decision was directed to the single and specific point just set out."

LORD SHAW formulated the following principle (75):

D " Once the relations of parties have been ascertained to be those in which a duty is laid upon one person of giving information or advice to another upon which that other is entitled to rely as the basis of a transaction, responsibility for error amounting to misrepresentation in any statement made will attach to the adviser or informer although the information and advice have been given, not fraudulently, but in good faith."

E LORD PARMOOR in his speech said (76) in reference to *Derry* v. *Peek* (72):

" That case decides that in an action founded on deceit and in which deceit is a necessary factor, actual dishonesty, involving mens rea, must be proved. The case, in my opinion, has no bearing whatever on actions founded on a breach of duty in which dishonesty is not a necessary factor."

F My lords, guided by the assistance given in *Nocton* v. *Ashburton* (77) I consider that it ought not to have been held in *Le Lievre* v. *Gould* (78) that *Cann* v. *Willson* (79) was wrongly decided. Independently of contract there may be circumstances where information is given or where advice is given which establish a relationship which creates a duty not only to be honest but also to be careful.

In his speech in *Heilbut, Symons & Co.* v. *Buckleton* LORD MOULTON (80) said

G that it was of the greatest importance to

" maintain in its full integrity the principle that a person is not liable in damages for an innocent misrepresentation, no matter in what way or under what form the attack is made."

That principle is, however, in no way impeached by recognition of the fact that

H if a duty exists there is a remedy for the breach of it. As LORD BOWEN said in *Low* v. *Bouverie* (81):

" the doctrine that negligent misrepresentation affords no cause of action is confined to cases in which there is no duty, such as the law recognises, to be careful."

The inquiry in the present case, and in similar cases, becomes therefore an inquiry as to whether there was a relationship between the parties which created a duty and if so whether such duty included a duty of care.

(72) (1889), 14 App. Cas. 337.
(73) [1914-15] All E.R. Rep. at p. 501; [1914] A.C. at p. 959.
(74) [1914-15] All E.R. Rep. at p. 61; [1914] A.C. at p. 970.
(75) [1914-15] All E.R. Rep. at p. 62; [1914] A.C. at p. 972.
(76) [1914] A.C. at p. 978.   (77) [1914-15] All E.R. Rep. 45; [1914] A.C. 932.
(78) [1893] 1 Q.B. 491.   (79) (1888), 39 Ch.D. 39.
(80) [1911-13] All E.R. Rep. 83 at p. 92; [1913] A.C. 30 at p. 51.
(81) [1891] 3 Ch. 82 at p. 105.

The guidance which LORD HALDANE gave in *Nocton* v. *Ashburton* (82) was A
repeated by him in his speech in *Robinson* v. *National Bank of Scotland* (83)
He clearly pointed out that *Derry* v. *Peek* (84) did not affect (a) the whole doctrine
as to fiduciary relationships (b) the duty of care arising from implied as well
as express contracts and (c) the duty of care arising from other special relationships which the courts may find to exist in particular cases.

My lords, I consider that it follows and that it should now be regarded as B
settled that if someone possessed of a special skill undertakes, quite irrespective
of contract, to apply that skill for the assistance of another person who relies
on such skill, a duty of care will arise. The fact that the service is to be given
by means of, or by the instrumentality of, words can make no difference. Furthermore if, in a sphere in which a person is so placed that others could reasonably
rely on his judgment or his skill or on his ability to make careful inquiry, a person C
takes it on himself to give information or advice to, or allows his information
or advice to be passed on to, another person who, as he knows or should know,
will place reliance on it, then a duty of care will arise.

I do not propose to examine the facts of particular situations or the facts
of recent decided cases in the light of this analysis, but I proceed to apply it to
the facts of the case now under review. As I have stated, I approach the case D
on the footing that the bank knew that what they said would in fact be passed
on to some unnamed person who was a customer of National Provincial Bank,
Ltd. The fact that it was said that " they ", i.e. National Provincial Bank,
Ltd., "wanted to know " does not prevent this conclusion. In these circumstances
I think that some duty towards the unnamed person, whoever it was, was owed by
the bank. There was a duty of honesty. The great question, however, is whether E
there was a duty of care. The bank need not have answered the inquiry from
National Provincial Bank, Ltd. It appears, however, that it is a matter of
banking convenience or courtesy and presumably of mutual business advantage
that inquiries as between banks will be answered. The fact that it is most
unlikely that the bank would have answered a direct inquiry from Hedleys
does not affect the question as to what the bank must have known as to the use F
that would be made of any answer that they gave but it cannot be left out
of account in considering what it was that the bank undertook to do. It does
not seem to me that they undertook before answering an inquiry to expend
time or trouble " in searching records, studying documents, weighing and com-
paring the favourable and unfavourable features and producing a well-balanced
and well-worded report." (I quote the words of PEARSON, L.J. (85)). Nor does G
it seem to me that the inquiring bank (nor therefore their customer) would expect
such a process. This was, I think, what was denoted by LORD HALDANE
in his speech in *Robinson* v. *National Bank of Scotland* (83) when he spoke of a
" mere inquiry " being made by one banker of another. In *Parsons* v. *Barclay
& Co., Ltd.* (86) COZENS-HARDY, M.R., expressed the view that it was no part
of a banker's duty, when asked for a reference, to make inquiries outside as to H
the solvency or otherwise of the person asked about or to do more than answer
the question put to him honestly from what he knew from the books and accounts
before him. There was in the present case no contemplation of receiving anything like a formal and detailed report such as might be given by some concern
charged with the duty (probably for reward) of making all proper and relevant
inquiries concerning the nature, scope and extent of a company's activities I
and of obtaining and marshalling all available evidence as to its credit, efficiency,
standing and business reputation. There is much to be said, therefore, for the view
that if a banker gives a reference in the form of a brief expression of opinion
in regard to credit-worthiness he does not accept, and there is not expected

(82) [1914-15] All E.R. Rep. 45; [1914] A.C. 932.   (83) 1916 S.C. (H.L.) 154.
(84) (1889), 14 App. Cas. 337.
(85) [1961] 3 All E.R. at p. 902. letter E; [1962] 1 Q.B. at p. 414.
(86) [1908-10] All E.R. Rep. 429.

A from him, any higher duty than that of giving an honest answer. I need not, however, seek to deal further with this aspect of the matter, which perhaps cannot be covered by any statement of general application, because in my judgment the bank in the present case, by the words which they employed, effectively disclaimed any assumption of a duty of care. They stated that they only responded to the inquiry on the basis that their reply was without respon-
B sibility. If the inquirers chose to receive and act upon the reply they cannot disregard the definite terms upon which it was given. They cannot accept a reply given with a stipulation and then reject the stipulation. Furthermore, within accepted principles (as illustrated in *Rutter* v. *Palmer* (87)) the words employed were apt to exclude any liability for negligence.

I would therefore dismiss the appeal.

C
LORD HODSON: My Lords, the appellants, who are advertising agents, claim damages for loss which they allege they have suffered through the negligence of the respondents, who are merchant bankers. The negligence attributed to the respondents consists of their failure to act with reasonable skill and care in giving references as to the credit-worthiness of a company called Easipower Ltd.,
D which went into liquidation after the references had been given, so that the appellants were unable to recover the bulk of the costs of advertising orders which Easipower Ltd. had placed with them.

The learned judge at the trial found that the respondent bankers had been negligent in the advice which they gave in the form of bankers references, the appellants being a company which acted in reliance on the references and suffered
E financial loss accordingly, but that he must enter judgment for the respondents since there was no duty imposed by law to exercise care in giving these references, the duty being only to act honestly in so doing. The respondents have at all times maintained that they were in no sense negligent, and further that no damage flowed from the giving of references, but first they took the point that, whether or no they were careless and whether or no the appellants suffered
F damage as a result of their carelessness, they must succeed on the footing that no duty was owed by them. This point has been taken throughout as being, if the respondents are right, decisive of the whole matter. I will deal with it first, although the underlying question is whether the respondent bankers, who at all times disclaimed responsibility, ever assumed any duty at all. The appellants depend on the existence of a duty said to be assumed by or imposed on the
G respondents when they gave a reference as to the credit-worthiness of Easipower Ltd., knowing that it would or might be relied on by the appellants or some other third party in like situation. The case has been argued first on the footing that the duty was imposed by the relationship between the parties recognised by law as being a special relationship derived either from the notion of proximity introduced by Lord Esher, M.R., in *Heaven* v. *Pender* (88), or from those cases firmly established in our law which show that those who hold themselves out as
H possessing a special skill are under a duty to exercise it with reasonable care.

The important case of *Donoghue* (or *McAlister*) v. *Stevenson* (89) shows that the area of negligence is extensive, for as Lord Macmillan said (90):

" The grounds of action may be as various and manifold as human errancy, and the conception of legal responsibility may develop in adaptation to
I altering social conditions and standards. The criterion of judgment must adjust and adapt itself to the changing circumstances of life. The categories of negligence are never closed . . . .Where there is room for diversity of view is in determining what circumstances will establish such relationship between the parties as to give rise on the one side to a duty to take care and on the other side to a right to have care taken."

---

(87) [1922] All E.R. Rep. 367; [1922] 2 K.B. 87.
(88) (1883), 11 Q.B.D. 503, 509.   (89) [1932] All E.R. Rep. 1; [1932] A.C. 562.
(90) [1932] All E.R. Rep. at p. 30; [1932] A.C. at p. 619.

In that case the necessary relationship was held to have been established where **A**
the manufacturer of an article, ginger beer in a bottle, sold by him to a distributor in circumstances which prevented the distributor or the ultimate purchaser
or consumer from discovering by inspection any defect.   He is under a legal
duty to the ultimate purchaser or consumer to take reasonable care that the
article is free from injurious defect.   No doubt that was the actual decision in
that case and indeed it was thought by WROTTESLEY, J., in *Old Gate Estates Ltd.* **B**
v. *Toplis and Harding and Russell* (91) that he was precluded from awarding
damages in tort for a negligent valuation made by a firm of valuers, which knew
it was to be used by the plaintiffs, since the doctrine of *Donoghue* v. *Stevenson* (92)
was confined to negligence which results in danger to life, limb or health.   I do
not think that this is the true view of *Donoghue* v. *Stevenson* (92), but the
decision itself, although its effect has been extended to cases where there was no **C**
expectation as contrasted with opportunity of inspection (see *Grant* v. *Australian
Knitting Mills, Ltd.* (93)), and to liability of repairers (see *Haseldine* v. *Daw
& Son, Ltd.* (94)), has never been applied to cases where damages are claimed
in tort for negligent statements producing damage.   The attempt so to apply it
failed as recently as 1951 when in *Candler* v. *Crane, Christmas & Co.* (95) the
Court of Appeal by a majority held that a false statement made carelessly as **D**
contrasted with fraudulently by one person to another, though acted on by that
other to his detriment, was not actionable in the absence of any contractual
or fiduciary relationship between the parties and that this principle had in no
way been modified by the decision in *Donoghue* v. *Stevenson* (92).   COHEN, L.J.,
one of the majority of the court, referred to the language of LORD ESHER, M.R., in
Le Lievre v. *Gould* (96) who, repeating the substance of what he had said in **E**
Heaven v. *Pender* (97) said (98):   " If one man is near to another or is near to
the property of another, a duty lies upon him not to do that which may cause
a personal injury to that other, or may injure his property ".   ASQUITH, L.J., the
other member of the majority of the court held that the " neighbour " doctrine
had not been applied where the damage complained of was not physical in its
incidence to either person or property.   The majority thus went no further than **F**
WROTTESLEY, J., in the *Old Gate Estates* case (91) save that injury to property
was said to be contemplated by the doctrine expounded in *Donoghue* v. *Stevenson*
(92).   It is desirable to consider the reasons given by the majority for their
decision in the *Candler* case (95) for the appellants rely on the dissenting judgment of DENNING, L.J., in the same case.   The majority, as also the learned
trial judge, held that they were bound by the decision of the Court of Appeal in **G**
Le Lievre v. *Gould* (96) in which the leading judgment was given by LORD
ESHER, M.R., and referred to as authoritative by LORD ATKIN in *Donoghue* v.
Stevenson (92).

It is true that LORD ESHER, M.R., refused to extend the proximity doctrine so
as to cover the relationship between the parties in that case and the majority in
Candler's case (95) were unable to draw a valid distinction between the facts of **H**
that case and the case of *Le Lievre* v. *Gould* (96).   DENNING, L.J., however,
accepted the argument for the appellant which has been repeated before your
lordships, that the facts in *Le Lievre* v. *Gould* (96) were not such as to impose a
liability, for the plaintiff mortgagees, who alleged that the owner's surveyor owed
a duty to them, not only had the opportunity but also had stipulated for inspection by their own surveyor.   The defendant's employee, who prepared the **I**
accounts in *Candler's* case (95), knew that the plaintiff was a potential investor
in the company of which the accounts were negligently prepared and that the

---

(91) [1939] 3 All E.R. 209.   (92) [1932] All E.R. Rep. 1; [1932] A.C. 562.
(93) [1935] All E.R. Rep. 209; [1936] A.C. 85.
(94) [1941] 3 All E.R. 156; [1941] 2 K.B. 343.
(95) [1951] 1 All E.R. 426; [1951] 2 K.B. 164.   (96) [1893] 1 Q.B. 491.
(97) (1883), 11 Q.B.D. 503, 509.
(98) [1893] 1 Q.B. at p. 497; [1951] 1 All E.R. at p. 445; [1951] 2 K.B. at p. 199.

A   accounts were required in order that they might be shown to the plaintiff. In these circumstances I agree with DENNING, L.J., that there is a valid distinction between the two cases. In *Le Lievre* v. *Gould* (99) it was held that an older case of *Cann* v. *Willson* (100) was overruled. That is a case where the facts were in pari materia with those in *Candler's* case (101) and CHITTY, J., held that the defendants were liable because (a) they, independently of contract, owed a duty

B   to the plaintiff, which they failed to discharge, and (b) they had made reckless statements on which the plaintiff had acted. This case was decided before this House in *Derry* v. *Peek* (102) overruled the Court of Appeal on the second proposition, but the first proposition was untouched by *Derry* v. *Peek* (102) and, in so far as it depended on the authority of *George* v. *Skivington* (103), the latter case was expressly affirmed in *Donoghue* v. *Stevenson* (104) although it had often

C   previously been impugned. It is true that, as ASQUITH, L.J., pointed out in referring to *George* v. *Skivington* (103), the hair wash put into circulation, knowing it was intended to be used by the purchaser's wife, was a negligently compounded hair wash, so that the case was so far on all fours with *Donoghue* v. *Stevenson* (104), but the declaration also averred that the defendant had said that the hair wash was safe. I cannot see that there is any valid distinction in this field between a

D   negligent statement, e.g. an incorrect label on a bottle, which leads to injury and a negligent compounding of ingredients which leads to the same result. It may well be that at the time when *Le Lievre* v. *Gould* (99) was decided the decision of this House in *Derry* v. *Peek* (102) was thought to go further than it did. It certainly decided that careless statements recklessly but honestly made by directors in a prospectus issued to the public were not actionable on

E   the basis of fraud and inferentially that such statements would not be actionable in negligence (which had not in fact been pleaded), but it was pointed out by this House in *Nocton* v. *Lord Ashburton* (105) that an action does lie for negligent misstatement where the circumstances disclose a duty to be careful. It is necessary in this connexion to quote the actual language of VISCOUNT HALDANE, L.C. (106):

F   " Such a special duty may arise from the circumstances and relations of the parties. These may give rise to an implied contract at law or to a fiduciary obligation in equity. If such a duty can be inferred in a particular case of a person issuing a prospectus, as, for instance, in the case of director issuing to the shareholders of the company which they direct a prospectus inviting the subscription by them of further capital, I do not find in *Derry* v. *Peek* (102) an authority for the suggestion that an action for damages for

G   misrepresentation without an actual intention to deceive may not lie. What was decided there was that from the facts proved in that case no such special duty to be careful in statement could be inferred, and that mere want of care therefore gave rise to no cause of action. In other words, it was decided that the directors stood in no fiduciary relation, and, therefore, were under no fiduciary duty to the public to whom they had addressed the

H   invitation to subscribe. I have only to add that the special relationship must, whenever it is alleged, be clearly shown to exist."

So far I have done no more than summarise the argument addressed to the Court of Appeal in *Candler's* case (101) to which effect was given in the dissenting judgment of DENNING, L.J., with which I respectfully agree in so far as it dealt

I   with the facts of that case. I am, therefore, of opinion that his judgment is to be preferred to that of the majority, although the opinion of the majority is undoubtedly supported by the ratio decidendi of *Le Lievre* v. *Gould* (99), which they cannot be criticised for following. This, however, does not carry the

(99) [1893] 1 Q.B. 491.   (100) (1888), 39 Ch.D. 39.
(101) [1951] 1 All E.R. 426; [1951] 2 K.B. 164.   (102) (1889), 14 App. Cas. 337.
(103) (1869), L.R. 5 Exch. 1.   (104) [1932] All E.R. Rep. 1; [1932] A.C. 562.
(105) [1914-15] All E.R. Rep. 45; [1914] A.C. 932.
(106) [1914-15] All E.R. Rep. at p. 53; [1914] A.C. at pp. 955, 956.

appellants further than this, that, provided that they can establish a special   **A**
duty, they are entitled to succeed in an action based on breach of that duty.

I shall later refer to certain cases which support the view that apart from what
are usually called fiduciary relationships such as those between trustee and
cestui que trust, solicitor and client, parent and child or guardian and ward there
are other circumstances in which the law imposes a duty to be careful, which is
not limited to a duty to be careful to avoid personal injury or injury to property   **B**
but covers a duty to avoid inflicting pecuniary loss provided always that there
is a sufficiently close relationship to give rise to a duty of care. The courts of
equity recognised that a fiduciary relationship exists " in almost every shape ",
to quote from FIELD, J., in *Plowright* v. *Lambert* (107). He went on to refer
to a case (108), which had said that the relationship could be created voluntarily,
as it were, by a person coming into a state of confidential relationship with   **C**
another by offering to give advice in a matter, and so being disabled thereafter
from purchasing.

It is difficult to see why liability as such should depend on the nature of the
damage. LORD ROCHE in *Morrison S.S. Co., Ltd.* v. *Greystoke Castle (Cargo
Owners)* (109) instanced damage to a lorry by the negligence of the driver of
another lorry which while it does no damage to the goods in the second lorry   **D**
causes the goods owner to be put to expense which is recoverable by direct
action against the negligent driver.

It is not to be supposed that the majority of the Court of Appeal, who decided
as they did in *Candler's* case (110), were unmindful of the decision in *Nocton* v.
Lord Ashburton (111), to which their attention was drawn, but they seem to have
been impressed with the view that, in the passage which I have quoted, LORD   **E**
HALDANE had in mind only fiduciary relationships in the strict sense, but in
my opinion the words need not be so limited. I am fortified in this opinion by
examples to be found in the old authorities such as *Shiells* v. *Blackburne* (112),
Wilkinson v. *Coverdale* (113) and *Gladwell* v. *Steggall* (114), which are illustrations
of cases where the law has held that a duty to exercise reasonable care (breach of
which is remediable in damages) has been imposed in the absence of a fiduciary   **F**
relationship where persons hold themselves out as possessing special skill and are
thus under a duty to exercise it with reasonable care. The statement of LORD
LOUGHBOROUGH in *Shiells* v. *Blackburne* (115) is always accepted as authoritative
and ought not to be dismissed as dictum, although the plaintiff failed to establish
facts which satisfied the standard he set. He said (115):

    " If a man gratuitously undertakes to do a thing to the best of his skill,   **G**
where the situation or profession is such as to imply skill, an omission of
that skill is imputable to him as gross negligence."

True that proximity is more difficult to establish where words are concerned than
in the case of other activities and mere casual observations are not to be relied
on, see *Fish* v. *Kelly* (116), but these matters go to difficulty of proof rather   **H**
than principle.

A modern instance is to be found in the case of *Woods* v. *Martins Bank Ltd.*
(117) where SALMON, J., held that on the facts of the case the defendant bank,
which had held itself out as being advisers on investments (which was within the
scope of its business) and had not given the plaintiff reasonably careful or skilful
advice, so that he suffered loss, was in breach of duty and so liable in damages,   **I**
even though the plaintiff might not have been a customer of the bank at the

(107) (1885), 52 L.T. 646 at p. 652.
(108) *Tate* v. *Williamson* (1866), 2 Ch. App. 55.
(109) [1946] 2 All E.R. 696, at p. 700; [1947] A.C. 265 at p. 280.
(110) [1951] 1 All E.R. 426; [1951] 2 K.B. 164.
(111) [1914-15] All E.R. Rep. 45; [1914] A.C. 932.   (112) (1789), 1 Hy. Bl. 158.
(113) (1793), 1 Esp. 74.   (114) (1839), 5 Bing. N.C. 733.
(115) (1789), 1 Hy. Bl. at p. 162.   (116) (1864), 17 C.B.N.S. 194.
    (117) [1958] 3 All E.R. 166; [1959] 1 Q.B. 55.

A material time. True that the learned judge based this part of his conclusion on a fiduciary relationship which he held to exist between the plaintiff and the bank (118) and thus brought himself within the scope of the decision in *Candler's case* (119) by which he was bound. For my part I should have thought that even if the learned judge put a strained interpretation on the word " fiduciary ", which is based on the idea of trust, the decision can be properly sustained as an

B example involving a special relationship.

I do not overlook the point forcefully made by HARMAN, L.J., in his judgment (120), and elaborated by counsel for the respondent before your lordships, that it may in certain cases appear to be strange that whereas innocent misrepresentation does not sound in damages yet in the special cases under consideration an injured party may sue in tort a third party whose negligent mis-

C representation has induced him to enter into the contract. As was pointed out by LORD WRENBURY, however, in *Banbury* v. *Bank of Montreal* (121), innocent misrepresentation is not the cause of action but evidence of the negligence which is the cause of action.

Was there then a special relationship here? I cannot exclude from consideration the actual terms in which the reference was given and I cannot see how the

D appellants can get over the difficulty which these words put in their way. They cannot say that the respondents are seeking to, as it were, contract out of their duty by the use of language which is insufficient for the purpose, if the truth of the matter is that the respondents never assumed a duty of care nor was such a duty imposed on them.

The first question is whether a duty was ever imposed and the language used

E must be considered before the question can be answered. In the case of a person giving a reference I see no objection in law or morals to the giver of the reference protecting himself by giving it without taking responsibility for anything more than the honesty of his opinion which must involve without taking responsibility for negligence in giving that opinion. I cannot accept the contention of the appellants that the responsibility disclaimed was limited to the bank to which

F the reference was given, nor can I agree that it referred only to responsibility for accuracy of detail. Similar words were present in the case of *Robinson* v. *National Bank of Scotland* (122), a case in which the facts cannot, I think, be distinguished in any material respect from this. Moreover in the Inner House the words of disclaimer were, I think, treated as not without significance. In this House the opinion was clearly expressed that the representations made

G were careless, inaccurate and misleading, but that the pursuer had no remedy since there was no special duty on the bank's representative towards the pursuer. This conclusion was reached quite apart from the disclaimer of responsibility contained in the defender bank's letters. VISCOUNT HALDANE, L.C., recalled the case of *Nocton* v. *Lord Ashburton* (123) in the following passage (124):

" In saying that I wish emphatically to repeat what I said in advising

H this House in the case of *Nocton* v. *Lord Ashburton* (123) that it is a great mistake to suppose that, because the principle in *Derry* v. *Peek* (125) clearly covers all cases of the class to which I have referred, therefore the freedom of action of the courts in recognising special duties arising out of other kinds of relationship which they find established by the evidence is in any way affected. I think, as I said in *Nocton's* case (123), that an exaggerated view

I was taken by a good many people of the scope of the decision in *Derry* v. *Peek* (125). The whole of the doctrine as to fiduciary relationships, as to the duty of care arising from implied as well as express contracts, as to the

(118) [1959] 1 Q.B. at p. 72; cf. [1958] 3 All E.R. at p. 174, [1958] W.L.R. at p. 1032.
(119) [1951] 1 All E.R. 426; [1951] 2 K.B. 164.
(120) [1961] 3 All E.R. at pp. 902, 903; [1962] 1 Q.B. at p. 415.
(121) [1918-19] All E.R. Rep. 1 at p. 28; [1918] A.C. 626 at p. 713.
(122) 1916 S.C. (H.L.) 154 at p. 159.
(123) [1914-15] All E.R. Rep. 45; [1914] A.C. 932.   (124) 1916 S.C. (H.L.) at p. 157.
(125) (1889), 14 App. Cas. 337.

duty of care arising from other special relationships which the courts may   A
find to exist in particular cases, still remains, and I should be very sorry if
any word fell from me which should suggest that the courts are in any
way hampered in recognising that the duty of care may be established when
such cases really occur."

This authority is, I think, conclusive against the appellants, and is not effectively
weakened by the fact that the case came to an end, before the matter had been   B
fully argued, on the House intimating that it was prepared to dismiss the appeal
without costs on either side, since the pursuer had in its opinion been badly
treated. Since no detailed reasons were given by the House for the view that
a banker's reference given honestly does not in the ordinary course carry with
it a duty to take reasonable care, that duty being based on a special relationship,
it will not, I hope, be out of place if I express my concurrence with the observa-   C
tions of PEARSON, L.J., who delivered the leading judgment in the Court of Appeal
and said (126):

> " Apart from authority, I am not satisfied that it would be reasonable
> to impose on a banker the obligation suggested, if that obligation really adds
> anything to the duty of giving an honest answer. It is conceded by counsel
> for the plaintiffs that the banker is not expected to make outside inquiries   D
> to supplement the information which he already has. Is he then expected,
> in business hours in the bank's time, to expend time and trouble in searching
> records, studying documents, weighing and comparing the favourable and
> unfavourable features and producing a well-balanced and well-worded report?
> That seems wholly unreasonable. Then, if he is not expected to do any of
> those things, and if he is permitted to give an impromptu answer in the   E
> words that immediately come to his mind on the basis of the facts which he
> happens to remember or is able to ascertain from a quick glance at the file
> or one of the files, the duty of care seems to add little, if anything, to the
> duty of honesty. If the answer given is seriously wrong, that is some evidence
> —of course, only some evidence—of dishonesty. Therefore, apart from
> authority, it is to my mind far from clear that the banker, in answering   F
> such an inquiry, could reasonably be supposed to be assuming any duty
> higher than that of giving an honest answer.'

This is to the same effect as the opinion of COZENS-HARDY, M.R., in *Parsons*
v. *Barclay & Co., Ltd.* (127) cited as follows:

> " His Lordship said he wished emphatically to repudiate the suggestion   G
> that, when a banker was asked for a reference of this kind, it was any part
> of his duty to make inquiries outside as to the solvency or otherwise of the
> person asked about, or to do anything more than answer the question put
> to him honestly from what he knew from the books and accounts before him.
> To hold otherwise would be a very dangerous thing to do and would put an
> end to a very wholesome and useful practice and long established custom   H
> which was now largely followed by bankers."

It would, I think, be unreasonable to impose an additional burden on persons,
such as bankers, who are asked to give references and might, if more than honesty
were required, be put to great trouble before all available material had been
explored and considered.

It was held in *Low* v. *Bouverie* (128) that if a trustee takes on himself to answer   I
the inquiries of a stranger about to deal with the cestui que trust, he is not under
a legal obligation to do more than to give honest answers to the best of his
actual knowledge and belief, he is not bound to make inquiries himself. I do
not think that a banker giving references in the ordinary exercise of business
should be in any worse position than the trustee. I have already pointed out

(126) [1961] 3 All E.R. at p. 902; [1962] 1 Q.B. at pp. 414, 415.
(127) (1910), 26 T.L.R. 628 at p. 629; cf. [1908-10] All E.R. Rep. 429 at pp. 432, 433.
(128) [1891] 3 Ch. 82.

A   that a banker like anyone else may find himself involved in a special relationship involving liability, as in *Woods* v. *Martins Bank Ltd.* (129), but there are no special features here which enable the appellants to succeed.

I do not think that it is possible to catalogue the special features which must be found to exist before the duty of care will arise in a given case, but since preparing this opinion I have had the opportunity of reading the speech which B   my noble and learned friend LORD MORRIS OF BORTH-Y-GEST has now delivered. I agree with him that if in a sphere where a person is so placed that others could reasonably rely on his judgment or his skill or on his ability to make careful inquiry such person takes it on himself to give information or advice to, or allows his information or advice to be passed on to, another person who, as he knows, or should know, will place reliance on it, then a duty of care will arise.

C   I would dismiss the appeal.

LORD DEVLIN (read by LORD PEARCE): My Lords, the bare facts of this case, stated sufficiently to raise the general point of law, are these. The appellants, being anxious to know whether they could safely extend credit to certain traders with whom they were dealing, sought a banker's reference about them. For this purpose their bank, National Provincial Bank, Ltd., approached D   the respondents who are the traders' bank. The respondents gave, without making any charge for it and in the usual way, a reference which was so carelessly phrased that it led the appellants to believe the traders to be creditworthy when in fact they were not. The appellants seek to recover from the respondents the consequent loss.

Counsel for the respondents has given your lordships three reasons why the E   appellants should not recover. The first is founded on a general statement of the law which, if true, is of immense effect. Its hypothesis is that there is no general duty not to make careless statements. No one challenges that hypothesis. There is no duty to be careful in speech, as there is a duty to be honest in speech. Nor indeed is there any general duty to be careful in action. The duty is limited to those who can establish some relationship of proximity such as was found to F   exist in *Donoghue* (*or McAlister*) v. *Stevenson* (130). A plaintiff cannot therefore recover for financial loss caused by a careless statement unless he can show that the maker of the statement was under a special duty to him to be careful. Counsel submits that this special duty must be brought under one of three categories. It must be contractual; or it must be fiduciary; or it must arise from the relationship of proximity, and the financial loss must flow from physical damage done G   to the person or the property of the plaintiff. The law is now settled, counsel submits, and these three categories are exhaustive. It was so decided in *Candler* v, *Crane, Christmas & Co.* (131) and that decision, counsel submits, is right in principle and in accordance with earlier authorities.

Counsel for the appellants agrees that outside contractual and fiduciary duty there must be a relationship of proximity—that is *Donoghue* v. *Stevenson* (130)— H   but he disputes that recovery is then limited to loss flowing from physical damage. He has not been able to cite a single case in which a defendant has been held liable for a careless statement leading, otherwise than through the channel of physical damage, to financial loss; but he submits that in principle such loss ought to be recoverable and that there is no authority which prevents your lordships from acting on that principle. Unless counsel for the appellants can I   persuade your lordships of this, his case fails at the outset. This therefore is the first and the most fundamental of the issues which the House is asked to decide.

Counsel for the respondents' second reason is that, if it is open to your lordships to declare that there are or can be special or proximate relationships outside the categories he has named, your lordships cannot formulate one to fit the case of a banker who gives a reference to a third party who is not his customer; and he

(129) [1958] 3 All E.R. 166; [1959] 1 Q.B. 55.
(130) [1932] All E.R. Rep. 1; [1932] A.C. 562.
(131) [1951] 1 All E.R. 426; [1951] 2 K.B. 164.

contends that your lordships have already decided that point in *Robinson* v. **A**
National Bank of Scotland (132). His third reason is that if there can be found in
cases such as this a special relationship between bankers and third parties, on the
facts of the present case the appellants fall outside it; and here he relies particularly on the fact that the reference was marked " Strictly confidential and given
on the express understanding that we incur no responsibility whatever in furnishing it."   **B**

My lords, I approach the consideration of the first and fundamental question
in the way in which LORD ATKIN approached the same sort of question—that is,
in essence the same sort, though in particulars very different—in *Donoghue* v.
Stevenson (133). If counsel for the respondents' proposition is the result of the
authorities, then, as LORD ATKIN said (134):

" I should consider the result a grave defect in the law and so contrary to   **C**
principle that I should hesitate long before following any decision to that
effect which had not the authority of this House."

So before I examine the authorities, I shall explain why I think that the law, if
settled as counsel for the respondents says that it is, would be defective. As well
as being defective in the sense that it would leave a man without a remedy where
he ought to have one and where it is well within the scope of the law to give him   **D**
one, it would also be profoundly illogical. The common law is tolerant of much
illogicality especially on the surface; but no system of law can be workable if it
has not got logic at the root of it.

Originally it was thought that the tort of negligence must be confined entirely
to deeds and could not extend to words. That was supposed to have been decided
by *Derry* v. *Peek* (135). I cannot imagine that anyone would now dispute that,   **E**
if this were the law, the law would be gravely defective. The practical proof of this
is that the supposed deficiency was, in relation to the facts in *Derry* v. *Peek* (135),
immediately made good by Act of Parliament. Today it is unthinkable that the
law could permit directors to be as careless as they liked in the statements that
they made in a prospectus.

A simple distinction between negligence in word and negligence in deed might   **F**
leave the law defective but at least it would be intelligible. This is not, however,
the distinction that is drawn in counsel for the respondents' argument and it is
one which would be unworkable. A defendant who is given a car to overhaul and
repair if necessary is liable to the injured driver (a) if he overhauls it and repairs
it negligently and tells the driver that it is safe when it is not; (b) if he overhauls it
and negligently finds it not to be in need of repair and tells the driver that it is   **G**
safe when it is not; and (c) if he negligently omits to overhaul it at all and tells the
driver that it is safe when it is not. It would be absurd in any of these cases to
argue that the proximate cause of the driver's injury was not what the defendant
did or failed to do but his negligent statement on the faith of which the driver
drove the car and for which he could not recover. In this type of case where if
there were a contract there would undoubtedly be a duty of service, it is not   **H**
practicable to distinguish between the inspection or examination, the acts done or
omitted to be done, and the advice or information given. So neither in this case
nor in *Candler* v. *Crane, Christmas & Co.* (136) (DENNING, L.J., noted the point
(137) when he gave the example of the analyst who negligently certifies food to be
harmless) has counsel for the respondents argued that the distinction lies there.

This is why the distinction is now said to depend on whether financial loss is   **I**
caused through physical injury or whether it is caused directly. The interposition
of the physical injury is said to make a difference of principle. I can find neither
logic nor commonsense in this. If irrespective of contract, a doctor negligently
advises a patient that he can safely pursue his occupation and he cannot and the

(132) 1916 S.C. (H.L.) 154.   (133) [1932] All E.R. Rep. 1; [1932] A.C. 562.
(134) [1932] All E.R. Rep. at p. 12; [1932] A.C. at p. 582.
(135) (1889), 14 App. Cas. 337.   (136) [1951] 1 All E.R. 426; [1951] 2 K.B. 164.
       (137) [1951] 1 All E.R. at p. 432; [1951] 2 K.B. at p. 179.

A patient's health suffers and he loses his livelihood, the patient has a remedy. But if the doctor negligently advises him that he cannot safely pursue his occupation when in fact he can and he loses his livelihood, there is said to be no remedy. Unless, of course, the patient was a private patient and the doctor accepted half a guinea for his trouble: then the patient can recover all. I am bound to say, my lords, that I think this to be nonsense. It is not the sort of nonsense that can

B arise even in the best system of law out of the need to draw nice distinctions between borderline cases. It arises, if it is the law, simply out of a refusal to make sense. The line is not drawn on any intelligible principle. It just happens to be the line which those who have been driven from the extreme assertion that negligent statements in the absence of contractual or fiduciary duty give no cause of action have in the course of their retreat so far reached.

C I shall now examine the relevant authorities and your lordships will, I hope, pardon me if, with one exception, I attend only to those that have been decided in this House, for I have made it plain that I will not in this matter yield to persuasion but only to compulsion. The exception is the case of *Le Lievre* v. *Gould* (138), for your lordships will not easily upset decisions of the Court of Appeal if they have stood unquestioned for as long as seventy years. The five relevant

D decisions of this House are *Derry* v. *Peek* (139), *Nocton* v. *Lord Ashburton* (140), *Robinson* v. *National Bank of Scotland* (141), *Donoghue* v. *Stevenson* (142), and *Morrison S.S. Co., Ltd.* v. *Greystoke Castle (Cargo Owners)* (143). The last of these I can deal with at once for it lies outside the main stream of authority on this point. It is a case in which damage was done to a ship as the result of a collision with another ship. The owners of cargo on the first ship, which cargo was not

E itself damaged, thus became liable to the owners of the first ship for a general average contribution. They sued the second ship as being partly to blame for the collision. Thus they were claiming for the financial loss caused to them by having to make the general average contribution although their property sustained no physical damage. This House held that they could recover. Their lordships did not in that case lay down any general principle about liability for financial loss in the

F absence of physical damage; but the case itself makes it impossible to argue that there is any general rule showing that such loss is of its nature irrecoverable.

I turn back to the earlier authorities beginning with *Derry* v. *Peek* (139). The facts in this case are so well known that I need not state them again. Nor need I state in my own words the effect of the decision. That has been done authoritatively by this House in *Nocton* v. *Lord Ashburton* (140). I quote Viscount

G Haldane, L.C., as stating most comprehensively the limits of the decision (noting that his view of the case is fully supported by Lord Shaw (144) and Lord Parmoor (145)) as follows (146):

"The discussion of the case by the noble and learned Lords who took part in the decision appears to me to exclude the hypothesis that they considered any other question to be before them than what was the necessary founda-

H tion of an ordinary action for deceit. They must indeed be taken to have thought that the facts proved as to the relationship of the parties in *Derry* v. *Peek* (139) were not enough to establish any special duty arising out of that relationship other than the general duty of honesty. But they do not say that where a different sort of relationship ought to be inferred from the circumstances the case is to be concluded by asking whether an action for

I deceit will lie."

There was in *Derry* v. *Peek* (139), as the report of the case shows, no plea of

(138) [1893] 1 Q.B. 491.   (139) (1889), 14 App. Cas. 337.
(140) [1914-15] All E.R. Rep. 45; [1914] A.C. 932.
(141) 1916 S.C. (H.L.) 154.   (142) [1932] All E.R. Rep. 1; [1932] A.C. 562.
(143) [1946] 2 All E.R. 696; [1947] A.C. 265.
(144) [1914-15] All E.R. Rep. at p. 61; [1914] A.C. at p. 970.
(145) [1914] A.C. at p. 978.
(146) [1914-15] All E.R. Rep. at p. 49; [1914] A.C. at p. 947.

innocent or negligent misrepresentation and so their lordships did not make any A
pronouncement on that. I am bound to say that had there been such a plea I am
sure that the House would have rejected it. As LORD HALDANE said, their
lordships must " be taken to have thought " that there was no liability in negligence. But what their lordships may be taken to have thought, though it may
exercise great influence on those who thereafter have to form their own opinion
on the subject, is not the law of England. It is impossible to say how their B
lordships would have formulated the principle if they had laid one down. They
might have made it general or they might have confined it to the facts of the case.
They might have made an exception of the sort indicated by LORD HERSCHELL
(147) or they might not. This is speculation. All that is certain is that on this
point the House laid down no law at all.

Clearly in *Le Lievre* v. *Gould* (148) it was thought that the House had done so. C
LORD ESHER, M.R. (149), treated *Derry* v. *Peek* (150) as restating the old law
" that, in the absence of contract, an action for negligence cannot be maintained
when there is no fraud ". A. L. SMITH, L.J., stated the law in the same way (151).
This is wrong and the House in effect said so in *Nocton* v. *Lord Ashburton* (152).

My lords, I need not consider how far thereafter a court of equal authority was
bound to follow *Le Lievre* v. *Gould* (148). It may be that the decision on the facts D
was correct even though the reasoning was too wide. There has been a difference
of opinion about the effect of the decision: compare ASQUITH, L.J., in *Candler* v.
Crane, Christmas & Co. (153) with DENNING, L.J. (154). Nor need I consider
what part of the reasoning, if any, should be held to survive *Nocton* v. *Lord
Ashburton* (152). It is clear that after 1914 it would be to *Nocton* v. *Lord Ashburton* (152) and not to *Le Lievre* v. *Gould* (148) that the lawyer would look in E
order to ascertain what the exceptions were to the general principle that a man is
not liable for careless misrepresentation. I cannot feel, therefore, that there is any
principle enunciated in *Le Lievre* v. *Gould* (148) which is now so deeply embedded
in the law that your lordships ought not to disturb it.

I come now to the case of *Nocton* v. *Lord Ashburton* (152) which both sides put
forward as the most important of the authorities which your lordships have to F
consider. The appellants say that it removed the restrictions which *Derry* v.
Peek (150) was thought to have put on liability for negligent misrepresentation.
The respondents say that it removed those restrictions only to a very limited
extent, that is to say, by adding fiduciary obligation to contract as a source of
special duty; and that it closed the door on any further expansion. I propose,
therefore, to examine it with some care because it is not at all easy to determine G
exactly what it decided. LORD HALDANE began his speech by saying (155):

" Owing to the mode in which this case has been treated both by the learned
judge who tried it and by the Court of Appeal, the question to be decided has
been the subject of some uncertainty and much argument."

He went on to say that the difficulties in giving relief were concerned with form H
and not with substance. The main difficulty, I think, lies in discovering from the
statement of claim what the cause of action was. Lord Ashburton sought relief
from the consequences of having advanced money on mortgage to several persons
of whom the defendant Nocton was one. The statement of claim consists of a long
narrative of events interspersed with complaints. Although in the end the vital
fact was that Nocton was Ashburton's solicitor, there is no allegation of any
retainer and nothing is pleaded in contract. The fact that Nocton was a solicitor I
emerges only in the framing of the complaint in para. 13 where it was said that
Nocton's advice to make the advance of £65,000 " was not that of a solicitor

(147) (1889), 14 App. Cas. at p. 360.   (148) [1893] 1 Q.B. 491.
(149) [1893] 1 Q.B. at p. 498.   (150) (1889), 14 App. Cas. 337.
(151) [1893] 1 Q.B. at p. 504.   (152) [1914-15] All E.R. Rep. 45; [1914] A.C. 932.
(153) [1951] 1 All E.R. 426 at p. 441; [1951] 2 K.B. 164 at p. 193.
(154) [1951] 1 All E.R. at p. 434; [1951] 2 K.B. at p. 181.
(155) [1914-15] All E.R. Rep. at p. 47; [1914] A.C. at p. 943.

A advising his client in good faith but was given for his own private ends ". The relief asked for in respect of this transaction is a declaration " that the plaintiff was improperly advised and induced by the defendant Nocton whilst acting as the plaintiff's confidential solicitor " to advance £65,000. In para. 31 to para. 33 of the statement of claim it is related that the plaintiff was asked to release part of his security for the loan; and it is said that " the defendant Nocton in advising

B the plaintiff to execute the said release allowed the plaintiff to believe that he was advising the plaintiff independently and in good faith and in the plaintiff's interest ". No separate relief was sought in respect of this transaction.

Until the case reached this House no substantial point of law was raised. NEVILLE, J., at the trial held that the only issue raised by the statement of claim was whether the defendant Nocton was guilty of fraud and that the plaintiff had

C failed to prove it. The Court of Appeal agreed with the judge's view of the pleadings. COZENS-HARDY, M.R., said that if damages had been claimed on the ground of negligence, the action would have been practically undefended. But it was then too late to amend the statement of claim if only because a new cause of action would have been statute-barred. On the facts the Court of Appeal reversed in part the judge's finding of fraud, holding that there was fraud in relation to the

D release.

In this House at the conclusion of the appellant's argument the respondent's counsel was told that the House was unlikely to differ from the judgment of NEVILLE, J., on fraud. The pith of the respondent's argument is reported as follows (156):

E " Assuming that fraud is out of the question, the allegations in the statement of claim are wide enough to found a claim for dereliction of duty by a person occupying a fiduciary relation. In the old cases in equity the term 'fraud' was frequently applied to cases of a breach of fiduciary obligation."

He was then stopped.

It can now be understood why LORD HALDANE regarded the question as

F one of form rather than of substance. The first question which the House had to consider was whether the statement of claim was wide enough to cover negligence. LORD PARMOOR thought that it was and (157) decided the appeal on that ground. So I think in the end did LORD DUNEDIN (158), but he also expressed his agreement with the opinion of LORD HALDANE. LORD HALDANE, with whom LORD ATKINSON concurred, thought that possibly negligence was covered but he did

G not take the view that the statement of claim must be interpreted either as an allegation of deceit or as an allegation of negligence. He said (159):

" There is a third form of procedure to which the statement of claim approximated very closely, and that is the old bill in Chancery to enforce compensation for breach of a fiduciary obligation. There appears to have been an impression that the necessity which recent authorities have estab-

H lished of proving moral fraud in order to succeed in an action of deceit has narrowed the scope of this remedy. For the reasons which I am about to offer to your lordships, I do not think that this is so."

The Lord Chancellor then went on to examine *Derry* v. *Peek* (160) in order to determine exactly what it had decided.

I I find most interest for present purposes in the speech of LORD SHAW OF DUNFERMLINE. He held that the pleadings disclosed (161)

" a claim for liability upon a ground quite independent of fraud, namely,

---

(156) [1914] A.C. at p. 943.
(157) [1914] A.C. at p. 978; [1914-15] All E.R. Rep. at p. 63.
(158) [1914-15] All E.R. Rep. at p. 58; [1914] A.C. at p. 965.
(159) [1914-15] All E.R. Rep. at pp. 48, 49; [1914] A.C. at p. 946.
(160) (1889), 14 App. Cas. 337.
(161) [1914-15] All E.R. Rep. at p. 59; [1914] A.C. at p. 967.

of misrepresentations and misstatements made by a person entrusted with a   A
duty to another, and in failure of that duty."

He posed what he considered to be the crucial question (162): "What was the
relation in which the parties stood to each other at the time of the transaction."
He stated (163) that the defendant was Lord Ashburton's solicitor and so under
a duty to advise. He concluded in the following terms (164):
                                                                             B
    "Once the relations of parties have been ascertained to be those in which a
    duty is laid upon one person of giving information or advice to another upon
    which that other is entitled to rely as the basis of a transaction, responsibility
    for error amounting to misrepresentation in any statement made will attach
    to the advisor or informer, although the information and advice have been
    given not fraudulently, but in good faith. It is admitted in the present case   C
    that misrepresentations were made; that they were material; that they were
    the cause of the loss; that they were made by a solicitor to his client in a
    situation in which the client was entitled to rely, and did rely, upon the infor-
    mation received. I, accordingly, think that that situation is plainly open for
    the application of the principle of liability to which I have referred, namely,
    liability for the consequences of a failure of duty in circumstances in which   D
    it was a matter equivalent to contract between the parties that that duty
    should be fulfilled."

LORD SHAW does not anywhere in his speech refer to the relationship as being of a
fiduciary character. LORD HALDANE laid down the general principle in much
the same terms. He said (165):

    "Although liability for negligence in word has in material respects been   E
    developed in our law differently from liability for negligence in act, it is
    none the less true that a man may come under a special duty to exercise care
    in giving information or advice. I should accordingly be sorry to be thought
    to lend countenance to the idea that recent decisions have been intended to
    stereotype the cases in which people can be held to have assumed such a
    special duty. Whether such a duty has been assumed must depend on the   F
    relationship of the parties, and it is at least certain that there are a good
    many cases in which that relationship may be properly treated as giving rise
    to a special duty of care in statement."

It is quite true that LORD HALDANE applied this principle only to cases of
breach of fiduciary duty. But that was inevitable on the facts of the case since
upon the view of the pleading on which he was proceeding it was necessary to   G
show equitable fraud.

In my judgment the effect of this case is as follows. The House clearly considered
the view of *Derry* v. *Peek* (166), exemplified in *Le Lievre* v. *Gould* (167), to be too
narrow. It considered that outside contract (for contract was not pleaded in the
case), there could be a special relationship between parties which imposed a duty
to give careful advice and accurate information. The majority of their lordships   H
did not extend the application of this principle beyond the breach of a fiduciary
obligation, but none of them said anything at all to show that it was limited to
fiduciary obligation. Your lordships can therefore proceed on the footing that
there is such a general principle and that it is for you to say to what cases, beyond
those of fiduciary obligation, it can properly be extended.

I shall not at this stage deal in any detail with *Robinson* v. *National Bank of*   I
Scotland (168). Its chief relevance is to counsel for the respondents' second point.
All that need be said about it on his first point is that it is no authority for the

(162) [1914-15] All E.R. Rep. at p. 60; [1914] A.C. at p. 968.
(163) [1914-15] All E.R. Rep. at p. 60; [1914] A.C. at p. 969.
(164) [1914-15] All E.R. Rep. at p. 62; [1914] A.C. at p. 972.
(165) [1914-15] All E.R. Rep. at p. 50; [1914] A.C. at p. 948.
(166) (1889), 14 App. Cas. 337.   (167) [1893] 1 Q.B. 491.
                (168) 1916 S.C. (H.L.) 154.

A proposition that those relationships which give rise to a special duty of care are limited to the contractual and the fiduciary. On the contrary, it is a clear authority for the view that LORD HALDANE did not mean the general principle he stated in *Nocton* v. *Lord Ashburton* (169) to be limited to fiduciary relationships. He said (170) that he wished emphatically to repeat what he had said in *Nocton* v. *Lord Ashburton* (169) that it would be a great mistake to suppose that the principle

B in *Derry* v. *Peek* (171) affected the freedom of action of the courts in recognising special duties arising out of other kinds of relationship. He went on (170):

> " The whole of the doctrine as to fiduciary relationships, as to the duty of care arising from implied as well as express contracts, as to the duty of care arising from special relationships which the courts may find to exist in particular cases, still remains, and I should be very sorry if any word fell from
C me which should suggest that the courts are in any way hampered in recognising that the duty of care may be established when such cases really occur."

I come next to *Donoghue (or McAlister)* v. *Stevenson* (172). In his celebrated speech in that case LORD ATKIN did two things. He stated (173) what he des-
D cribed as a general conception and from that conception he formulated (174) a specific proposition of law. In between he gave a warning (175)

> " against the danger of stating propositions of law in wider terms than is necessary, lest essential factors be omitted in a wider survey and the inherent adaptability of English law be unduly restricted."

What LORD ATKIN called a " general conception of relations giving rise to a duty
E of care " is now often referred to as the principle of proximity. You must take reasonable care to avoid acts or omissions which you can reasonably foresee would be likely to injure your neighbour. In the eyes of the law your neighbour is a person who is so closely and directly affected by your act that you ought reasonably to have him in contemplation as being so affected when you are direct-ing your mind to the acts or omissions which are called in question. The specific
F proposition arising out of this conception is that (176)

> " a manufacturer of products, which he sells in such a form as to show that he intends them to reach the ultimate consumer in the form in which they left him, with no reasonable possibility of intermediate examination, and with the knowledge that the absence of reasonable care in the preparation or putting up of the products will result in an injury to the consumer's life or
G property, owes a duty to the consumer to take that reasonable care."

Now it is not in my opinion a sensible application of what LORD ATKIN was saying for a judge to be invited on the facts of any particular case to say whether or not there was " proximity " between the plaintiff and the defendant. That would be a misuse of a general conception and it is not the way in which English
H law develops. What LORD ATKIN did was to use his general conception to open up a category of cases giving rise to a special duty. It was already clear that the law recognised the existence of such duty in the category of articles that were dangerous in themselves. What *Donoghue* v. *Stevenson* (177) did may be described either as the widening of an old category or as the creation of a new and similar one. The general conception can be used to produce other categories in the same way. An existing category grows as instances of its application multiply, until the time comes when the cell divides.

---

(169) [1914-15] All E.R. Rep. 45; [1914] A.C. 932.
(170) 1916 S.C. (H.L.) at p. 157.   (171) (1889), 14 App. Cas. 337.
(172) [1932] All E.R. Rep. 1; [1932] A.C. 562.
(173) [1932] All E.R. Rep. at p. 11; [1932] A.C. at p. 580.
(174) [1932] All E.R. Rep. at p. 20; [1932] A.C. at p. 599.
(175) [1932] All E.R. Rep. at p. 13; [1932] A.C. at p. 584.
(176) [1932] All E.R. Rep. at p. 20; [1932] A.C. at p. 599.
(177) [1932] All E.R. Rep. 1; [1932] A.C. 562.

LORD THANKERTON and LORD MACMILLAN approached the problem funda-   **A**
mentally in the same way, though they left any general conception on which they
were acting to be implied. They inquired directly (178) whether the relationship
between the plaintiff and the defendant was such as to give rise to a duty to take
care. It is significant, whether it is a coincidence or not, that the term " special
relationship " used by LORD THANKERTON is also the one used by LORD HALDANE
in *Nocton* v. *Lord Ashburton* (179). The field is very different but the object of the   **B**
search is the same.

In my opinion the appellants in their argument tried to press *Donoghue* v.
Stevenson (108) too hard. They asked whether the principle of proximity should
not apply as well to words as to deeds. I think that it should, but as it is only a
general conception it does not get them very far. Then they take the specific
proposition laid down by *Donoghue* v. *Stevenson* (180) and try to apply it literally   **C**
to a certificate or a banker's reference. That will not do, for a general conception
cannot be applied to pieces of paper in the same way as to articles of commerce,
or to writers in the same way as to manufacturers. An inquiry into the possibili-
ties of intermediate examination of a certificate will not be fruitful. The real value
of *Donoghue* v. *Stevenson* (180) to the argument in this case is that it shows how
the law can be developed to solve particular problems. Is the relationship   **D**
between the parties in this case such that it can be brought within a category
giving rise to a special duty? As always in English law the first step in such an
inquiry is to see how far the authorities have gone, for new categories in the law
do not spring into existence overnight.

It would be surprising if the sort of problem that is created by the facts of this
case had never until recently arisen in English law. As a problem it is a by-   **E**
product of the doctrine of consideration. If the respondents had made a nominal
charge for the reference, the problem would not exist. If it were possible in
English law to construct a contract without consideration, the problem would
move at once out of the first and general phase into the particular; and the
question would be, not whether on the facts of the case there was a special relationship, but whether on the facts of the case there was a contract.   **F**

The respondents in this case cannot deny that they were performing a service.
Their sheet anchor is that they were performing it gratuitously and therefore no
liability for its performance can arise. My lords, in my opinion this is not the law.
A promise given without consideration to perform a service cannot be enforced as
a contract by the promisee; but if the service is in fact performed and done
negligently, the promisee can recover in an action in tort. This is the foundation   **G**
of the liability of a gratuitous bailee. In the famous case of *Coggs* v. *Bernard* (181),
where the defendant had charge of brandy belonging to the plaintiff and had
spilt a quantity of it, there was a motion in arrest of judgment " for that it was not
alleged in the declaration that the defendant was a common porter, nor averred
that he had anything for his pains ". The declaration was held to be good notwithstanding that there was not any consideration laid. GOULD, J., said (181):   **H**

" The reason of the action is, the particular trust reposed in the defendant,
to which he has concurred by his assumption, and in the executing which he
has miscarried by his neglect."

This proposition is not limited to the law of bailment. In *Skelton* v. *London &
North Western Ry. Co.* (182) WILLES, J., applied it generally to the law of negli-   **I**
gence. He said (183):

---

(178) [1932] All E.R. Rep. at pp. 22, 30; [1932] A.C. at pp. 603, 619, 620.
(179) [1914-15] All E.R. Rep. 45; [1914] A.C. 932.
(180) [1932] All E.R. Rep. 1; [1932] A.C. 562.
(181) (1703), 2 Ld. Raym. 909.   (182) (1867), L.R. 2 C.P. 631.
          (183) (1867), L.R. 2 C.P. at p. 636.

A "Actionable negligence must consist in the breach of some duty . . . if a person undertakes to perform a voluntary act, he is liable if he performs it improperly, but not if he neglects to perform it. Such is the result of the decision in the case of *Coggs* v. *Bernard* (184)."

Likewise in *Banbury* v. *Bank of Montreal* (185), where the bank had advised a
B customer on his investments, Lord Finlay, L.C., said (186): "He is under no obligation to advise, but if he takes upon himself to do so, he will incur liability if he does so negligently."

The principle has been applied to cases where as a result of the negligence no damage was done to person or to property and the consequential loss was purely financial. In *Wilkinson* v. *Coverdale* (187) the defendant undertook gratuitously
C to get a fire policy renewed for the plaintiff, but, in doing so, neglected formalities, the omission of which rendered the policy inoperative. It was held that an action would lie. In two similar cases the defendants succeeded on the ground that negligence was not proved in fact. Both cases were thus decided on the basis that in law an action would lie. In the first of them, *Shiells* v. *Blackburne* (188), the defendant had, acting voluntarily and without reward, made an entry of the
D plaintiff's leather as wrought leather instead of dressed leather, with the result that the leather was seized. In *Dartnall* v. *Howard* (189) the defendants purchased an annuity for the plaintiff but on the personal security of two insolvent persons. The court, after verdict, arrested the judgment on the ground that the defendants appeared to be gratuitous agents and that it was not averred that they had acted either with negligence or dishonesty.
E Many cases could be cited in which the same result has been achieved by setting up some nominal consideration and suing in contract instead of in tort. In *Coggs* v. *Bernard* (190) Holt, C.J., put the obligation on both grounds. He said (191):

F "Secondly it is objected, that there is no consideration to ground this promise upon, and therefore the undertaking is but nudum pactum. But to this I answer, that the owner's trusting him with the goods is a sufficient consideration to oblige him to a careful management. Indeed if the agreement had been executory, to carry these brandies from the one place to the other such a day, the defendant had not been bound to carry them. But this is a different case, for assumpsit does not only signify a future
G agreement, but in such a case as this, it signifies an actual entry upon the thing, and taking the trust upon himself. And if a man will do that, and miscarries in the performance of his trust, an action will lie against him for that, though nobody could have compelled him to do the thing."

De la Bere v. *Pearson, Ltd.* (192) is an example of a case of this sort decided
H on the ground that there was a sufficiency of consideration. The defendants advertised in their newspaper that their city editor would answer inquiries from readers of the paper desiring financial advice. The plaintiff asked for the name of a good stockbroker. The editor recommended the name of a person whom he knew to be an outside broker and whom he ought to have known, if he had made proper inquiries, to be an undischarged bankrupt. The plaintiff dealt with him
I and lost his money. The case being brought in contract, Vaughan Williams, L.J., thought (193) that there was sufficient consideration in the fact that the

(184) (1703), 2 Ld. Raym. 909.   (185) [1918-19] All E.R. Rep. 1; [1918] A.C. 626.
(186) [1918] A.C. at p. 654.   (187) (1793), 1 Esp. 74.   (188) (1789), 1 Hy. Bl. 158.
(189) (1825), 4 B. & C. 345.   (190) (1703), 2 Ld. Raym. 909.
(191) (1703), 2 Ld. Raym. at p. 919.
(192) [1904-7] All E.R. Rep. 755; [1908] 1 K.B. 280.
(193) [1904-7] All E.R. Rep. at p. 756; [1908] 1 K.B. at p. 287.

plaintiff consented to the publication of his question in the defendants' paper if **A**
the defendants so chose. For BARNES, P., the consideration appears to have lain
in the plaintiff addressing an inquiry as invited (194). In the same way when in
Everett v. *Griffiths* (195) the Court of Appeal was considering the liability of a
doctor towards the person he was certifying, SCRUTTON, L.J. (196), said that the
submission to treatment would be a good consideration.

My lords, I have cited these instances so as to show that in one way or another **B**
the law has ensured that in this type of case a just result has been reached. But
I think that today the result can and should be achieved by the application of
the law of negligence and that it is unnecessary and undesirable to construct an
artificial consideration. I agree with Sir Frederick Pollock's note on the case of
De la Bere v. *Pearson, Ltd.* (197), where he wrote in POLLOCK ON CONTRACT
(13th Edn.) 140 (note 31) that "the cause of action is better regarded as arising **C**
from default in the performance of a voluntary undertaking independent of contract".

My lords, it is true that this principle of law has not yet been clearly applied
to a case where the service which the defendant undertakes to perform is or
includes the obtaining and imparting of information. But I cannot see why it
should not be: and if it had not been thought erroneously that *Derry* v. *Peek* **D**
(198) negatived any liability for negligent statements, I think that by now it
probably would have been. It cannot matter whether the information consists
of fact or of opinion or is a mixture of both, nor whether it was obtained as a result
of special inquiries or comes direct from facts already in the defendant's possession
or from his general store of professional knowledge. One cannot, as I have already
endeavoured to show, distinguish in this respect between a duty to inquire and a **E**
duty to state.

I think, therefore, that there is ample authority to justify your lordships in
saying now that the categories of special relationships, which may give rise to a
duty to take care in word as well as in deed, are not limited to contractual relationships or to relationships of fiduciary duty, but include also relationships which in
the words of LORD SHAW in *Nocton* v. *Lord Ashburton* (199) are "equivalent to **F**
contract" that is, where there is an assumption of responsibility in circumstances
in which, but for the absence of consideration, there would be a contract. Where
there is an express undertaking, an express warranty as distinct from mere
representation, there can be little difficulty. The difficulty arises in discerning
those cases in which the undertaking is to be implied. In this respect the absence
of consideration is not irrelevant. Payment for information or advice is very good **G**
evidence that it is being relied on and that the informer or adviser knows that it is.
Where there is no consideration, it will be necessary to exercise greater care in
distinguishing between social and professional relationships and between those
which are of a contractual character and those which are not. It may often be
material to consider whether the adviser is acting purely out of good nature or
whether he is getting his reward in some indirect form. The service that a bank **H**
performs in giving a reference is not done simply out of a desire to assist commerce.
It would discourage the customers of the bank if their deals fell through because
the bank had refused to testify to their credit when it was good.

I have had the advantage of reading all the opinions prepared by your lordships
and of studying the terms which your lordships have framed by way of definition
of the sort of relationship which gives rise to a responsibility towards those who
act on information or advice and so creates a duty of care towards them. I do not

---

(194) [1904-7] All E.R. Rep. at p. 757; [1908] 1 K.B. at p. 289.
(195) [1920] 3 K.B. 163; *affd.* [1921] 1 A.C. 631.
(196) [1920] 3 K.B. at p. 191.
(197) [1904-7] All E.R. Rep. 755; [1908] 1 K.B. 280.
(198) (1889), 14 App. Cas. 337.
(199) [1914-15] All E.R. Rep. at p. 62; [1914] A.C. at p. 972.

A understand any of your lordships to hold that it is a responsibility imposed by law on certain types of persons or in certain sorts of situations. It is a responsibility that is voluntarily accepted or undertaken either generally where a general relationship, such as that of solicitor and client or banker and customer, is created, or specifically in relation to a particular transaction. In the present case the appellants were not, as in *Woods* v. *Martins Bank, Ltd.* (200) the customers

B or potential customers of the bank. Responsibility can attach only to the single act, i.e., the giving of the reference, and only if the doing of that act implied a voluntary undertaking to assume responsibility. This is a point of great importance because it is, as I understand it, the foundation for the ground on which in the end the House dismisses the appeal. I do not think it possible to formulate with exactitude all the conditions under which the law will in a specific case

C imply a voluntary undertaking, any more than it is possible to formulate those in which the law will imply a contract. But in so far as your lordships describe the circumstances in which an implication will ordinarily be drawn, I am prepared to adopt any one of your lordships' statements as showing the general rule; and I pay the same respect to the statement by Denning, L.J., in his dissenting judgment in *Candler* v. *Crane, Christmas & Co.* (201) about the circumstances

D in which he says a duty to use care in making a statement exists.

I do not go further than this for two reasons. The first is that I have found in the speech of Lord Shaw in *Nocton* v. *Lord Ashburton* (202) and in the idea of a relationship that is equivalent to contract all that is necessary to cover the situation that arises in this case. Counsel for the appellants does not claim to succeed unless he can establish that the reference was intended by the respondents to be

E communicated by National Provincial Bank, Ltd. to some unnamed customer of theirs, whose identity was immaterial to the respondents, for that customer's use. All that was lacking was formal consideration. The case is well within the authorities that I have already cited and of which *Wilkinson* v. *Coverdale* (203) is the most apposite example.

I shall therefore content myself with the proposition that wherever there

F is a relationship equivalent to contract there is a duty of care. Such a relationship may be either general or particular. Examples of a general relationship are those of solicitor and client and of banker and customer. For the former *Nocton* v. *Lord Ashburton* (202) has long stood as the authority and for the latter there is the decision of Salmon, J., in *Woods* v. *Martins Bank, Ltd.* (204) which I respectfully approve. There may well be others yet to be established. Where there is a general

G relationship of this sort it is unnecessary to do more than prove its existence and the duty follows. Where, as in the present case, what is relied on is a particular relationship created ad hoc, it will be necessary to examine the particular facts to see whether there is an express or implied undertaking of responsibility.

I regard this proposition as an application of the general conception of proximity. Cases may arise in the future in which a new and wider proposition,

H quite independent of any notion of contract, will be needed. There may, for example, be cases in which a statement is not supplied for the use of any particular person, any more than in *Donoghue* v. *Stevenson* (205) the ginger beer was supplied for consumption by any particular person; and it will then be necessary to return to the general conception of proximity and to see whether there can be evolved from it, as was done in *Donoghue* v. *Stevenson* (205), a specific proposition to fit

I the case. When that has to be done, the speeches of your lordships today as well as the judgment of Denning, L.J., to which I have referred—and also, I may add,

(200) [1958] 3 All E.R. 166; [1959] 1 Q.B. 55.
(201) [1951] 1 All E.R. 426 at p. 433; [1951] 2 K.B. 164 at p. 179.
(202) [1914-15] All E.R. Rep. 45; [1914] A.C. 932.   (203) (1793), 1 Esp. 74.
(204) [1958] 3 All E.R. 166; [1959] 1 Q.B. 55.
(205) [1932] All E.R. Rep. 1; [1932] A.C. 562.

the proposition in the " Restatement " (206), and the cases which exemplify it, will **A**
afford good guidance as to what ought to be said. I prefer to see what shape such
cases take before committing myself to any formulation, for I bear in mind
LORD ATKIN's warning, which I have quoted, against placing unnecessary
restrictions on the adaptability of English law. I have, I hope, made it clear that
I take quite literally the dictum of LORD MACMILLAN, so often quoted from
the same case, that (207) " the categories of negligence are never closed ". **B**
English law is wide enough to embrace any new category or proposition that
exemplifies the principle of proximity.

I have another reason for caution. Since the essence of the matter in the present
case and in others of the same type is the acceptance of responsibility, I should
like to guard against the imposition of restrictive terms notwithstanding that the
essential condition is fulfilled. If a defendant says to a plaintiff:—" Let me **C**
do this for you, do not waste your money in employing a professional, I will do
it for nothing and you can rely on me ", I do not think that he could escape
liability simply because he belonged to no profession or calling, had no qualifications or special skill and did not hold himself out as having any. The relevance
of these factors is to show the unlikelihood of a defendant in such circumstances
assuming a legal responsibility and as such they may often be decisive. But they **D**
are not theoretically conclusive, and so cannot be the subject of definition. It
would be unfortunate if they were. For it would mean that plaintiffs would
seek to avoid the rigidity of the definition by bringing the action in contract
as in *De la Bere* v. *Pearson, Ltd.* (208) and setting up something that would do for
consideration. That to my mind would be an undesirable development in the law;
and the best way of avoiding it is to settle the law so that the presence or absence **E**
of consideration makes no difference.

Your lordships' attention was called to a number of cases in courts of first
instance or of appeal which it was said would have been decided differently if the
appellants' main contention was correct. I do not propose to go through them in
order to consider whether on the facts of each it should or should not be upheld.
I shall content myself with saying that in my opinion *Le Lievre* v. *Gould* (209) **F**
and all decisions based on its reasoning (in which I specifically include, lest
otherwise it might be thought that generalia specialibus non derogant, the decision
of DEVLIN, J., in *Heskell* v. *Continental Express, Ltd.* (210)) can no longer be
regarded as authoritative; and when similar facts arise in the future, the case
will have to be judged afresh in the light of the principles which the House has
now laid down. **G**

My lords, I have devoted much time and thought to considering the first
reason given by counsel for the respondents for rejecting the appellants' claim. I
have done so, not only because his reason was based on a ground so fundamental
that it called for a full refutation, but also because it is impossible to find the correct answer on the facts to the appellants' claim until the relevant criteria for
ascertaining whether or not there is a duty to take care have been clearly estab- **H**
lished. Once that is done their application to the facts of this case can be done
very shortly, for the case then becomes a very simple one.

I am satisfied for the reasons which I have given that a person for whose use
a banker's reference is furnished is not, simply because no consideration has
passed, prevented from contending that the banker is responsible to him for what

---

(206) See 65 CORPUS JURIS SECUNDUM title Negligence, pp. 428, 429, §20, which begins
" A false statement negligently made may be the basis of a recovery of damages for
injury or loss sustained in consequence of reliance thereon, the American rule, in this
respect, being more liberal than the rule in England."
(207) [1932] All E.R. Rep. at p. 30; [1932] A.C. at p. 619.
(208) [1904-7] All E.R. Rep. 755; [1908] 1 K.B. 280.
(209) [1893] 1 Q.B. 491.
(210) [1950] 1 All E.R. 1033 at p. 1044.

A he has said. The question is whether the appellants can set up a claim equivalent to contract and rely on an implied undertaking to accept responsibility. Counsel for the respondents' second point is that in *Robinson* v. *National Bank of Scotland* (211) this House has already laid it down as a general rule that in the case of a banker furnishing a reference that cannot be done. I do not agree. The facts in that case have been stated by my noble and learned friend LORD REID and I

B need not repeat them. I think it is plain on those facts that the bank in that case was not furnishing the reference for the use of the pursuer; he was not a person for whose use of the reference they were undertaking any responsibility, and that quite apart from their general disclaimer. Furthermore, the pursuer never saw the reference; he was given only what the Lord Justice-Clerk described (212) as

C "a gloss of it". This makes the connexion between the pursuer and the defendants far too remote to constitute a relationship of a contractual character.

On the facts of the present case counsel for the respondents has, under his third head, argued for the same result. He submits, first, that it ought not to be inferred that the respondents knew that National Provincial Bank, Ltd. were asking for the reference for the use of a customer. If the respondents did know

D that, then counsel submits that they did not intend that the reference itself should be communicated to the customer; it was intended only as material upon which the customer's bank could advise the customer on its own responsibility. I should consider it necessary to examine these contentions were it not for the general disclaimer of responsibility which appears to me in any event to be conclusive. I agree entirely with the reasoning and conclusion on this point of my noble and

E learned friend LORD REID. A man cannot be said voluntarily to be undertaking a responsibility if at the very moment when he is said to be accepting it he declares that in fact he is not. The problem of reconciling words of exemption with the existence of a duty arises only when a party is claiming exemption from a responsibility which he has already undertaken or which he is contracting to undertake.

F For this reason alone, I would dismiss the appeal.

LORD PEARCE: My Lords, VISCOUNT HALDANE, L.C., in *Nocton* v. *Lord Ashburton* (213) said:

G " Although liability for negligence in word has in material respects been developed in our law differently from liability for negligence in act, it is none the less true that a man may come under a special duty to exercise care in giving information or advice. I should accordingly be sorry to be thought to lend countenance to the idea that recent decisions have been intended to stereotype the cases in which people can be held to have assumed such a special duty. Whether such a duty has been assumed must depend

H on the relationship of the parties, and it is at least certain that there are a good many cases in which that relationship may be properly treated as giving rise to a special duty of care in statement."

The law of negligence has been deliberately limited in its range by the courts' insistence that there can be no actionable negligence in vacuo without the exist-

I ence of some duty to the plaintiff. For it would be impracticable to grant relief to everybody who suffers damage through the carelessness of another.

The reason for some divergence between the law of negligence in word and that of negligence in act is clear. Negligence in word creates problems different from those of negligence in act. Words are more volatile than deeds. They travel fast and far afield. They are used without being expended and take effect

---

(211) 1916 S.C. (H.L.) 154.   (212) 1916 S.C. at p. 58.
    (213) [1914-15] All E.R. Rep. 45 at p. 50; [1914] A.C. 932 at p. 948.

in combination with innumerable facts and other words. Yet they are dangerous A and can cause vast financial damage. How far they are relied on unchecked (by analogy with there being no probability of intermediate inspection—see *Grant* v. *Australian Knitting Mills, Ltd.* (214)) must in many cases be a matter of doubt and difficulty. If the mere hearing or reading of words were held to create proximity, there might be no limit to the persons to whom the speaker or writer could be liable. Damage by negligent acts to persons or property on the other hand is more B visible and obvious; its limits are more easily defined and it is with this damage that the earlier cases were more concerned. It was not until 1789 that *Pasley* v. *Freeman* (215) recognised and laid down a duty of honesty in words to the world at large—thus creating a remedy designed to protect the economic as opposed to the physical interests of the community. Any attempts to extend this remedy C by imposing a duty of care as well as a duty of honesty in representations by word were curbed by *Derry* v. *Peek* (216).

In *Cann* v. *Willson* (217) it had been held that a valuer was liable in respect of a negligent valuation which he had been employed by the owner of property to make for the purpose of raising a mortgage, and which the valuer himself put before the proposed mortgagee's solicitor. CHITTY, J., there said (218): D

" It seems to me that the defendants knowingly placed themselves in that position, and in point of law incurred a duty towards him to use reasonable care in the preparation of the document called a valuation. I think it is like the case of an article—the supply of the hairwash in the case of *George* v. *Skivington* (219)." E

George v. *Skivington* was later approved in *Donoghue (or McAlister)* v. *Stevenson* (220). Thus in the case of economic damage alone he was drawing an analogy from a case where physical damage to the wife of a purchaser was held to give rise to an action for negligence.

Cann v. *Willson* (217) was, however, overruled by *Le Lievre* v. *Gould* (221) F on the ground, erroneous as it seems to me, that it could not stand with *Derry* v. *Peek* (216). The particular facts in *Le Lievre* v. *Gould* (221) justified the particular decision, as DENNING, L.J., explained in *Candler* v. *Crane, Christmas & Co.* (222). But the ratio decidendi was wrong since it attributed to *Derry* v. *Peek* (216) more than that case decided. In *Nocton* v. *Lord Ashburton* (223) this House pointed out that too much had been ascribed to *Derry* v. *Peek* (216). VISCOUNT G HALDANE, L.C., said (224):

" The discussion of the case by the noble and learned lords who took part in the decision appears to me to exclude the hypothesis that they considered any other question to be before them than what was the necessary foundation of an ordinary action for deceit. They must indeed be taken to have H thought that the facts proved as to the relationship of the parties in *Derry* v. *Peek* (216) were not enough to establish any special duty arising out of that relationship other than the general duty of honesty. But they do not say that where a different sort of relationship ought to be inferred from the circumstances the case is to be concluded by asking whether an action

---

(214) [1935] All E.R. Rep. 209; [1936] A.C. 85.
(215) (1789), 3 Term. Rep. 51.   (216) (1889), 14 App. Cas. 337.
(217) (1888), 39 Ch.D. 39.   (218) (1888), 39 Ch.D. at pp. 42, 43.
(219) (1869), L.R. 5 Exch. 1.
(220) [1932] All E.R. Rep. 1; [1932] A.C. 562.
(221) [1893] 1 Q.B. 491.   (222) [1951] 1 All E.R. 426; [1951] 2 K.B. 164.
(223) [1914-15] All E.R. Rep. 45; [1914] A.C. 932.
(224) [1914-15] All E.R. Rep. at p. 49; [1914] A.C. at p. 947.

A   of deceit will lie. I think that the authorities, subsequent to the decision of the House of Lords shew a tendency to assume that it was intended to mean more than it did. In reality the judgment covered only a part of the field in which liabilities may arise. There are other obligations besides that on honesty, the breach of which may give rise to damages. These obligations depend on principles which the judges have worked out in the

B   fashion that is characteristic of a system where much of the law has always been judge-made and unwritten."

Lord Haldane spoke to a like effect in *Robinson* v. *National Bank of Scotland* (225):

C   " I think, as I said in *Nocton's* case (226) that an exaggerated view was taken by a good many people of the scope of the decision in *Derry* v. *Peek* (227). The whole of the doctrine as to fiducary relationships, as to the duty of care arising from implied as well as express contracts, as to the duty of care arising from other special relationships which the courts may find to exist in particular cases, still remains and I should be very sorry if any

D   word fell from me which should suggest that the courts are in any way hampered in recognising that the duty of care may be established when such cases really occur."

Lord Haldane was thus in terms preserving unencumbered the area of special relationships which created a duty of care; and he was not restricting the

E   area to cases where courts of equity would find a fiduciary duty.

The range of negligence in act was greatly extended in *Donoghue* v. *Stevenson* (228) on the wide principle of the good neighbour—sic utere tuo alienum non laedas. It is argued that the principles enunciated in *Donoghue* v. *Stevenson* (228) apply fully to negligence in word. It may well be that Wrottesley, J., in *Old Gate Estates Ltd.* v. *Toplis and Harding and Russell* (229) put the matter too

F   narrowly when he confined the applicability of the principles laid down in *Donoghue* v. *Stevenson* (228) to negligence which caused damage to life, limb or health. But they were certainly not purporting to deal with such issues as, for instance, how far economic loss alone without some physical or material damage to support it, can afford a cause of action in negligence by act (see *Morrison Steamship Co., Ltd.* v. *Greystoke Castle (Cargo Owners)* (230) where it was held that it could do

G   so). The House in *Donoghue* v. *Stevenson* (228) was, in fact, dealing with negligent acts causing physical damage and the opinions cannot be read as if they were dealing with negligence in word causing economic damage. Had it been otherwise some consideration would have been given to problems peculiar to negligence in words. That case, therefore, can give no more help in this sphere than by affording

H   some analogy from the broad outlook which it imposed on the law relating to physical negligence.

How wide the sphere of the duty of care in negligence is to be laid depends ultimately on the courts' assessment of the demands of society for protection from the carelessness of others. Economic protection has lagged behind protection in physical matters where there is injury to person and property. It may be that

I   the size and the width of the range of possible claims has acted as a deterrent to extension of economic protection. In this sphere the law was developed in the United States in *Glanzer* v. *Shepard* (231), where a public weigher employed by a vendor was held liable to a purchaser for giving him a certificate which negli-

---

(225) 1916 S.C. 154 at p. 157.   (226) [1914-15] All E.R. Rep. 45; [1914] A.C. 932.
(227) (1889), 14 App. Cas. 337.   (228) [1932] All E.R. Rep. 1; [1932] A.C. 562.
(229) [1939] 3 All E.R. 209.   (230) [1946] 2 All E.R. 696; [1947] A.C. 265.
(231) (1922), 233 N.Y. 236.

gently overstated the amount of the goods supplied to him. The defendant was **A**
thus engaged on a task in which, as he knew, vendor and purchaser alike depended
on his skill and care and the fact that it was the vendor who paid him was merely
an accident of commerce. This case was followed and developed in later cases.

In the *Ultramares* case (232) however, the court felt the undesirability of
exposing defendants to a potential liability " in an indeterminate amount for an
indefinite time to an indeterminate class ". It decided that auditors were not **B**
liable for negligence in the preparation of their accounts (of which they supplied
thirty copies although they were not aware of the specific purpose, namely, to
obtain financial help) to a plaintiff who lent money on the strength of them. In
South Africa, under a different system of law, two cases show a similar advance
and subsequent restriction (*Perlman* v. *Zoutendyk* (233) and *Herschel* v. *Mrupe*
(234).   **C**

Some guidance may be obtained from the case of *Shiells* v. *Blackburne* (235).
There a general merchant undertook, voluntarily and without reward, to enter a
parcel of the goods of another, together with a parcel of his own of the same
sort, at the Customs House for exportation. Acting, it was contended, with gross
negligence, he made the entry under a wrong denomination, whereby both parcels
were seized. The plaintiff failed on the facts to make out a case of gross negligence. **D**
But LORD LOUGHBOROUGH said (236):

". . . where a bailee undertakes to perform a gratuitous act, from which
the bailor alone is to receive benefit, there the bailee is only liable for gross
negligence, but if a man gratuitously undertakes to do a thing to the best
of his skill, where his situation or profession is such as to imply skill, an **E**
omission of that skill is imputable to him as gross negligence. If in this case
a ship broker or a clerk in the Custom-House, had undertaken to enter the
goods, a wrong entry would in them be gross negligence, because their situation and employment necessarily imply a competent degree of knowledge in
making such entries."

HEATH, J., said (237):   **F**

". . . the surgeon would also be liable for such negligence, if he undertook
gratis to attend a sick person, because his situation implies skill in surgery;
but if the patient applies to a man of a different employment or occupation
for his gratuitous assistance, who either does not exert all his skill, or
administers improper remedies to the best of his ability, such person is not **G**
liable."

In *Gladwell* v. *Stegall* (238) an infant plaintiff, ten years old, recovered damages
for injury to health from a surgeon and apothecary who had treated her. She did
not sue in contract but brought an action ex delicto alleging a breach of duty
arising out of his employment by her, although it was her father to whom the bill **H**
was made out. In *Wilkinson* v. *Coverdale* (239) LORD KENYON accepted the proposition that a defendant who had gratuitously undertaken to take out an insurance
policy and who did it negligently could be liable in damages. In those cases there
was no dichotomy between negligence in act and in word, nor between physical
and economic loss. The basis underlying them is that if persons holding themselves
out in a calling or situation or profession take on a task within that calling or **I**
situation or profession they have a duty of skill and care. In terms of proximity
one might say that they are in particularly close proximity to those who, as they
know, are relying on their skill and care, although the proximity is not contractual.

(232) (1931), 255 N.Y. 170.   (233) 1934 C.P.D. 151.
(234) 1954 (3) S.A. 464.   (235) (1789), 1 Hy. Bl. 158.
(236) (1789), 1 Hy. Bl. at p. 162.   (237) (1789), 1 Hy. Bl. at p. 161.
(238) (1839), 5 Bing. N.C. 733.   (239) (1793), 1 Esp. 74.

A The reasoning of *Shiells* v. *Blackburne* (240) was applied in *Everett* v. *Griffiths* (241) where the Court of Appeal held that a doctor owed a duty of care to a man by whom he was not employed but whom he had a duty to examine under the Lunacy Act, 1890. It was also relied on by DENNING, L.J., in his dissenting judgment in *Candler* v. *Crane, Christmas & Co.* (242). He reached the conclusion that in respect of reports and work that resulted in such reports there was a duty of

B care laid on (243)

> " those persons such as accountants, surveyors, valuers and analysts, whose profession and occupation it is to examine books, accounts, and other things and to make reports on which other people—other than their clients— rely in the ordinary course of business."

C The duty is in his opinion owed (apart from contractual duty to their employer) (244)

> " to any third person to whom they themselves show the accounts, or to whom they know their employer is going to show the accounts so as to induce him to invest money or take some other action on them."

D He excludes strangers of whom they have heard nothing and to whom their employer without their knowledge may choose to hand their accounts, and continues (245):

> " The test of proximity in these cases is: did the accountants know that the accounts were required for submission to the plaintiff and use by him? "

E (It is to be noted that these expressions of opinion produce a result somewhat' similar to the Restatement para. 552 (246). I agree with those words. In my opinion they are consonant with the earlier cases and with the observations of LORD HALDANE.

It is argued that so to hold would create confusion in many aspects of the law

F and infringe the established rule that innocent misrepresentation gives no right to damages. I cannot accept that argument. The true rule is that innocent misrepresentation per se gives no right to damages. If the misrepresentation was intended by the parties to form a warranty between two contracting parties, it gives on that ground a right to damages (*Heilbut, Symons & Co.* v. *Buckleton* (247). If an innocent misrepresentation is made between parties in a fiduciary relation-

G ship it may, on that ground, give a right to claim damages for negligence. There is also in my opinion a duty of care created by special relationships which, though not fiduciary, give rise to an assumption that care as well as honesty is demanded.

Was there such a special relationship in the present case as to impose on the respondents a duty of care to the appellants as the undisclosed principals for whom National Provincial Bank, Ltd. was making the inquiry? The answer to

H that question depends on the circumstances of the transaction. If, for instance, they disclosed a casual social approach to the inquiry no such special relationship or duty of care would be assumed (see *Fish* v. *Kelly* (248)). To import such a duty the representation must normally, I think, concern a business or professional transaction whose nature makes clear the gravity of the inquiry and the importance and influence attached to the answer. It is conceded that SALMON, J.,

---

(240) (1789), 1 Hy. Bl. 158.
(241) [1920] 3 K.B. 163, particularly at pp. 182, 217.
(242) [1951] 1 All E.R. 426; [1951] 2 K.B. 164.
(243) [1951] 1 All E.R. at p. 433; [1951] 2 K.B. at p. 179.
(244) [1951] 1 All E.R. at p. 434; [1951] 2 K.B. at pp. 180, 181.
(245) [1951] 1 All E.R. at p. 434; [1951] 2 K.B. at p. 181.
(246) Compare p. 612 note (206), ante.
(247) [1911-13] All E.R. Rep. 83; [1913] A.C. 30.
(248) (1864), 17 C.B.N.S. 194.

rightly found a duty of care in *Woods* v. *Martins Bank, Ltd.* (249), but the facts A
in that case were wholly different from those in the present case. A most important circumstance is the form of the inquiry and of the answer. Both were here
plainly stated to be without liability. Counsel for the appellants argues that those
words are not sufficiently precise to exclude liability for negligence. Nothing,
however, except negligence could, in the facts of this case, create a liability
(apart from fraud to which they cannot have been intended to refer and against B
which the words would be no protection since they would be part of the fraud).
I do not, therefore, accept that, even if the parties were already in contractual or
other special relationship, the words would give no immunity to a negligent
answer. But in any event they clearly prevent a special relationship from arising.
They are part of the material from which one deduces whether a duty of care and
a liability for negligence was assumed. If both parties say expressly (in a case C
where neither is deliberately taking advantage of the other) that there shall be no
liability, I do not find it possible to say that a liability was assumed.

In *Robinson* v. *National Bank of Scotland* (250) also the correspondence expressly
excluded responsibility. Possibly that factor weighed with LORD HALDANE when
he said (251):

D

"But when a mere inquiry is made by one banker of another, who stands
in no special relation to him, then, in the absence of special circumstances
from which a contract to be careful can be inferred, I think there is no duty
excepting the duty of common honesty to which I have referred."

I appreciate counsel for the appellants' emphasis on the general importance to
the business world of bankers' references and the desirability that in an inte- E
grated banking system there should be a duty of care with regard to them, but on
the facts before us it is in my opinion not possible to hold that there was a special
duty of care and a liability for negligence.

I would, therefore, dismiss the appeal.

Appeal dismissed.

Solicitors: *Evill & Coleman* (for the appellants); *Franks, Charlesly & Co.* (for
the respondents).

[*Reported by* C. G. LEONARD, ESQ., *Barrister-at-Law.*]

---

(249) [1958] 3 All E.R. 166; [1959] 1 Q.B. 55.   (250) 1916 S.C. (H.L.) 154.
          (251) 1916 S.C. (H.L.) at p. 157.

Extended right to recover damages
to relations likely to suffer
shock from the aftermath of
an accident etc at which they
were not present.

McLoughlin v O'Brian and others

HOUSE OF LORDS

LORD WILBERFORCE, LORD EDMUND-DAVIES, LORD RUSSELL OF KILLOWEN, LORD SCARMAN AND
LORD BRIDGE OF HARWICH

15, 16 FEBRUARY, 6 MAY 1982

Negligence – Duty to take care – Foreseeable harm – Duty to take care to avoid injury to persons who might foreseeably suffer injury from want of care – Driver of motor vehicle – Duty to other road users and owners of property – Nervous shock – Plaintiff suffering nervous shock on hearing that family involved in road accident – Plaintiff at home at time of accident – Whether duty of care owed to plaintiff by driver causing accident.

Damages – Personal injury – Nervous shock – Plaintiff's family killed or badly injured in road accident caused by defendant's negligence – Plaintiff at home at time of accident – Plaintiff informed of accident and going to hospital – Plaintiff suffering nervous shock as a result – Whether defendant owing duty of care to plaintiff – Whether plaintiff's injury reasonably foreseeable – Whether as matter of policy court would not impose duty of care on defendant to plaintiff.

Damages – Personal injury – Nervous shock – Public policy – Whether public policy requiring legal limitations on recovery of damages for nervous shock.

The plaintiff's husband and three children were involved in a road accident caused by the negligence of the defendants. One of the plaintiff's children was killed and her husband and other two children were severely injured. At the time of the accident the plaintiff was at home two miles away. She was told of the accident by a motorist who had been at the scene of the accident and was taken to hospital where she saw the injured members of her family and the extent of their injuries and shock and heard that her daughter had been killed. As a results of hearing, and seeing the results of, the accident the plaintiff suffered severe and persisting nervous shock. The plaintiff claimed damages against the defendants for the nervous shock, distress and injury to her health caused by the defendants' negligence. The judge dismissed her claim on the ground that her injury was not reasonably foreseeable. On appeal, the Court of Appeal held that the plaintiff was not entitled to claim against the defendants either because as a matter of policy a duty of care was not to be imposed on a negligent defendant beyond that owed to persons in close proximity, both in time and place, to an accident, even though the injuries received by the plaintiff might be reasonably foreseeable as being a consequence of the defendants' negligence, or because the duty of care owed by a driver of a motor vehicle was limited to persons on or near the road. The plaintiff appealed to the House of Lords.

Held – The test of liability for damages for nervous shock was reasonable foreseeability of the plaintiff being injured by nervous shock as a result of the defendant's negligence. Applying that test, the plaintiff was entitled to recover damages from the defendants because even though the plaintiff was not at or near the scene of the accident at the time or shortly afterwards the nervous shock suffered by her was a reasonably foreseeable consequence of the defendant's negligence. The appeal would accordingly be allowed (see p 301 *j*, p 302 *a b* and *h* to p 303 *a*, p 305 *e* to *g*, p 306 *f g*, p 309 *g*, p 310 *a d e*, p 311 *f g*, p 313 *b c* and p 320 *h j*, post).

Dictum of Denning LJ in *King v Phillips* [1953] 1 All ER at 623 approved.

Dictum of Bankes LJ in *Hambrook v Stokes Bros* [1924] All ER Rep at 113 and of Lord Wright in *Hay (or Bourhill) v Young* [1942] 2 All ER at 405–406 applied.

Dillon v Legg (1968) 68 C 2d 728 considered.

Chester v Waverley Municipal Council (1939) 62 CLR 1 not followed.

Per Lord Russell, Lord Scarman and Lord Bridge (Lord Edmund-Davies not con-

a curring). In the area of nervous shock caused by negligence on the highway, the sole test of liability is reasonable foreseeability without any legal limitation in terms of space, time, distance, the nature of the injuries sustained or the relationship of the plaintiff to the victim (although those are factors to be considered), since (per Lord Bridge) there are no policy considerations sufficient to justify limiting the liability of negligent tortfeasors by some narrower criterion than that of reasonable foreseeability. If (per Lord Scarman) public policy requires such a limitation, the policy issue where to draw the line is not
b justiciable but a matter for legislation (see p 310 *b* to *h*, p 311 *c* to *g*, p 317 *h j*, p 319 *f* to *j* and p 320 *e* to *g*, post).

Per Lord Wilberforce. The application of the reasonable foreseeability test in nervous shock claims ought to be limited, in terms of proximity, so that what is foreseeable is circumscribed by the proximity of the tie or relationship between the plaintiff and the injured person, the proximity of the plaintiff to the accident both in time and place, and
c the proximity of communication of the accident to the plaintiff through sight or hearing of the event or its immediate aftermath (see p 303 *d* to *f* and p 304 *f* to p 305 *e*, post).

Decision of the Court of Appeal [1981] 1 All ER 809 reversed.

Notes

For liability for nervous shock, see 34 Halsbury's Laws (4th edn) para 8, and for cases on
d the subject, see 17 Digest (Reissue) 145–147, 377–391.

For remoteness of damage, see 12 Halsbury's Laws (4th edn) para 1127, and for cases on the subject, see 36(1) Digest (Reissue) 63–65, 306–307, 227–236, 1232–1236.

Cases referred to in opinions

Abramʒik v Brenner (1967) 65 DLR (2d) 651, 17 Digest (Reissue) 152, *283.
e *Anns v Merton London Borough* [1977] 2 All ER 492, [1978] AC 728, [1977] 2 WLR 1024, HL, 1(1) Digest (Reissue) 128, 721.
Bell v Great Northern Rly Co of Ireland (1890) 26 LR Ir 428, 36(1) Digest (Reissue) 310, *2558.
Benson v Lee [1972] VR 879, 17 Digest (Reissue) 151, *277.
Boardman v Sanderson [1964] 1 WLR 1317, CA, 17 Digest (Reissue) 145, 378.
f *British Rlys Board v Herrington* [1972] 1 All ER 749, [1972] AC 877, [1972] 2 WLR 537, HL, 36(1) Digest (Reissue) 121, 466.
Byrne v Great Southern and Western Rly Co of Ireland (1884) unreported, cited in 26 LR Ir at 428, 36(1) Digest (Reissue) 310, *2557.
Chadwick v British Transport Commission [1967] 2 All ER 945, [1967] 1 WLR 912, 17 Digest (Reissue) 147, 390.
g *Chester v Waverley Municipal Council* (1939) 62 CLR 1, 36(1) Digest (Reissue) 33, *103.
Dillon v Legg (1968) 68 C 2d 728, Cal SC.
Donoghue (or M'Alister) v Stevenson [1932] AC 562, [1932] All ER Rep 1, HL, 36(1) Digest (Reissue) 144, 562.
Dulieu v White & Sons [1901] 2 KB 669, [1900–3] All ER Rep 353, DC, 17 Digest (Reissue) 146, 385.
h *Fender v Mildmay* [1937] 3 All ER 402, [1938] AC 1, HL, 12 Digest (Reissue) 325, 2352.
Hambrook v Stokes Bros [1925] 1 KB 141, [1924] All ER Rep 110, CA, 17 Digest (Reissue) 145, 377.
Hay (or Bourhill) v Young [1942] 2 All ER 396, [1943] AC 92, HL; *affg* 1941 SC 395, 17 Digest (Reissue) 146, 388.
Haynes v Harwood [1935] 1 KB 146, [1934] All ER Rep 103, CA, 36(1) Digest (Reissue) 245, 953.
j *Hedley Byrne & Co Ltd v Heller & Partners Ltd* [1963] 2 All ER 575, [1964] AC 465, [1963] 3 WLR 101, HL, 36(1) Digest (Reissue) 24, 84.
Hinʒ v Berry [1970] 1 All ER 1074, [1970] 2 QB 40, [1970] 2 WLR 684, CA, 17 Digest (Reissue) 147, 391.
Home Office v Dorset Yacht Co Ltd [1970] 2 All ER 294, [1970] AC 1004, [1970] 2 WLR 1140, HL, 36(1) Digest (Reissue) 27, 93.

Janson v Driefontein Consolidated Mines Ltd [1902] AC 484, [1900–3] All ER Rep 426, HL,
12 Digest (Reissue) 296, 2132.

King v Phillips [1953] 1 All ER 617, [1953] 1 QB 429, [1953] 2 WLR 526, CA, 17 Digest
(Reissue) 147, 389.

Lambert v Lewis [1980] 1 All ER 978, [1980] 2 WLR 299, CA; *rvsd in part* [1981] 1 All ER
1185, [1981] 2 WLR 713, HL.

Marshall v Lionel Enterprises Inc (1971) 25 DLR (3d) 141, 17 Digest (Reissue) 152, *284.

McKew v Holland & Hannen & Cubitts (Scotland) Ltd [1969] 3 All ER 1621, HL, 17 Digest
(Reissue) 115, 187.

Morgans v Launchbury [1972] 2 All ER 606, [1973] AC 127, [1972] 2 WLR 1217, HL,
36(1) Digest (Reissue) 173, 643.

Nova Mink Ltd v Trans-Canada Airlines [1951] 2 DLR 241, 36(1) Digest (Reissue) 47, *208.

Overseas Tankship (UK) Ltd v Morts Dock and Engineering Co Ltd, The Wagon Mound (No 1)
[1961] 1 All ER 404, [1961] AC 388, [1961] 2 WLR 126, DC, 36(1) Digest (Reissue) 63,
227.

Rondel v Worsley [1967] 3 All ER 993, [1969] 1 AC 191, [1967] 3 WLR 1666, HL, 3 Digest
(Reissue) 786, 4877.

Smith v Johnson & Co (1897) unreported, cited in [1897] 2 QB at 61, DC, 36(1) Digest
(Reissue) 308, 1241.

Victorian Rlys Comrs v Coultas (1888) 13 App Cas 222, PC, 36(1) Digest (Reissue) 308,
1239.

Wagner v International Rlys Co (1921) 232 NY Rep 176.

Appeal

The plaintiff, Rosina McLoughlin, appealed against the judgment of the Court of Appeal
(Stephenson, Cumming-Bruce and Griffiths LJJ) ([1981] 1 All ER 809, [1981] QB 599)
given on 16 December 1980 dismissing her appeal against the judgment of Boreham J
on 11 December 1978 whereby the judge dismissed her claim against the defendants,
Thomas Alan O'Brian, A E Docker & Sons Ltd, Raymond Sygrove and Ernest Doe & Sons
Ltd, the respondents to the appeal, for damages for shock, distress and injury to her
health. The facts are set out in the opinion of Lord Wilberforce.

Michael Ogden QC and *Jonathan Haworth* for the appellant.
Michael Turner QC and *John Leighton Williams* for the respondents.

Their Lordships took time for consideration.

6 May. The following opinions were delivered.

LORD WILBERFORCE. My Lords, this appeal arises from a very serious and tragic
road accident which occurred on 19 October 1973 near Withersfield, Suffolk. The
appellant's husband, Thomas McLoughlin, and three of her children, George, aged 17,
Kathleen, aged 7, and Gillian, nearly 3, were in a Ford motor car; George was driving.
A fourth child, Michael, then aged 11, was a passenger in a following motor car driven
by Mr Pilgrim; this car did not become involved in the accident. The Ford car was in
collision with a lorry driven by the first respondent and owned by the second
respondent. That lorry had been in collision with another lorry driven by the third
respondent and owned by the fourth respondent. It is admitted that the accident to the
Ford car was caused by the respondents' negligence. It is necessary to state what followed
in full detail.

As a result of the accident, the appellant's husband suffered bruising and shock; George
suffered injuries to his head and face, cerebral concussion, fractures of both scapulae and
bruising and abrasions; Kathleen suffered concussion, fracture of the right clavicle,
bruising, abrasions and shock; Gillian was so seriously injured that she died almost
immediately.

At the time, the appellant was at her home about two miles away; an hour or so
afterwards the accident was reported to her by Mr Pilgrim, who told her that he thought

a

George was dying, and that he did not know the whereabouts of her husband or the condition of her daughter. He then drove her to Addenbrooke's hospital, Cambridge. There she saw Michael, who told her that Gillian was dead. She was taken down a corridor and through a window she saw Kathleen, crying, with her face cut and begrimed with dirt and oil. She could hear George shouting and screaming. She was taken to her husband who was sitting with his head in his hands. His shirt was hanging off him and he was covered in mud and oil. He saw the appellant and started sobbing. The appellant

b

was then taken to see George. The whole of his left face and left side was covered. He appeared to recognise the appellant and then lapsed into unconsciousness. Finally, the appellant was taken to Kathleen who by now had been cleaned up. The child was too upset to speak and simply clung to her mother. There can be no doubt that these circumstances, witnessed by the appellant, were distressing in the extreme and were capable of producing an effect going well beyond that of grief and sorrow.

c

The appellant subsequently brought proceedings against the respondents. At the trial, the judge assumed, for the purpose of enabling him to decide the issue of legal liability, that the appellant subsequently suffered the condition of which she complained. This was described as severe shock, organic depression and a change of personality. Numerous symptoms of a physiological character are said to have been manifested. The details were not investigated at the trial, the court being asked to assume that the appellant's condition

d

had been caused or contributed to by shock, as distinct from grief or sorrow, and that the appellant was a person of reasonable fortitude.

On these facts, or assumed facts, the trial judge, Boreham J, gave judgment for the respondents holding, in a most careful judgment reviewing the authorities, that the respondents owed no duty of care to the appellant because the possibility of her suffering injury by nervous shock, in the circumstances, was not reasonably foreseeable.

e

On appeal by the appellant, the judgment of Boreham J was upheld, but not on the same ground (see [1981] 1 All ER 809, [1981] QB 599). Stephenson LJ took the view that the possibility of injury to the appellant by nervous shock *was* reasonably foreseeable and that the respondents owed the appellant a duty of care. However, he held that considerations of policy prevented the appellant from recovering. Griffiths LJ held that injury by nervous shock to the appellant was 'readily foreseeable' but that the respondents

f

owed no duty of care to the appellant. The duty was limited to those on the road nearby. Cumming-Bruce LJ agreed with both judgments. The appellant now appeals to this House. The critical question to be decided is whether a person in the position of the appellant, ie one who was not present at the scene of grievous injuries to her family but who comes on those injuries at an interval of time and space, can recover damages for nervous shock.

g

Although we continue to use the hallowed expression 'nervous shock', English law, and common understanding, have moved some distance since recognition was given to this symptom as a basis for liability. Whatever is unknown about the mind-body relationship (and the area of ignorance seems to expand with that of knowledge), it is now accepted by medical science that recognisable and severe physical damage to the human body and system may be caused by the impact, through the senses, of external

h

events on the mind. There may thus be produced what is as identifiable an illness as any that may be caused by direct physical impact. It is safe to say that this, in general terms, is understood by the ordinary man or woman who is hypothesised by the courts in situations where claims for negligence are made. Although in the only case which has reached this House (*Hay (or Bourhill) v Young* [1942] 2 All ER 396, [1943] AC 92) a claim for damages in respect of 'nervous shock' was rejected on its facts, the House gave clear

j

recognition to the legitimacy, in principle, of claims of that character. As the result of that and other cases, assuming that they are accepted as correct, the following position has been reached:

1. While damages cannot, at common law, be awarded for grief and sorrow, a claim for damages for 'nervous shock' caused by negligence can be made without the necessity of showing direct impact or fear of immediate personal injuries for oneself. The reservation made by Kennedy J in *Dulieu v White & Sons* [1901] 2 KB 669, [1900–3] All ER Rep 353, though taken up by Sargant LJ in *Hambrook v Stokes Bros* [1925] 1 KB 141,

[1924] All ER Rep 110, has not gained acceptance, and although the respondents, in the
courts below, reserved their right to revive it, they did not do so in argument. I think *a*
that it is now too late to do so. The arguments on this issue were fully and admirably
stated by the Supreme Court of California in *Dillon v Legg* (1968) 29 ALR 3d 1316.

2. A plaintiff may recover damages for 'nervous shock' brought on by injury caused
not to him or herself but to a near relative, or by the fear of such injury. So far (subject
to 5 below), the cases do not extend beyond the spouse or children of the plaintiff
(*Hambrook v Stokes Bros* [1925] 1 KB 141, [1924] All ER Rep 110, *Boardman v Sanderson* *b*
[1964] 1 WLR 1317, *Hinz v Berry* [1970] 1 All ER 1074, [1970] 2 QB 40, including foster
children (where liability was assumed), and see *King v Phillips* [1953] 1 All ER 617, [1953]
1 QB 429).

3. Subject to the next paragraph, there is no English case in which a plaintiff has been
able to recover nervous shock damages where the injury to the near relative occurred out
of sight and earshot of the plaintiff. In *Hambrook v Stokes Bros* an express distinction was *c*
made between shock caused by what the mother saw with her own eyes and what she
might have been told by bystanders, liability being excluded in the latter case.

4. An exception from, or I would prefer to call it an extension of, the latter case has
been made where the plaintiff does not see or hear the incident but comes on its
immediate aftermath. In *Boardman v Sanderson* the father was within earshot of the
accident to his child and likely to come on the scene; he did so and suffered damage from *d*
what he then saw. In *Marshall v Lionel Enterprises* (1971) 25 DLR (3d) 141 the wife came
immediately on the badly injured body of her husband. And in *Benson v Lee* [1972] VR
879 a situation existed with some similarity to the present case. The mother was in her
home 100 yards away, and, on communication by a third party, ran out to the scene of
the accident and there suffered shock. Your Lordships have to decide whether or not to
validate these extensions. *e*

5. A remedy on account of nervous shock has been given to a man who came on a
serious accident involving people immediately thereafter and acted as a rescuer of those
involved (*Chadwick v British Transport Commission* [1967] 2 All ER 945, [1967] 1 WLR
912). 'Shock' was caused neither by fear for himself nor by fear or horror on account of
a near relative. The principle of 'rescuer' cases was not challenged by the respondents and
ought, in my opinion, to be accepted. But we have to consider whether, and how far, it *f*
can be applied to such cases as the present.

Throughout these developments, as can be seen, the courts have proceeded in the
traditional manner of the common law from case to case, on a basis of logical necessity.
If a mother, with or without accompanying children, could recover on account of fear for
herself, how can she be denied recovery on account of fear for her accompanying
children? If a father could recover had he seen his child run over by a backing car, how *g*
can he be denied recovery if he is in the immediate vicinity and runs to the child's
assistance? If a wife and mother could recover if she had witnessed a serious accident to
her husband and children, does she fail because she was a short distance away and
immediately rushes to the scene? (cf *Benson v Lee*). I think that, unless the law is to draw
an arbitrary line at the point of direct sight and sound, these arguments require
acceptance of the extension mentioned above under principle 4 in the interests of justice. *h*

If one continues to follow the process of logical progression, it is hard to see why the
present plaintiff also should not succeed. She was not present at the accident, but she
came very soon after on its aftermath. If, from a distance of some 100 yards (cf *Benson v
Lee*), she had found her family by the roadside, she would have come within principle 4
above. Can it make any difference that she comes on them in an ambulance, or, as here,
in a nearby hospital, when, as the evidence shows, they were in the same condition, *j*
covered with oil and mud, and distraught with pain? If Mr Chadwick can recover when,
acting in accordance with normal and irresistible human instinct, and indeed moral
compulsion, he goes to the scene of an accident, may not a mother recover if, acting
under the same motives, she goes to where her family can be found?

I could agree that a line can be drawn above her case with less hardship than would
have been apparent in *Boardman's* and *Hinz's* cases, but so to draw it would not appeal to
most people's sense of justice. To allow her claim may be, I think it is, on the margin of

what the process of logical progression would allow. But where the facts are strong and
a exceptional, and, as I think, fairly analogous, her case ought, prima facie, to be assimilated
to those which have passed the test.

   To argue from one factual situation to another and to decide by analogy is a natural
tendency of the human and legal mind. But the lawyer still has to inquire whether, in
so doing, he has crossed some critical line behind which he ought to stop. That is said to
be the present case. The reasoning by which the Lords Justices decided not to grant relief
b to the plaintiff is instructive. Both Stephenson and Griffiths LJJ accepted that the 'shock'
to the plaintiff was foreseeable; but from this, at least in presentation, they diverge.
Stephenson LJ considered that the defendants owed a duty of care to the plaintiff, but
that for reasons of policy the law should stop short of giving her damages: it should limit
relief to those on or near the highway at or near the time of the accident caused by the
defendants' negligence. He was influenced by the fact that the courts of this country,
c and of other common law jurisdictions, had stopped at this point: it was indicated by the
barrier of commercial sense and practical convenience. Griffiths LJ took the view that,
although the injury to the plaintiff was foreseeable, there was no duty of care. The duty
of care of drivers of motor vehicles was, according to decided cases, limited to persons and
owners of property on the road or near to it who might be directly affected. The line
should be drawn at this point. It was not even in the interest of those suffering from
d shock as a class to extend the scope of the defendants' liability: to do so would quite likely
delay their recovery by immersing them in the anxiety of litigation.

   I am deeply impressed by both of these arguments, which I have only briefly
summarised. Though differing in expression, in the end, in my opinion, the two
presentations rest on a common principle, namely that, at the margin, the boundaries of
a man's responsibility for acts of negligence have to be fixed as a matter of policy.
e Whatever is the correct jurisprudential analysis, it does not make any essential difference
whether one says, with Stephenson LJ, that there is a duty but, as a matter of policy, the
consequences of breach of it ought to be limited at a certain point, or whether, with
Griffiths LJ, one says that the fact that consequences may be foreseeable does not
automatically impose a duty of care, does not do so in fact where policy indicates the
contrary. This is an approach which one can see very clearly from the way in which Lord
f Atkin stated the neighbour principle in *Donoghue v Stevenson* [1932] AC 462 at 580,
[1932] All ER Rep 1 at 11: '. . . persons who are so closely and directly affected by my act
that I ought reasonably to have them in contemplation as being so affected . . .'

   This is saying that foreseeability must be accompanied and limited by the law's
judgment as to persons who ought, according to its standards of value or justice, to have
been in contemplation. Foreseeability, which involves a hypothetical person, looking
g with hindsight at an event which has occurred, is a formula adopted by English law, not
merely for defining, but also for limiting the persons to whom duty may be owed, and
the consequences for which an actor may be held responsible. It is not merely an issue
of fact to be left to be found as such. When it is said to result in a duty of care being owed
to a person or a class, the statement that there is a 'duty of care' denotes a conclusion into
the forming of which considerations of policy have entered. That foreseeability does not
h of itself, and automatically, lead to a duty of care is, I think, clear. I gave some examples
in *Anns v Merton London Borough* [1977] 2 All ER 492 at 498, [1978] AC 728 at 752, *Anns*
itself being one. I may add what Lord Reid said in *McKew v Holland & Hannen & Cubitts
(Scotland) Ltd* [1969] 3 All ER 1621 at 1623: 'A defender is not liable for a consequence of
a kind which is not foreseeable. But it does not follow that he is liable for every
consequence which a reasonable man could foresee.'
j   We must then consider the policy arguments. In doing so we must bear in mind that
cases of 'nervous shock' and the possibility of claiming damages for it are not necessarily
confined to those arising out of accidents in public roads. To state, therefore, a rule that
recoverable damages must be confined to persons on or near the highway is to state not
a principle in itself but only an example of a more general rule that recoverable damages
must be confined to those within sight and sound of an event caused by negligence or,
at least, to those in close, or very close, proximity to such a situation.

   The policy arguments against a wider extension can be stated under four heads. First, it may be said that such extension may lead to a proliferation of claims, and possibly *a* fraudulent claims, to the establishment of an industry of lawyers and psychiatrists who will formulate a claim for nervous shock damages, including what in America is called the customary miscarriage, for all, or many, road accidents and industrial accidents. Second, it may be claimed that an extension of liability would be unfair to defendants, as imposing damages out of proportion to the negligent conduct complained of. In so far as such defendants are insured, a large additional burden will be placed on insurers, and ultimately on the class of persons insured: road users or employers. Third, to extend *b* liability beyond the most direct and plain cases would greatly increase evidentiary difficulties and tend to lengthen litigation. Fourth, it may be said (and the Court of Appeal agreed with this) that an extension of the scope of liability ought only to be made by the legislature, after careful research. This is the course which has been taken in New South Wales and the Australian Capital Territory.

The whole argument has been well summed up by Dean Prosser in *The Law of Torts* *c* (4th edn, 1971) p 256:

> 'The reluctance of courts to enter this zone even where the mental injury is clearly foreseeable, and the frequent mention of the difficulties of proof, the facility of fraud and the problem of finding a place to stop and draw the line, suggest that here it is the nature of the interest invaded and the type of damages which is the real *d* obstacle.'

Since he wrote, the type of damage has, in this country at least, become more familiar and less deterrent to recovery. And some of the arguments are susceptible of answer. Fraudulent claims can be contained by the courts, which, also, can cope with evidentiary difficulties. The scarcity of cases which have occurred in the past, and the modest sums recovered, give some indication that fears of a flood of litigation may be exaggerated: *e* experience in other fields suggests that such fears usually are. If some increase does occur, that may only reveal the existence of a genuine social need; that legislation has been found necessary in Australia may indicate the same thing.

But, these discounts accepted, there remains, in my opinion, just because 'shock' in its nature is capable of affecting so wide a range of people, a real need for the law to place some limitation on the extent of admissible claims. It is necessary to consider three *f* elements inherent in any claim: the class of persons whose claims should be recognised; the proximity of such persons to the accident; and the means by which the shock is caused. As regards the class of persons, the possible range is between the closest of family ties, of parent and child, or husband and wife, and the ordinary bystander. Existing law recognises the claims of the first; it denies that of the second, either on the basis that such persons must be assumed to be possessed of fortitude sufficient to enable them to endure *g* the calamities of modern life or that defendants cannot be expected to compensate the world at large. In my opinion, these positions are justifiable, and since the present case falls within the first class it is strictly unnecessary to say more. I think, however, that it should follow that other cases involving less close relationships must be very carefully scrutinised. I cannot say that they should never be admitted. The closer the tie (not merely in relationship, but in care) the greater the claim for consideration. The claim, *h* in any case, has to be judged in the light of the other factors, such as proximity to the scene in time and place, and the nature of the accident.

As regards proximity to the accident, it is obvious that this must be close in both time and space. It is after all, the fact and consequence of the defendant's negligence that must be proved to have caused the 'nervous shock'. Experience has shown that to insist on direct and immediate sight or hearing would be impractical and unjust and that under *j* what may be called the 'aftermath' doctrine, one who, from close proximity comes very soon on the scene, should not be excluded. In my opinion, the result in *Benson v Lee* [1972] VR 879 was correct and indeed inescapable. It was based, soundly, on 'direct perception of some of the events which go to make up the accident as an entire event, and this includes . . . the immediate aftermath'. The High Court of Australia's majority decision in *Chester v Waverley Municipal Council* (1939) 62 CLR 1, where a child's body a   was found floating in a trench after a prolonged search, may perhaps be placed on the other side of a recognisable line (Evatt J in a powerful dissent placed it on the same side), but in addition, I find the conclusion of Lush J in *Benson v Lee* to reflect developments in the law.

b   Finally, and by way of reinforcement of 'aftermath' cases, I would accept, by analogy with 'rescue' situations, that a person of whom it could be said that one could expect nothing else than that he or she would come immediately to the scene (normally a parent or a spouse) could be regarded as being within the scope of foresight and duty. Where there is not immediate presence, account must be taken of the possibility of alterations in the circumstances, for which the defendant should not be responsible.

Subject only to these qualifications, I think that a strict test of proximity by sight or hearing should be applied by the courts.

c   Lastly, as regards communication, there is no case in which the law has compensated shock brought about by communication by a third party. In *Hambrook v Stokes Bros* [1925] 1 KB 141, [1924] All ER Rep 110, indeed, it was said that liability would not arise in such a case, and this is surely right. It was so decided in *Abramzik v Brenner* (1967) 65 DLR (2d) 651. The shock must come through sight or hearing of the event or of its immediate aftermath. Whether some equivalent of sight or hearing, eg through simultaneous television, would suffice may have to be considered.

d   My Lords, I believe that these indications, imperfectly sketched, and certainly to be applied with common sense to individual situations in their entirety, represent either the existing law, or the existing law with only such circumstantial extension as the common law process may legitimately make. They do not introduce a new principle. Nor do I see any reason why the law should retreat behind the lines already drawn. I find on this appeal that the appellant's case falls within the boundaries of the law so drawn. I would allow her appeal.

e

LORD EDMUND-DAVIES. My Lords, I am for allowing this appeal. The facts giving rise to it have been related in detail by my noble and learned friend, Lord Wilberforce, and both he and my noble and learned friend Lord Bridge have spaciously reviewed the case law relating to the recovery of damages for personal injury resulting f   from nervous shock. My own observations can, in the circumstances, be substantially briefer than I had originally planned.

It is common ground in the appeal that, the appellant's claim being based on shock, '... there can be no doubt since *Hay (or Bourhill) v Young* ([1942] 2 All ER 396, [1943] AC 92 that the test of liability ... is foreseeability of injury by shock' (per Denning LJ in *King v Phillips* [1953] 1 All ER 617 at 623, [1953] 1 QB 429 at 441). But this was not always g   the law, and great confusion arose in the cases from applying to claims based on shock restrictions hedging negligence actions based on the infliction of *physical* injuries. In the same year as that in which *King v Phillips* was decided, Goodhart perceptively asked why it was considered that the area of possible physical injury should be relevant to a case based on the unlawful infliction of shock, and continued (16 MLR, p 22):

h   'A woman standing at the window of a second-floor room is just as likely to receive a shock when witnessing an accident as she would be if she were standing on the pavement. To say that the careless driver of a motor-car could not reasonably foresee such a self-evident fact is to hide the truth behind a fiction which must disappear as soon as we examine it. The driver obviously cannot foresee that the woman at the window will receive a physical injury, but it does not follow from this that he cannot foresee that she will receive a shock. As the cause of action is based j   on shock it is only foresight of shock which is relevant.'

Indeed, in *King v Phillips* itself Denning LJ expressly held that the fact that the plaintiff was in an upstairs room 80 yards away from the scene of the accident was immaterial.

It is true that, as Goodhart observed, in most cases the foresight concerning emotional injury and that concerning physical injury are identical, the shock following the physical injury, and the result was that, in the early development of this branch of the law, the

courts tended to assume that this must be so in all cases. But in fact, as Goodhart
laconically put it, 'The area of risk of physical injury may extend to only X yards, while *a*
the area of risk of emotional injury may extend to Y yards'. That error still persists is
indicated by the holding of Stephenson LJ in the instant case that the ambit of duty of
care owed by a motorist is restricted to persons 'on or near the highway at or near the
time of the accident' (see [1981] 1 All ER 809 at 820, [1981] QB 599 at 614), and by
Griffiths LJ to those 'on the road or near to it who may be directly affected by the bad
driving. It is not owed to those who are nowhere near the scene' (see [1981] 1 All ER 809 *b*
at 827, [1981] QB 599 at 623). The most striking feature in the present case is that such
limits on the duty of care were imposed notwithstanding the unanimous conclusion of
the Court of Appeal that it was reasonably foreseeable (and even 'readily' so in the
judgment of Griffiths LJ) that injury by shock could be caused to a person in the position
of the appellant.

Similar restrictions were unsuccessfully sought to be imposed in *Haynes v Harwood* *c*
[1935] 1 KB 146, [1934] All ER Rep 103, the plaintiff having been inside a police station
when he first saw the bolting horses and therefore out of sight and seemingly out of
danger. And they were again rejected in *Chadwick v British Transport Commission* [1967]
2 All ER 945, [1967] 1 WLR 912, where the plaintiff was in his home 200 yards away
when the Lewisham railway accident occurred. Griffiths LJ expressed himself as 'quite
unable to include in the category of rescuers to whom a duty [of care] is owed a relative *d*
visiting victims in hospital' (see [1981] 1 All ER 809 at 827, [1981] QB 599 at 623). I do
not share the difficulty, and in my respectful judgment none exists. I am here content
to repeat once more the noble words of Cardozo J in *Wagner v International Rlys Co* (1921)
232 NY Rep 176 at 180:

> 'Danger invites rescue. The cry of distress is the summons to relief. The law does
> not ignore these reactions of the mind in tracing conduct to its consequences. It *e*
> recognises them as normal. It places their effect within the range of the natural and
> probable. The wrong that imperils life is a wrong to the imperilled victim; it is
> wrong also to his rescuer.'

Was not the action of the appellant in visiting her family in hospital immediately she
heard of the accident basically indistinguishable from that of a 'rescuer', being intent on *f*
comforting the injured? And was not her action 'natural and probable' in the
circumstances? I regard the questions as capable only of affirmative answers, and,
indeed, Stephenson LJ so answered them.

I turn to consider the sole basis on which the Court of Appeal dismissed the claim, that
of public policy. They did so on the ground of what, for short, may be called the
'floodgates' argument. Griffiths LJ presented it in the following way ([1981] 1 All ER *g*
809 at 823, [1981] QB 599 at 617):

> 'If the [appellant's] argument is right it will certainly have far-reaching
> consequences, for it will not only apply to road traffic accidents. Whenever anybody
> is injured it is foreseeable that the relatives will be told and will visit them in
> hospital, and it is further foreseeable that in cases of grave injury and death some of *h*
> those relatives are likely to have a severe reaction causing illness. Of course, the
> closer the relationship the more readily it is foreseeable that they may be so affected,
> but if we just confine our consideration to parents and children and husbands and
> wives, it is clear that the potential liability of the tortfeasor is vastly increased if he
> has to compensate the relatives as well as the immediate victims of his carelessness.'

He continued ([1981] 1 All ER 809 at 827, [1981] QB 599 at 623): *j*

> 'Every system of law must set some bounds to the consequences for which a
> wrongdoer must make reparation. If the burden is too great it cannot and will not
> be met, the law will fall into disrepute, and it will be a disservice to those victims
> who might reasonably have expected compensation. In any state of society it is
> ultimately a question of policy to decide the limits of liability.'

Stephenson LJ expressed the same view by citing his own observation when giving the judgment of the Court of Appeal in *Lambert v Lewis* [1980] 1 All ER 978 at 1006, [1980] 2 WLR 299 at 331 that 'There comes a point where the logical extension of the boundaries of duty and damage is halted by the barrier of commercial sense and practical convenience'.

My Lords, the experiences of a long life in the law have made me very familiar with this 'floodgates' argument. I do not, of course, suggest that it can invariably be dismissed as lacking cogency; on the contrary, it has to be weighed carefully, but I have often seen it disproved by later events. It was urged when abolition of the doctrine of common employment was being canvassed, and it raised its head again when the abolition of contributory negligence as a total bar to a claim in negligence was being urged. And, even before my time, on the basis of conjecture later shown to be ill-founded it provided a fatal stumbling-block to the plaintiff's claim in the 'shock' case of *Victorian Rlys Comrs v Coultas* (1888) 13 App Cas 222, where Sir Richard Couch sounded the 'floodgates' alarm in stirring words which are quoted in the speech of my noble and learned friend Lord Bridge.

My Lords, for such reasons as those developed in the speech of my noble and learned friend Lord Wilberforce and which it would serve no purpose for me to repeat in less felicitous words of my own, I remain unconvinced that the number and area of claims in 'shock' cases would be substantially increased or enlarged were the respondents here held liable. It is a question which Kennedy J answered in *Dulieu v White & Sons* [1901] 2 KB 669 at 681, [1900–3] All ER Rep 353 at 360 in the following terms, which commend themselves strongly to me:

> 'I should be sorry to adopt a rule which would bar all such claims on grounds of policy alone, and in order to prevent the possible success of unrighteous or groundless actions. Such a course involves the denial of redress in meritorious cases, and it necessarily implies a certain amount of distrust, which I do not share, in the capacity of legal tribunals to get at the truth in this class of claim.'

My Lords, in the present case two totally different points arising from the speeches of two of your Lordships call for further attention. Both relate to the Court of Appeal's invoking public policy. Unless I have completely misunderstood my noble and learned friend Lord Bridge, he doubts that any regard should have been had to such a consideration, and seemingly considered the Court of Appeal went wrong in paying any attention to it. The sole test of liability, I read him as saying, is the reasonable foreseeability of injury to the plaintiff through nervous shock resulting from the defendant's conceded default. And, such foreseeability having been established to their unanimous satisfaction, it followed that in law no other course was open to the Court of Appeal than to allow this appeal. I have respectfully to say that I cannot accept this approach. It is true that no decision was cited to your Lordships in which the contrary has been held, but that is not to say that reasonable foreseeability is the *only* test of the validity of a claim brought in negligence. If it is surmounted, the defendant would probably be hard put to escape liability.

Lord Wright found it difficult to conceive that any new head of public policy could be discovered (see *Fender v Mildmay* [1937] 3 All ER 402 at 427, [1938] AC 1 at 41), and, were Lord Halsbury LC sound in denying that any court could invent a new head of policy (see *Janson v Driefontein Consolidated Mines* [1902] AC 484 at 491, [1900–3] All ER Rep 426 at 429), I should have been in the happy position of accepting the standpoint adopted by my noble and learned friend Lord Bridge. But, as I shall later indicate, the more recent view which has found favour in your Lordships' House is that public policy is not immutable. Accordingly, whilst I would have strongly preferred indicating with clarity where the limit of liability should be drawn in such cases as the present, in my judgment the possibility of a wholly new type of policy being raised renders the attainment of such finality unfortunately unattainable.

As I think, all we can say is that any invocation of public policy calls for the closest scrutiny, and the defendant might well fail to discharge the burden of making it good, as indeed, happened in *Rondel v Worsley* [1967] 3 All ER 993, [1969] 1 AC 191. But that is not to say that success for the defendant would be unthinkable, for, in the words of *a* MacDonald J in *Nova Mink Ltd v Trans-Canada Airlines* [1951] 2 DLR 241 at 254:

> '. . . there is always a large element of judicial policy and social expediency involved in the determination of the duty-problem, however it may be obscured by the use of traditional formulae.'

I accordingly hold, as Griffiths LJ did, that 'The test of foreseeability is not a universal *b* touchstone to determine the extent of liability for the consequences of wrongdoing' (see [1981] 1 All ER 809 at 823 [1981] QB 599 at 618). Authority for that proposition is both ample in quantity and exalted in status. My noble and learned friend Lord Wilberforce has already quoted in this context the observation of Lord Reid in *McKew v Holland & Hannen & Cubitts (Scotland) Ltd* [1969] 3 All ER 1621 at 1623, and referred to his own treatment of the topic in *Anns v Merton London Borough* [1977] 2 All ER 492 at 498, [1978] *c* AC 728 at 752, where further citations are furnished. To add yet another, let me conclude by recalling that in *Hedley Byrne & Co Ltd v Heller & Partners Ltd* [1963] 2 All ER 575 at 615, [1964] AC 465 at 536 Lord Pearce observed:

> 'How wide the sphere of the duty of care in negligence is to be laid depends *ultimately* on the courts' assessment of the demands of society for protection from the carelessness of others.' (My emphasis.)   *d*

I finally turn to consider the following passage in the speech of my noble and learned friend Lord Scarman:

> 'Policy considerations will have to be weighed; but the objective of the judges is the formulation of principle. And, if principle inexorably requires a decision which entails a degree of policy risk, the court's function is to adjudicate according to *e* principle, leaving policy curtailment to the judgment of Parliament . . . If principle leads to results which are thought to be socially unacceptable, Parliament can legislate to draw a line or map out a new path.'

And at a later stage my noble and learned friend adds:

> 'Why then should not the courts draw the line, as the Court of Appeal manfully *f* tried to do in this case? Simply, because the policy issue where to draw the line is not justiciable.'

My understanding of these words is that my noble and learned friend shares (though for a different reason) the conclusion of my noble and learned friend Lord Bridge that, in adverting to public policy, the Court of Appeal here embarked on a sleeveless errand, *g* for public policy has no relevance to liability at law. In my judgment, the proposition that '. . . the policy issue . . . is not justiciable' is as novel as it is startling. So novel is it in relation to this appeal that it was never mentioned during the hearing before your Lordships. And it is startling because in my respectful judgment it runs counter to well-established and wholly acceptable law.

I restrict myself to recent decisions of your Lordships' House. In *Rondel v Worsley* *h* [1967] 3 All ER 993, [1969] 1 AC 191 their Lordships unanimously held that public policy required that a barrister should be immune from an action for negligence in respect of his conduct and management of a case in court and the work preliminary thereto, Lord Reid saying ([1967] 3 All ER 993 at 998, [1969] 1 AC 191 at 228):

> 'Is it in the public interest that barristers and advocates should be protected *j* against such actions? Like so many questions which raise the public interest, a decision one way will cause hardships to individuals while a decision the other way will involve disadvantage to the public interest . . . So the issue appears to me to be whether the abolition of the rule would probably be attended by such disadvantage to the public interest as to make its retention clearly justifiable.'

In *Home Office v Dorset Yacht Co* [1970] 2 All ER 294, [1970] AC 1004 your Lordships'

House was called on to decide whether the English law of civil wrongs should be
a extended to impose legal liability for loss caused by conduct of a kind which had not
hitherto been recognised by the courts as entailing liability. In expressing the view that
it did, Lord Diplock said ([1970] 2 All ER 294 at 324, [1970] AC 1004 at 1058):

> '... I agree with Lord Denning MR that what we are concerned with in this
> appeal "is ... at bottom a matter of public policy which we, as judges, must
> resolve".'

b
And in *British Rlys Board v Herrington* [1972] 1 All ER 749 at 756–757, [1972] AC 877
at 897, dealing with an occupier's duty to trespassing children, Lord Reid said:

> 'Legal principles cannot solve the problem. How far occupiers are to be required
> by law to take steps to safeguard such children must be a matter of public policy.'

c   My Lords, in accordance with such a line of authorities, I hold that public policy issues
are 'justiciable'. Their invocation calls for close scrutiny, and the conclusion may be that
its nature and existence have not been established with the clarity and cogency required
before recognition can be granted to any legal doctrine and before any litigant can
properly be deprived of what would otherwise be his manifest legal rights. Or the
conclusion may be that adoption of the public policy relied on would involve the
d introduction of new legal principles so fundamental that they are best left to the
legislature: see, for example, *Morgans v Launchbury* [1972] 2 All ER 606 esp at 615, [1973]
AC 127 esp at 142, per Lord Pearson. And 'Public policy is not immutable' (per Lord
Reid in *Rondel v Worsley* [1967] 3 All ER 993 at 998, [1969] 1 AC 199 at 227). Indeed,
Winfield described it as '*necessarily* variable', and wisely added ((1928) 42 Harv LR at 93):

> 'This variability ... is a stone in the edifice of the doctrine, and not a missile to be
e > flung at it. Public policy would be almost useless without it. The march of
> civilization and the difficulty of ascertaining public policy at any given time make
> it essential ... How is public policy evidenced? If it is so variable, if it depends on
> the welfare of the community at any given time, how are the courts to ascertain
> it? Some judges have thought this difficulty so great that they have urged that it
> would be solved much better by the legislature and have considered it to be the
f > main reason why the courts should leave public policy alone ... This admonition
> is a wise one and judges are not likely to forget it. But the better view seems to be
> that the difficulty of discovering what public policy is at any given moment
> certainly does not absolve the bench from the duty of doing so. The judges are
> bound to take notice of it and of the changes which it undergoes, and it is immaterial
> that the question may be one of ethics rather than of law.'

g
In the present case the Court of Appeal did just that, and in my judgment they were
right in doing so. But they concluded that public policy required them to dismiss what
they clearly regarded as an otherwise irrefragable claim. In so concluding, I respectfully
hold that they were wrong, and I would accordingly allow the appeal.

h **LORD RUSSELL OF KILLOWEN.** My Lords, I make two comments at the
outset. First, we are not concerned with any problem that might have been posed had
the accident been not wholly attributable to the negligence of the defendants, but partly
attributable to negligent driving by the injured son of the plaintiff. Second, the plaintiff
is to be regarded as of normal disposition or phlegm; we are therefore not concerned to
investigate the applicability of the 'thin skull' cases to this type of case.

j   The facts in this case, and the physical illness suffered by the plaintiff as a result of
mental trauma caused to her by what she learned, heard and saw at the hospital have
been set out in the speech of my noble and learned friend Lord Wilberforce and I do not
repeat them.

All members of the Court of Appeal concluded that that which happened to the
plaintiff was reasonably foreseeable by the defendants as a consequence of their negligence
on the road. (In some cases, and at all levels, a reasonable *bystander* seems to be introduced

as a relevant mind; I do not understand why: reasonable foreseeability must surely be something to be attributed to the person guilty of negligence.)

But, if the effect on this wife and mother of the results of the negligence is considered to have been reasonably foreseeable, I do not see the justification for not finding the defendants liable in damages therefor. I would not shrink from regarding in an appropriate case policy as something which may feature in a judicial decision. But in this case what policy should inhibit a decision in favour of liability to the plaintiff? Negligent driving on the highway is only one form of negligence which may cause wounding or death and thus induce a relevant mental trauma in a person such as the plaintiff. There seems to be no policy requirement that the damage to the plaintiff should be on or adjacent to the highway. In the last analysis any policy consideration seems to be rooted in a fear of floodgates opening, the tacit question: what next? I am not impressed by that fear, certainly not sufficiently to deprive this plaintiff of just compensation for the reasonably foreseeable damage done to her. I do not consider that such deprivation is justified by trying to answer in advance the question posed, What next? by a consideration of relationships of plaintiff to the sufferers or deceased, or other circumstances; to attempt in advance solutions, or even guidelines, in hypothetical cases may well, it seems to me, in this field, do more harm than good.

I also would allow this appeal.

LORD SCARMAN. My Lords, I have had the advantage of reading in draft the speech of my noble and learned friend Lord Bridge. It cannot be strengthened or improved by any words of mine. I accept his approach to the law and the conclusion he reaches. But I also share the anxieties of the Court of Appeal. I differ, however, from the Court of Appeal in that I am persuaded that in this branch of the law it is not for the courts but for the legislature to set limits, if any be needed, to the law's development.

The appeal raises directly a question as to the balance in our law between the functions of judge and legislature. The common law, which in a constitutional context includes judicially developed equity, covers everything which is not covered by statute. It knows no gaps: there can be no casus omissus. The function of the court is to decide the case before it, even though the decision may require the extension or adaptation of a principle or in some cases the creation of new law to meet the justice of the case. But, whatever the court decides to do, it starts from a baseline of existing principle and seeks a solution consistent with or analogous to a principle or principles already recognised.

The distinguishing feature of the common law is this judicial development and formulation of principle. Policy considerations will have to be weighed; but the objective of the judges is the formulation of principle. And, if principle inexorably requires a decision which entails a degree of policy risk, the court's function is to adjudicate according to principle, leaving policy curtailment to the judgment of Parliament. Here lies the true role of the two law-making institutions in our constitution. By concentrating on principle the judges can keep the common law alive, flexible and consistent, and can keep the legal system clear of policy problems which neither they, nor the forensic process which it is their duty to operate, are equipped to resolve. If principle leads to results which are thought to be socially unacceptable, Parliament can legislate to draw a line or map out a new path.

The real risk to the common law is not its movement to cover new situations and new knowledge but lest it should stand still, halted by a conservative judicial approach. If that should happen, and since the 1966 practice direction of the House (see Note [1966] 3 All ER 77, [1966] 1 WLR 1234) it has become less likely, there would be a danger of the law becoming irrelevant to the consideration, and inept in its treatment, of modern social problems. Justice would be defeated. The common law has, however, avoided this catastrophe by the flexibility given it by generations of judges. Flexibility carries with it, of course, certain risks, notably a degree of uncertainty in the law and the 'floodgates' risk which so impressed the Court of Appeal in the present case.

The importance to be attached to certainty and the size of the 'floodgates' risk vary from one branch of the law to another. What is required of the law in its approach to a

commercial transaction will be very different from the approach appropriate to problems
a of tortious liability for personal injuries. In some branches of the law, notably that now
under consideration, the search for certainty can obstruct the law's pursuit of justice, and
can become the enemy of the good.

The present case is a good illustration. Certainty could have been achieved by leaving
the law as it was left by *Victorian Rlys Comrs v Coultas* (1888) 13 App Cas 222 or, again, by
holding the line drawn in 1901 by *Dulieu v White & Sons* [1901] 1 KB 669, [1900–3] All
b ER Rep 353 or today by confining the law to what was regarded by Lord Denning MR
in *Hinz v Berry* [1970] 1 All ER 1074 at 1075, [1970] 2 QB 40 at 42 as 'settled law', namely
that 'damages can be given for nervous shock caused by the sight of an accident, at any
rate to a close relative'.

But at each landmark stage common law principle, when considered in the context of
developing medical science, has beckoned the judges on. And now, as has been made
c clear by Evatt J, dissenting in *Chester v Waverley Municipal Council* (1939) 62 CLR 1 in the
High Court of Australia, by Tobriner J, giving the majority judgment in the Californian
case of *Dillon v Legg* (1968) 68 C 2d 728, and by my noble and learned friend in this case,
common law principle requires the judges to follow the logic of the 'reasonably
foreseeable test' so as, in circumstances where it is appropriate, to apply it untrammelled
by spatial, physical or temporal limits. Space, time, distance, the nature of the injuries
d sustained and the relationship of the plaintiff to the immediate victim of the accident are
factors to be weighed, but not legal limitations, when the test of reasonable foreseeability
is to be applied.

But I am by no means sure that the result is socially desirable. The 'floodgates'
argument may be exaggerated. Time alone will tell; but I foresee social and financial
problems if damages for 'nervous shock' should be made available to persons other than
e parents and children who without seeing or hearing the accident, or being present in the
immediate aftermath, suffer nervous shock in consequence of it. There is, I think, a
powerful case for legislation such as has been enacted in New South Wales and the
Australian Capital Territory.

Why then should not the courts draw the line, as the Court of Appeal manfully tried
to do in this case? Simply, because the policy issue where to draw the line is not
f justiciable. The problem is one of social, economic, and financial policy. The
considerations relevant to a decision are not such as to be capable of being handled within
the limits of the forensic process.

My Lords, I would allow the appeal for the reasons developed by my noble and learned
friend Lord Bridge, while putting on record my view that there is here a case for
legislation.

g

LORD BRIDGE OF HARWICH. My Lords, I gratefully adopt the account given by
my noble and learned friend Lord Wilberforce of the facts giving rise to this appeal.

This is only the second case ever to reach your Lordships' House concerning the
liability of a tortfeasor who has negligently killed or physically injured A to pay damages
to B for a psychiatric illness resulting from A's death or injury. The previous case was
h *Hay (or Bourhill) v Young* [1942] 2 All ER 396, [1943] AC 92. The impression with which
I am left, after being taken in argument through all the relevant English authorities, a
number of Commonwealth authorities and one important decision of the Supreme
Court of California, is that this whole area of English law stands in urgent need of review.

The basic difficulty of the subject arises from the fact that the crucial answers to the
questions which it raises lie in the difficult field of psychiatric medicine. The common
j law gives no damages for the emotional distress which any normal person experiences
when someone he loves is killed or injured. Anxiety and depression are normal human
emotions. Yet an anxiety neurosis or a reactive depression may be recognisable
psychiatric illnesses, with or without psychosomatic symptoms. So, the first hurdle
which a plaintiff claiming damages of the kind in question must surmount is to establish
that he is suffering, not merely grief, distress or any other normal emotion, but a positive
psychiatric illness. That is here not in issue. A plaintiff must then establish the necessary

chain of causation in fact between his psychiatric illness and the death or injury of one
or more third parties negligently caused by the defendant. Here again, this is not in   *a*
dispute in the instant case. But, when causation in fact is in issue, it must no doubt be
determined by the judge on the basis of the evidence of psychiatrists. Then, here comes
the all important question. Given the fact of the plaintiff's psychiatric illness cased by
the defendant's negligence in killing or physically injuring another, was the chain of
causation from the one event to the other, considered ex post facto in the light of all that
has happened, 'reasonably foreseeable' by the 'reasonable man'? A moment's thought   *b*
will show that the answer to that question depends on what knowledge is to be attributed
to the hypothetical reasonable man of the operation of cause and effect in medicine.
There are at least two theoretically possible approaches. The first is that the judge should
receive the evidence of psychiatrists as to the degree of probability that the particular
cause would produce the particular effect, and apply to that the appropriate legal test of
reasonable foreseeability as the criterion of the defendant's duty of care. The second is   *c*
that the judge, relying on his own opinion of the operation of cause and effect in
psychiatric medicine, as fairly representative of that of the educated layman, should treat
himself as the reasonable man and form his own view from the primary facts whether
the proven chain of cause and effect was reasonably foreseeable. In principle, I think
there is much to be said for the first approach. Foreseeability, in any given set of
circumstances, is ultimately a question of fact. If a claim in negligence depends on   *d*
whether some defect in a complicated piece of machinery was foreseeably a cause of
injury, I apprehend that the judge will decide that question on the basis of the expert
evidence of engineers. But the authorities give no support to this approach in relation to
the foreseeability of psychiatric illness. The judges, in all the decisions we have been
referred to, have assumed that it lay within their own competence to determine whether
the plaintiff's 'nervous shock' (as lawyers quaintly persist in calling it) was in any given   *e*
circumstances a sufficiently foreseeable consequence of the defendant's act or omission
relied on as negligent to bring the plaintiff within the scope of those to whom the
defendant owed a duty of care. To depart from this practice and treat the question of
foreseeable causation in this field, and hence the scope of the defendant's duty, as a
question of fact to be determined in the light of the expert evidence adduced in each case
would, no doubt, be too large an innovation in the law to be regarded as properly within   *f*
the competence, even since the liberating 1966 practice direction (see *Note* [1966] 3 All
ER 77, [1966] 1 WLR 1234), of your Lordships' House. Moreover, psychiatric medicine
is far from being an exact science. The opinions of its practitioners may differ widely.
Clearly it is desirable in this, as in any other, field that the law should achieve such a
measure of certainty as is consistent with the demands of justice. It would seem that the
consensus of informed judicial opinion is probably the best yardstick available to   *g*
determine whether, in any given circumstances, the emotional trauma resulting from
the death or injury of third parties, or indeed the threat of such death or injury, ex
hypothesi attributable to the defendant's negligence, was a foreseeable cause in law, as
well as the actual cause in fact, of the plaintiff's psychiatric or psychosomatic illness. But
the word I would emphasise in the foregoing sentence is 'informed'. For too long earlier
generations of judges have regarded psychiatry and psychiatrists with suspicion, if not   *h*
hostility. Now, I venture to hope, that attitude has quite disappeared. No judge who has
spent any length of time trying personal injury claims in recent years would doubt that
physical injuries can give rise not only to organic but also to psychiatric disorders. The
sufferings of the patient from the latter are no less real and frequently no less painful and
disabling than from the former. Likewise, I would suppose that the legal profession well
understands that an acute emotional trauma, like a physical trauma, can well cause a   *j*
psychiatric illness in a wide range of circumstances and in a wide range of individuals
whom it would be wrong to regard as having any abnormal psychological make-up. It
is in comparatively recent times that these insights have come to be generally accepted
by the judiciary. It is only by giving effect to these insights in the developing law of

negligence that we can do justice to an important, though no doubt small, class of
a plaintiffs whose genuine psychiatric illnesses are caused by negligent defendants.

My Lords, in the instant case I cannot help thinking that the learned trial judge's
conclusion that the appellant's illness was not the foreseeable consequence of the
respondents' negligence was one to which, understandably, he felt himself driven by the
authorities. Free of authority, and applying the ordinary criterion of reasonable
foreseeability to the facts, with an eye 'enlightened by progressive awareness of mental
b illness' (the language of Stephenson LJ (see [1981] 1 All ER 809 at 819, [1981] QB 599 at
612)), any judge must, I would think, share the view of all three members of the Court
of Appeal, with which I understand all your Lordships agree, that, in the words of
Griffiths LJ, it was 'readily foreseeable that a significant number of mothers exposed to
such an experience might break down under the shock of the event and suffer illness' (see
[1981] 1 All ER 809 at 822, [1981] QB 599 at 617).

c   The question, then, for your Lordships' decision is whether the law, as a matter of
policy, draws a line which exempts from liability a defendant whose negligent act or
omission was actually and foreseeably the cause of the plaintiff's psychiatric illness and,
if so, where that line is to be drawn. In thus formulating the question, I do not, of course,
use the word 'negligent' as prejudging the question whether the defendant owes the
plaintiff a duty, but I do use the word 'foreseeably' as connoting the normally accepted
d criterion of such a duty.

Before attempting to answer the question, it is instructive to consider the historical
development of the subject as illustrated by the authorities, and to note, in particular,
three features of that development. First, it will be seen that successive attempts have
been made to draw a line beyond which liability should not extend, each of which has in
due course had to be abandoned. Second, the ostensible justification for drawing the line
e has been related to the current criterion of a defendant's duty of care, which, however
expressed in earlier judgments, we should now describe as that of reasonable
foreseeability. But, third, in so far as policy considerations can be seen to have influenced
any of the decisions, they appear to have sprung from the fear that to cross the chosen line
would be to open the floodgates to claims without limit and largely without merit.

Perhaps the most vivid illustration of all three features is in the very first case in the
f series, the decision of the Privy Council in *Victorian Rlys Comrs v Coultas* (1888) 13 App
Cas 222. The plaintiff, a pregnant lady, was a passenger in a buggy which was negligently
allowed by the defendants' gatekeeper to cross the railway line when a train was
approaching. The buggy crossed just in time, ahead of the train, but only narrowly
escaped collision. The plaintiff was so alarmed that she suffered what was described as
'a severe nervous shock'. She fainted, and subsequently miscarried. She succeeded in her
g claim for damages in the courts below. Delivering the judgment of the Privy Council,
allowing the appeal, Sir Richard Couch said (at 225–226):

'According to the evidence of the female plaintiff her fright was caused by seeing
the train approaching, and thinking they were going to be killed. Damages arising
from mere sudden terror unaccompanied by an actual physical injury, but
h occasioning a nervous or mental shock, cannot under such circumstances, their
Lordships think, be considered a consequence which, in the ordinary course of
things, would flow from the negligence of the gate-keeper. If it were held that they
can, it appears to their Lordships that it would be extending the liability for
negligence much beyond what that liability has hitherto been held to be. Not only
in such a case as the present, but in every case where an accident caused by
j negligence had given a person a serious nervous shock, there might be a claim for
damages on account of mental injury. The difficulty which now often exists in case
of alleged physical injuries of determining whether they were caused by the
negligent act would be greatly increased, and a wide field opened for imaginary
claims.'

Two Irish courts declined to follow this decision: *Bell v Great Northern Rly Co of Ireland* (1890) 26 LR Ir 428, following *Byrne v Great Southern and Western Rly Co of Ireland* (1884) unreported. The next English case followed the Irish courts' lead. This was *Dulieu v White & Sons* [1901] 2 KB 669, [1900–3] All ER Rep 353. The case was argued on a preliminary point of law. The plaintiff, again a pregnant lady, pleaded that she had suffered nervous shock when the defendants' horse-drawn van was negligently driven into the public house where she was behind the bar. Kennedy J gave the leading judgment of the Divisional Court in the plaintiff's favour. It is worth quoting the passage which is central to his decision, if only to show how far we have travelled in the last eighty years in the judicial approach to the kind of medical question presently under consideration. He said ([1901] 2 KB 669 at 677, [1900–3] All ER Rep 353 at 358):

'For my own part, I should not like to assume it to be scientifically true that a nervous shock which causes serious bodily illness is not actually accompanied by physical injury, although it may be impossible, or at least difficult, to detect the injury at the time in the living subject. I should not be surprised if the surgeon or the physiologist told us that nervous shock is or may be in itself an injurious affection of the physical organism. Let it be assumed, however, that the physical injury follows the shock, but that the jury are satisfied upon proper and sufficient medical evidence that it follows the shock as its direct and natural effect, is there any legal reason for saying that the damage is less proximate in the legal sense than damage which arises contemporaneously?'

But earlier in his judgment Kennedy J had drawn a new line of limitation when he said ([1901] 2 KB 669 at 675; cf [1900–3] All ER Rep 353 at 357): 'The shock, where it operates through the mind, must be a shock which arises from a reasonable fear of immediate personal injury to oneself.' He supported this by reference to an earlier case (*Smith v Johnson & Co* (1898) unreported), where the unsuccessful plaintiff suffered from the shock of seeing another person killed and said of such a case:

'I should myself . . . have been inclined to go a step further, and to hold . . . that, as the defendant neither intended to affect the plaintiff injuriously nor did anything which could reasonably or naturally be expected to affect him injuriously, there was no evidence of any breach of legal duty towards the plaintiff . . .'

The next landmark is *Hambrook v Stokes Bros* [1925] 1 KB 141, [1924] All ER Rep 110. This was the case which turned on whether 'nervous shock' caused to a mother by fear for her children, who had just disappeared round a corner going up a hill when a runaway lorry appeared round the corner going downhill, and when, as it turned out, one of her children was injured, gave a cause of action against the driver whose negligence allowed the lorry to run down the hill. The court by a majority held that it did. The leading judgment of Bankes LJ sought to demonstrate the absurdity of maintaining the boundary of a defendant's liability for 'nervous shock' on the line drawn by Kennedy J, saying ([1925] 1 KB 141 at 151, [1924] All ER Rep 110 at 113):

'Assume two mothers crossing the street at the same time when this lorry comes thundering down, each holding a small child by the hand. One mother is courageous and devoted to her child. She is terrified, but thinks only of the damage to the child, and not at all about herself. The other woman is timid and lacking in the motherly instinct. She also is terrified, but thinks only of the damage to herself and not at all about her child. The health of both mothers is seriously affected by the mental shock occasioned by the fright. Can any real distinction be drawn between the two cases? Will the law recognise a cause of action in the case of the less deserving mother, and none in the case of the more deserving one? Does the law say that the defendant ought reasonably to have anticipated the non-natural feeling of the timid mother, and not the natural feeling of the courageous mother? I think not.'

Sargant LJ, in his dissenting judgment, nevertheless sought to uphold the distinction

a essentially on the basis that 'nervous shock' caused to a plaintiff by fear of injury to himself occasioned by a 'near miss' is indistinguishable, so far as the defendant's duty is concerned, from injury by direct impact, whereas 'nervous shock' caused by the fear or sight of injury to another is beyond the defendant's anticipation and hence beyond the range of his duty.

When one comes to the decision of your Lordships' House in *Hay (or Bourhill) v Young*

b [1942] 2 All ER 396, [1943] AC 92 it is important to bear in mind, as the speeches delivered show, that the difference of judicial opinion in *Hambrook v Stokes Bros* remained unresolved, and indeed that their Lordships did not purport to resolve it. Furthermore, on the facts of that case, the result was surely a foregone conclusion. The pursuer was alighting from a tram when she heard, but did not see, the impact of a collision between a motor cyclist (on whose negligence in driving too fast her claim was based) and a car.

c The motor cyclist, a stranger to the pursuer, was killed. There is nothing in the report to indicate that she ever saw the body, but after the body had been removed she saw the blood left on the road. In these circumstances I cannot suppose that any judge today would dissent from the view that 'nervous shock' to the pursuer was not reasonably foreseeable. Nor would anyone, I think, quarrel with the following passage from the speech of Lord Porter as expressing a view of the law as acceptable in 1982 as it was in

d 1942 ([1942] 2 All ER 396 at 409, [1943] AC 92 at 117):

> 'The question whether emotional disturbance or shock, which a defender ought reasonably to have anticipated as likely to follow from his reckless driving, can ever form the basis of a claim is not in issue. It is not every emotional disturbance or every shock which should have been foreseen. The driver of a car or vehicle even though careless is entitled to assume that the ordinary frequenter of the streets has
> *e* sufficient fortitude to endure such incidents as may from time to time be expected to occur in them, including the noise of a collision and the sight of injury to others, and is not to be considered negligent towards one who does not possess the customary phlegm.'

On the difference of opinion in *Hambrook v Stokes Bros* Lord Russell in terms expressed

f a preference for the dissenting view of Sargant LJ. Lord Thankerton and Lord Macmillan, although not saying so in terms, appear by necessary implication to support the same view by confining a driver's duty of care to those in the area of potential physical danger which may arise from the manner of his driving. Lord Porter's speech is neutral. Lord Wright expressed provisional agreement with the majority decision in *Hambrook v Stokes Bros*. His speech also contained the following and, as I think, far-

g sighted passage ([1942] 2 All ER 396 at 405–406, [1943] AC 92 at 110):

> 'What is now being considered is the question of liability, and this, I think, in a question whether there is a duty owing to members of the public who come within the ambit of the act, must generally depend on a normal standard of susceptibility. This, it may be said, is somewhat vague. That is true; but definition involves limitation, which it is desirable to avoid further than is necessary in a
> *h* principle of law like negligence, which is widely ranging and is still in the stage of development. It is here, as elsewhere, a question of what the hypothetical reasonable man, viewing the position, I suppose *ex post facto*, would say it was proper to foresee. What danger of particular infirmity that would include must depend on all the circumstances; but generally, I think, a reasonably normal condition, if medical evidence is capable of defining it, would be the standard. The test of the plaintiff's
> *j* extraordinary susceptibility, if unknown to the defendant, would in effect make the defendant an insurer. The lawyer likes to draw fixed and definite lines and is apt to ask where the thing is to stop. I should reply it should stop where in the particular case the good sense of the jury, or of the judge, decides ... I cannot, however, forbear referring to a most important case in the High Court of Australia, *Chester* v.

Waverley Municipal Council ((1939) 62 CLR 1), where the court by a majority held that no duty was made out. The dissenting judgment of EVATT, J., will demand the consideration of any judge who is called upon to consider these questions.'

I shall return later to the judgment of Evatt J to which Lord Wright there refers.

I need not consider in detail the subsequent English Court of Appeal decisions in *King v Phillips* [1953] 1 All ER 617, [1953] 1 QB 429, *Boardman v Sanderson* [1964] 1 WLR 1317 and *Hinz v Berry* [1970] 1 All ER 1074, [1970] 2 QB 40. In *King v Phillips* [1953] 1 All ER 617 at 623, [1953] 1 QB 429 at 441, Denning LJ said: '. . . there can be no doubt since *Hay (or Bourhill) v Young* that the test of liability for shock is foreseeability of injury by shock.'

This observation was cited with approval in *Overseas Tankship (UK) Ltd v Morts Dock and Engineering Co Ltd The Wagon Mound (No 1)* [1961] 1 All ER 404 at 415, [1961] AC 388 at 426. I would add, however, that *King v Phillips*, a case in which the plaintiff failed, would, as I think, clearly be decided differently today. By 1970 it was clear that no one could any longer contend for the limitation of liability for 'nervous shock' to those who were themselves put in danger by the defendant's negligence, so much so that in *Hinz v Berry* a mother who witnessed from one side of the road a terrible accident to her family picnicking on the other side of the road recovered damages for her resulting psychiatric illness without dispute on the issue of liability, and the case reached the Court of Appeal on the issue of quantum of damages only. Lord Denning MR said ([1970] 1 All ER 1074 at 1075, [1970] 2 QB 40 at 42):

'The law at one time said that there could not be damages for nervous shock; but for these last 25 years, it has been settled that damages can be given for nervous shock caused by the sight of an accident, at any rate to a close relative.'

The only other important English decision is *Chadwick v British Transport Commission* [1967] 2 All ER 945, [1967] 1 WLR 912. The plaintiff's husband lived 200 yards from the scene of the terrible Lewisham railway accident in 1957 in which 90 people were killed. On hearing of the accident in the evening he went at once to the scene and assisted in the rescue work through the night until early next morning. As a result of his experiences of the night he developed an acute anxiety neurosis for which he required hospital treatment as an in-patient for over six months. After his death from unrelated causes his wife, as administratrix of his estate, recovered damages for his psychiatric illness. This was a decision of Waller J. It was not challenged on appeal and no one, I believe, has ever doubted that it was rightly decided.

I should mention two Commonwealth decisions of first instance. In *Benson v Lee* [1972] VR 879 Lush J, in the Supreme Court of Victoria, held that a mother who did not witness, but was told of, an accident to her son 100 yards from her home, went to the scene and accompanied the child in an ambulance to hospital where he died, was entitled to damages for 'nervous shock' notwithstanding evidence that she was prone to mental illness from stress. In *Marshal v Lionel Enterprises Inc* (1971) 25 DLR (3d) 141 Haines J, in the Ontario High Court, held that a wife who found her husband seriously injured shortly after an accident caused by defective machinery was not, as a matter of law, disentitled to damages for the 'nervous shock' which she claimed to have suffered as a result. On the other hand in *Abramzik v Brenner* (1967) 65 DLR (2d) 651 the Saskatchewan Court of Appeal held that a mother who suffered 'nervous shock' on being informed by her husband that two of her children had been killed in a road accident was not entitled to recover.

Chester v Waverley Municipal Council (1939) 62 CLR 1, referred to by Lord Wright in the passage quoted above, was a decision of the High Court of Australia. The plaintiff's seven-year-old son having been out to play, failed to return home when expected. A search was mounted which continued for some hours. Eventually, in the presence of the plaintiff, his mother, the child's dead body was recovered from a flooded trench which the defendant authority had left inadequately fenced. The plaintiff claimed damages for 'nervous shock'. The majority of the court (Latham CJ, Rich and Starke JJ) rejected the a claim. The decision was based squarely on the ground that, the plaintiff's injury not being a foreseeable consequence of the defendant's omission to fence the trench, they owed her no duty. But the judgment of Latham CJ contains an interesting example of the 'floodgates' argument. He said (at 7-8):

b 'But in this case the plaintiff must establish a duty owed by the defendant to herself and a breach of that duty. The duty which it is suggested the defendant owed to the plaintiff was a duty not to injure her child so as to cause her a nervous shock when she saw, not the happening of the injury, but the result of the injury, namely, the dead body of the child. It is rather difficult to state the limit of the alleged duty. If a duty of the character suggested exists at all it is not really said that it should be confined to mothers of children who are injured. It must extend to some wider class—but to what class? There appears to be no reason why it should not extend to other relatives or to all other persons, whether they are relatives or not. If this is the true principle of law, then a person who is guilty of negligence with the result that A is injured will be liable in damages to B, C, D and any other persons who receive a nervous shock (as distinguished from passing fright or distress) at any time upon perceiving the results of the negligence, whether in disfigurement of person, physical injury, or death.'

d In a powerful dissenting judgment, which I find wholly convincing, Evatt J drew a vivid picture of the mother's agony of mind as the search continued, culminating in the gruesome discovery in her presence of the child's drowned body. I cannot for a moment doubt the correctness of his conclusion that the mother's mental illness was the reasonably foreseeable consequence of the defendant's negligence. This was a case from New South Wales and I cannot help wondering whether it was not the manifest injustice of the result which led, a few years later, to the intervention of the New South Wales legislature, to enable the parent, husband or wife of a person 'killed, injured or put in peril' by another's negligence to recover damages for 'mental or nervous shock' irrespective of any spatial or temporal relationship to the accident in which the death, injury or peril occurred.

f My Lords, looking back I think it is possible to discern that there only ever were two clear lines of limitation of a defendant's liability for 'nervous shock' for which any rational justification could be advanced, in the light both of the state of the law of negligence and the state of medical science as judicially understood, at the time when those limitations were propounded. In 1888 it was, no doubt, perfectly sensible to say:

g 'Damages arising from mere sudden terror unaccompanied by any actual physical injury, but occasioning a nervous or mental shock, cannot ... be considered a consequence which, in the ordinary course of things, would flow from ... negligence.'

(See *Victorian Rlys Comrs v Coultas* 13 App Cas 222 at 225.) Here the test, whether of duty or of remoteness, can be recognised as a relatively distant ancestor of the modern criterion of reasonable foreseeability. Again, in 1901 it was, I would suppose, equally
h sensible to limit a defendant's liability for 'nervous shock' which could 'reasonably or naturally be expected' to be such as was suffered by a plaintiff who was himself physically endangered by the defendant's negligence (see *Dulieu v White & Sons* [1901] 2 KB 669 at 675; cf [1900-3] All ER Rep 353 at 357). But once that line of limitation has been crossed, as it was by the majority in *Hambrook v Stokes Bros*, there can be no logical reason whatever for limiting the defendant's duty to persons in physical proximity to the place
j where the accident, caused by the defendant's negligence, occurred. Much of the confusion in the authorities since *Hay (or Bourhill) v Young*, including, if I may say so, the judgments of the courts below in the instant case, has arisen, as it seems to me, from the deference still accorded, notwithstanding the acceptance of the *Hambrook* principle, to dicta of their Lordships in *Hay (or Bourhill) v Young* which only make sense if understood as based on the limited principle of liability propounded by Kennedy J in *Dulieu v White*

& *Sons*, and adopted in the dissenting judgment of Sargant LJ in *Hambrook v Stokes Bros*.

My Lords, before returning to the policy question, it is, I think, highly instructive to *a* consider the decision of the Supreme Court of California in *Dillon v Legg* (1968) 68 C 2d 728. Before this decision the law of California, and evidently of other states of the Union, had adhered to the English position before *Hambrook v Stokes Bros* that damages for nervous shock could only be recovered if resulting from the plaintiff's apprehension of danger to himself, and, indeed, this view had been affirmed by the Californian Supreme Court only five years earlier. The majority in *Dillon v Legg* adopted a contrary view in *b* refusing a motion to dismiss a mother's claim for damages for emotional trauma caused by seeing her infant daughter killed by a car as she crossed the road.

In delivering the majority judgment of the court, Tobriner J said (at 740–741):

'Since the chief element in determining whether defendant owes a duty or an obligation to plaintiff is the foreseeability of the risk, that factor will be of prime concern in every case. Because it is inherently intertwined with foreseeability such *c* duty or obligation must necessarily be adjudicated only upon a case-by-case basis. We cannot now predetermine defendant's obligation in every situation by a fixed category; no immutable rule can establish the extent of that obligation for every circumstance of the future. We can, however, define guidelines which will aid in the resolution of such an issue as the instant one. We note, first, that we deal here with a case in which plaintiff suffered a shock which resulted in physical injury and *d* we confine our ruling to that case. In determining, in such a case, whether defendant should reasonably foresee the injury to plaintiff, or, in other terminology, whether defendant owes plaintiff a duty of due care, the courts will take into account such factors as the following: (1) Whether plaintiff was located near the scene of the accident as contrasted with one who was a distance away from it. (2) Whether the shock resulted from a direct emotional impact upon plaintiff from the *e* sensory and contemporaneous observance of the accident, as contrasted with learning of the accident from others after its occurrence. (3) Whether plaintiff and the victim were closely related, as contrasted with an absence of any relationship or the presence of only a distant relationship. The evaluation of these factors will indicate the *degree* of the defendant's foreseeability: obviously defendant is more likely to foresee that a mother who observes an accident affecting her child will *f* suffer harm than to foretell that a stranger witness will do so. Similarly, the degree of foreseeability of the third person's injury is far greater in the case of his contemporaneous observance of the accident than that in which he subsequently learns of it. The defendant is more likely to foresee that shock to the nearby, witnessing mother will cause physical harm than to anticipate that someone distant from the accident will suffer more than a temporary emotional reaction. All these *g* elements, of course, shade into each other; the fixing of obligation, intimately tied into the facts, depends upon each case. In light of these factors the court will determine whether the accident and harm was *reasonably* foreseeable. Such reasonable foreseeability does not turn on whether the particular plaintiff as an individual would have in actuality foreseen the exact accident and loss; it contemplates that courts, on a case-to-case basis, analyzing all the circumstances, will *h* decide what the ordinary man under such circumstances should reasonably have foreseen. The courts thus mark out the areas of liability, excluding the remote and unexpected. In the instant case, the presence of all the above factors indicates that plaintiff has alleged a sufficient prima facie case. Surely the negligent driver who causes the death of a young child may reasonably expect that the mother will not be *j* far distant and will upon witnessing the accident suffer emotional trauma. As Dean Prosser has stated: "when a child is endangered, it is not beyond contemplation that its mother will be somewhere in the vicinity, and will suffer serious shock." (Prosser, The Law of Torts (3rd edn, 1964) p 353. See also 2 Harper & James, The Law of Torts (1956) p 1039.) We are not now called upon to decide whether, in the *a* absence or reduced weight of some of the above factors, we would conclude that the accident and injury were not reasonably foreseeable and that therefore defendant owed no duty of due care to plaintiff. In future cases the courts will draw lines of demarcation upon facts more subtle than the compelling one alleged in the complaint before us.'

b The leading minority judgment castigated the majority for embarking on a first excursion into the 'fantastic realm of infinite liability', a colourful variant of the familiar 'floodgates' argument.

In approaching the question whether the law should, as a matter of policy, define the criterion of liability in negligence for causing psychiatric illness by reference to some test other than that of reasonable foreseeability it is well to remember that we are concerned only with the question of liability of a defendant who is, ex hypothesi, guilty of fault in causing the death, injury or danger which has in turn triggered the psychiatric illness.
c A policy which is to be relied on to narrow the scope of the negligent tortfeasor's duty must be justified by cogent and readily intelligible considerations, and must be capable of defining the appropriate limits of liability by reference to factors which are not purely arbitrary. A number of policy considerations which have been suggested as satisfying these requirements appear to me, with respect, to be wholly insufficient. I can see no ground whatever for suggesting that to make the defendant liable for reasonably
d foreseeable psychiatric illness caused by his negligence would be to impose a crushing burden on him out of proportion to his moral responsibility. However liberally the criterion of reasonable foreseeability is interpreted, both the number of successful claims in this field and the quantum of damages they will attract are likely to be moderate. I cannot accept as relevant the well-known phenomenon that litigation may delay recovery from a psychiatric illness. If this were a valid policy consideration, it would lead to the
e conclusion that psychiatric illness should be excluded altogether from the heads of damage which the law will recognise. It cannot justify limiting the cases in which damages will be awarded for psychiatric illness by reference to the circumstances of its causation. To attempt to draw a line at the furthest point which any of the decided cases happen to have reached, and to say that it is for the legislature, not the courts, to extend the limits of liability any further, would be, to my mind, an unwarranted abdication of
f the court's function of developing and adapting principles of the common law to changing conditions, in a particular corner of the common law which exemplifies, par excellence, the important and indeed necessary part which that function has to play. In the end I believe that the policy question depends on weighing against each other two conflicting considerations. On the one hand, if the criterion of liability is to be reasonable foreseeability simpliciter, this must, precisely because questions of causation in psychiatric
g medicine give rise to difficulty and uncertainty, introduce an element of uncertainty into the law and open the way to a number of arguable claims which a more precisely fixed criterion of liability would exclude. I accept that the element of uncertainty is an important factor. I believe that the 'floodgates' argument, however, is, as it always has been, greatly exaggerated. On the other hand, it seems to me inescapable that any attempt to define the limit of liability by requiring, in addition to reasonable
h foreseeability, that the plaintiff claiming damages for psychiatric illness should have witnessed the relevant accident, should have been present at or near the place where it happened, should have come on its aftermath and thus have some direct perception of it, as opposed to merely learning of it after the event, should be related in some particular degree to the accident victim—to draw a line by reference to any of these criteria must impose a largely arbitrary limit of liability. I accept, of course, the importance of the
j factors indicated in the guidelines suggested by Tobriner J in *Dillon v Legg* as bearing on the *degree* of foreseeability of the plaintiff's psychiatric illness. But let me give two examples to illustrate what injustice would be wrought by any such hard and fast lines of policy as have been suggested. First, consider the plaintiff who learned after the event of the relevant accident. Take the case of a mother who knows that her husband and

children are staying in a certain hotel. She reads in her morning newspaper that it has
been the scene of a disastrous fire. She sees in the paper a photograph of unidentifiable
victims trapped on the top floor waving for help from the windows. She learns shortly
afterwards that all her family have perished. She suffers an acute psychiatric illness.
That her illness in these circumstances was a reasonably foreseeable consequence of the
events resulting from the fire is undeniable. Yet, is the law to deny her damages as
against a defendant whose negligence was responsible for the fire simply on the ground
that an important link in the chain of causation of her psychiatric illness was supplied by
her imagination of the agonies of mind and body in which her family died, rather than
by direct perception of the event? Second, consider the plaintiff who is unrelated to the
victims of the relevant accident. If rigidly applied, an exclusion of liability to him would
have defeated the plaintiff's claim in *Chadwick v British Transport Commission*. The Court
of Appeal treated that case as in a special category because Mr Chadwick was a rescuer.
Now, the special duty owed to a rescuer who voluntarily places himself in physical
danger to save others is well understood, and is illustrated by *Haynes v Harwood* [1935] 1
KB 146, [1934] All ER Rep 103, the case of the constable injured in stopping a runaway
horse in a crowded street. But, in relation to the psychiatric consequences of witnessing
such terrible carnage as must have resulted from the Lewisham train disaster, I would
find it difficult to distinguish in principle the position of a rescuer, like Mr Chadwick,
from a mere spectator, as, for example, an uninjured or only slightly injured passenger
in the train, who took no part in the rescue operations but was present at the scene after
the accident for some time, perforce observing the rescue operations while he waited for
transport to take him home.

My Lords, I have no doubt that this is an area of the law of negligence where we should
resist the temptation to try yet once more to freeze the law in a rigid posture which
would deny justice to some who, in the application of the classic principles of negligence
derived from *Donoghue v Stevenson* [1932] AC 562, [1932] All ER Rep 1, ought to succeed,
in the interests of certainty, where the very subject matter is uncertain and continuously
developing, or in the interests of saving defendants and their insurers from the burden
of having sometimes to resist doubtful claims. I find myself in complete agreement with
Tobriner J that the defendant's duty must depend on reasonable foreseeability and—

> 'must necessarily be adjudicated only upon a case-by-case basis. We cannot now
> predetermine defendant's obligation in every situation by a fixed category; no
> immutable rule can establish the extent of that obligation for every circumstance of
> the future.'

To put the matter in another way, if asked where the thing is to stop, I should answer,
in an adaptation of the language of Lord Wright and Stephenson LJ, 'Where in the
particular case the good sense of the judge, enlightened by progressive awareness of
mental illness, decides'.

I regret that my noble and learned friend Lord Edmund-Davies, who criticises my
conclusion that in this area of the law there are no policy considerations sufficient to
justify limiting the liability of negligent tortfeasors by reference to some narrower
criterion than that of reasonable foreseeability, stops short of indicating his view where
the limit of liability should be drawn or the nature of the policy considerations (other
than the 'floodgates' argument, which I understand he rejects) which he would invoke to
justify such a limit.

My Lords, I would accordingly allow the appeal.

Appeal allowed.

Solicitors: *Vinters*, Cambridge (for the appellant); *Hextall, Erskine & Co* (for the
respondents).

Mary Rose Plummer   Barrister.

Anns and others v
London Borough of Merton

[1977] 2 All ER 492

HOUSE OF LORDS

LORD WILBERFORCE, LORD DIPLOCK, LORD SIMON OF GLAISDALE, LORD SALMON AND LORD RUSSELL OF KILLOWEN

3rd, 7th, 8th, 9th, 10th, 14th, 15th, 16th, 17th FEBRUARY, 12th MAY 1977

b

Ultra vires

Negligence – Duty to take care – Statutory powers – Act performed in exercise of powers – Local authority – Building operations – Legislation giving authority control over building operations – Byelaws requiring approval of foundations of building by authority's inspector before being covered up – Inspector carrying out inspection but failing to take reasonable care to ensure that foundations adequate – Building constructed on inadequate foundations – Subsequent damage to structure of building resulting from inadequate foundations – Whether local authority in breach of duty of care to owner or occupier of building at time damage occurs.

c

Negligence – Duty to take care – Statutory powers – Non-exercise of power – Circumstances in which non-exercise of power capable of amounting to a breach of duty of care – Local authority – Building operations – Legislation giving authority control over building operations – Byelaws requiring approval of foundations of building by authority's inspector before being covered up – Authority not carrying out inspection of foundations – Building constructed on inadequate foundations – Subsequent damage to structure of buildings resulting from inadequate foundations – Local authority not under statutory duty to inspect foundations – Whether failure to carry out inspection capable of amounting to breach of duty of care.

d

Limitation of action – When time begins to run – Actions of tort – Accrual of cause of action – Negligence – Damage – Lapse of time between negligent act and occurrence of damage – Action against local authority for breach of duty to secure compliance with building byelaws – Construction of block of maisonettes – Block built on inadequate foundations – Consequent damage to structure occurring more than six years after first conveyance of maisonettes – Writ issued within six years of discovery of damage – Whether cause of action accrued on date of first conveyance or on date when damage occurred – Whether action 'brought after expiration of six years from the date on which the cause of action accrued' – Limitation Act 1939, s 2(1)(a).

e

f

Negligence – Duty to take care – Owner of realty – Builder – Duty to subsequent purchaser in respect of hidden defects – Negligence in construction of house – Inadequate foundations – Defect causing damage to house after purchase by subsequent purchaser – Builder in breach of duty of care to subsequent purchaser – Immaterial that builder owner of house when defect created.

g

Damages – Measure of damages – Negligence – Damage to building – Damage resulting from hidden defects – Inadequate foundations – Failure to comply with building byelaws – Purpose of byelaws to prevent danger to health and safety of occupants – Recoverable damages including amount of expenditure necessary to restore building to condition in which it is no longer a danger to health and safety of occupants.

h

The Public Health Act 1936 imposed and conferred a wide range of duties and powers on local authorities for the purpose of safeguarding and promoting the health of the public at large. In particular local authorities were enabled through building byelaws made under s 61 of the 1936 Act to supervise and control the construction of buildings in their area and in particular the foundations of buildings. Building byelaws were duly made under these powers by a local authority ('the council') in 1953. The byelaws contained provision for the deposit of plans and the inspection of work. Byelaw 18(1)(b) provided that the foundation of every building should be taken down to such depth or be so designed and constructed as to safeguard the building against damage

j

by swelling and shrinking of the subsoil. In February 1962 the council approved
building plans for the erection of a two storey block of maisonettes which were
deposited under the byelaws. The approved plans showed, inter alia, the base wall
and concrete foundations of the block '3 feet or deeper to the approval of local
authority'. The written notice of approval drew attention to the requirement of the
byelaws that notice should be given to the council surveyor both at the commencement of the work and when the foundations were ready to be covered. When the
foundations were ready the council had the power to inspect and to insist on any
corrections necessary to bring the work into conformity with the byelaws but were
not under any obligation to inspect the foundations. On completion of the block
in 1962 the builder, who was also the owner of the block, granted a long lease of
each of the maisonettes, the last conveyance being made on 5th November 1965.
In February 1970 structural movements began to occur resulting in cracks in the
walls, sloping of floors and other defects. On 21st February 1972 the plaintiffs, who
were the lessees of the maisonettes, issued writs against the builder and the council
claiming damages. Two of the plaintiffs were the original lessees of their maisonettes
and the other plaintiffs had acquired their leases by assignment in 1967 and 1968.
The plaintiffs claimed that the damage to the maisonettes was attributable to the
fact that the block had been built on inadequate foundations, there being a depth
of two feet six inches only instead of three feet or deeper as shown on the deposited
plans. As against the council the plaintiffs claimed damages for negligence by their
servants or agents in approving the foundations on which the block had been erected
and/or in failing to inspect the foundations. A preliminary issue was tried on the
question whether the plaintiffs' claims were barred under s 2(1)(a)ᵃ of the Limitation Act 1939. The official referee held that the plaintiffs' cause of action had
accrued on the date of the first conveyance of each of the maisonettes, i e more than
six years before the issue of the writs, and that accordingly the claims were barred
under s 2(1)(a). The Court of Appeal, however, allowed appeals by the plaintiffs,
holding that a cause of action did not accrue before a person capable of suing discovered, or ought to have discovered, the damage. The council appealed to the
House of Lords and obtained leave to argue the question whether it was under a duty
of care to the plaintiffs at all.

Held – The appeal would be dismissed for the following reasons—

(i) The question whether the council were under a duty of care towards the plaintiffs
had to be considered in relation to the duties, powers and discretions arising under the
Public Health Act 1936. The fact that an act had been performed in the exercise of a
statutory power did not exclude the possibility that the act might be a breach of the
common law duty of care. It was irrelevant to the existence of a duty of care whether
what was created by the statute was a duty or a power: the duty of care might exist in
either case. The difference was that, in the case of a power, liability could not exist
unless the act complained of was outside the ambit of the power (see p 503 e to p 504 a,
p 506 b and c, p 509 j to p 510 a and g, p 511 d to f and p 515 b, post); *Geddis v Bann
Reservoir Proprietors* (1878) 3 App Cas 430 and *Home Office v Dorset Yacht Co Ltd* [1970]
2 All ER 294 applied; *East Suffolk Rivers Catchment Board v Kent* [1940] 4 All ER 527
distinguished.

(ii) (per Lord Wilberforce, Lord Diplock, Lord Simon of Glaisdale and Lord Russell
of Killowen) Although the 1936 Act and the byelaws did not impose a duty on the
council to inspect the foundations, it did not follow that a failure to inspect could
not constitute a breach of the duty of care; it was the duty of the council to give proper
consideration of the question whether they should inspect or not (see p 501 e, p 506
b and c, and p 515 b, post).

---

a   Section 2(1), so far as material, provides: 'The following actions shall not be brought after
    the expiration of six years from the date on which the cause of action accrued, that is to say:
    —(a) actions founded on simple contract or on tort . . .'

(iii) It followed that the council were under a duty to take reasonable care to secure that a builder did not cover in foundations which did not comply with byelaws. That *a* duty was owed to owners and occupiers of the building, other than the builder, who might suffer damage as a result of the construction of inadequate foundations. A right of action would, however, only accrue to a person who was an owner or occupier of the building when the damage occurred. Accordingly the council would be liable to the plaintiffs if it were proved that, in failing to carry out an inspection, they had not properly exercised their discretion and had failed to exercise reasonable care in their *b* acts or omissions to secure that the byelaws applicable to foundations were complied with, or that the inspector having assumed the duty of inspecting the foundations, and acting otherwise than in the bona fide exercise of any discretion under the 1936 Act, had failed to take reasonable care to ensure that the byelaws were complied with, and that, in either case, the damage suffered by the plaintiffs was a consequence of that breach of duty (see p 500 *e*, p 504 *a* to *d*, p 505 *h* to p 506 *c*, p 508 *f*, p 511 *b* to *d* and p *c* 515 *b*, post); *Dutton v Bognor Regis United Building Co Ltd* [1972] 1 All ER 462 explained and applied.

(iv) On the assumption that there had been a breach of duty as alleged, the cause of action accrued on the date when the damage was sustained as a result of the negligent act, i.e, on the date when the state of the building became such that there was a present or imminent danger to the health and safety of persons occupying it. If it was the case *d* that the defects to the maisonettes had first appeared in 1970 then, since the writs had been issued in 1972, none of the actions was statute-barred (see p 506 *a* to *c*, p 513 *g* and *h* and p 515 *b*, post); *Sparham-Souter v Town and Country Developments (Essex) Ltd* [1976] 2 All ER 65 approved; *Higgins v Arfon Borough Council* [1975] 2 All ER 589 overruled.

Per Curiam. (i) A builder who is also the owner of a house is not immune from *e* liability in negligence for defects in the building to a person who subsequently acquires it. Alternatively, since it is the duty of the builder, whether owner or not, to comply with the byelaws, an action may be brought against him for breach of statutory duty by any person for whose benefit or protection the byelaw was made (see p 504 *g* to p 505 *a*, p 506 *b* and c and p 512 *e* and *f*, post); *Gallagher v N McDowell Ltd* [1961] NI 26 and dictum of Lord Denning MR in *Dutton v Bognor Regis United Building Co Ltd* *f* [1972] 1 All ER at 471,472 applied; *Bottomley v Bannister* [1931] All ER Rep 99 disapproved.

(ii) The damages recoverable include all those which foreseeably arise from the breach of the duty of care. Subject always to adequate proof of causation, those damages may include damages for personal injury and damage to property. They may also include damage to the dwelling-house itself, for the whole purpose of the byelaws in requiring foundations to be of certain standard is to prevent damage arising *g* from weakness of the foundations which is certain to endanger the health or safety of occupants. The relevant damage to the house is physical damage, and what is recoverable is the amount of expenditure necessary to restore the dwelling to a condition in which it is no longer a danger to the health or safety of persons occupying it and possibly (depending on the circumstances) expenses arising from necessary displacement (see p 505 *a* to *e* and p 514 *f* and *g*, post). *h*

Notes

For the duty to take care, see 28 Halsbury's Laws (3rd Edn) 7-9, paras 4-7, and for cases on the subject, see 36(1) Digest (Reissue) 17-55, *34-177*.

For when a limitation period begins to run, see 24 Halsbury's Laws (3rd Edn) 193-196, paras 347-349, and for cases on the subject, see 32 Digest (Repl) 384-386, *j* 400-404, *147-156, 255-277*.

For the Limitation Act 1939, s 2, see 19 Halsbury's Statutes (3rd Edn) 61.

Cases referred to in opinions

Ayr Harbour Trustees v Oswald (1883) 8 App Cas 623, HL, 11 Digest (Reissue) 103, *5*.

Bagot v Stevens Scanlan & Co [1964] 3 All ER 577, [1966] 1 QB 197, [1964] 3 WLR 1162,
a   [1964] 2 Lloyd's Rep 353, Digest (Cont Vol B) 68, 486Aa.

Bottomley v Bannister [1932] 1 KB 458, [1931] All ER Rep 99, 101 LJKB 46, 146 LT 68, CA,
36(1) Digest (Reissue) 136, 526.

Bowen v Paramount Builders (Hamilton) Ltd and McKay (22nd December 1976) unreported,
CA (NZ).

Cartledge v E Jopling & Sons Ltd [1963] 1 All ER 341, [1963] AC 758, [1963] 2 WLR 210,
b   [1963] 1 Lloyd's Rep 1, HL, 32 Digest (Repl) 401, 259.

Cavalier v Pope [1906] AC 428, 75 LJKB 609, 95 LT 65, HL, 31(2) Digest (Reissue) 651,
5273.

Clay v A J Crump & Sons Ltd [1963] 3 All ER 687, [1964] 1 QB 533, [1963] 3 WLR 866,
CA, Digest (Cont Vol A) 75, 486b.

Clayton v Woodman & Son (Builders) Ltd [1962] 2 All ER 33, [1962] 1 WLR 585, CA,
c   Digest (Cont Vol A) 75, 486a.

Davie v New Merton Board Mills Ltd [1959] 1 All ER 346, [1959] AC 604, [1959] 2 WLR
331, HL, 36(1) Digest (Reissue) 146, 565.

Donoghue v Stevenson [1932] AC 562, [1932] All ER Rep 1, 101 LJPC 119, 147 LT 281, 37
Com Cas 350, HL, 36(1) Digest (Reissue) 144, 562.

Dutton v Bognor Regis United Building Co Ltd [1972] 1 All ER 462, [1972] 1 QB 373, [1972]
d   2 WLR 299, 36 JP 201, [1972] 1 Lloyd's Rep 227, 70 LGR 57, CA, 36(1) Digest (Reissue)
30, 98.

East Suffolk Rivers Catchment Board v Kent [1940] 4 All ER 527, [1941] AC 74, 110 LJKB
252, 165 LT 65, 105 JP 129, 39 LGR 79, HL; *rvsg sub nom Kent and Porter v East
Suffolk Rivers Catchment Board* [1939] 4 All ER 174, [1940] 1 KB 319, CA; *affg* [1939] 2
All ER 207, 41 Digest (Repl) 57, 370.

e   *Gallagher v N McDowell Ltd* [1961] NI 26.

Geddis v Bann Reservoir Proprietors (1878) 3 App Cas 430, HL, 38 Digest (Repl) 16, 64.

Great Central Railway Co v Hewlett [1916] 2 AC 511, 85 LJKB 1705, 115 LT 349, 14 LGR
1015, HL, 38 Digest (Repl) 6, 14.

Hedley Byrne & Co Ltd v Heller & Partners Ltd [1963] 2 All ER 575, [1964] AC 465, [1963]
3 WLR 101, [1963] 1 Lloyd's Rep 485, HL, 36(1) Digest (Reissue) 24, 84.

f   *Higgins v Arfon Borough Council* [1975] 2 All ER 589, [1975] 1 WLR 524, [1975] 2 Lloyd's
Rep 330, Digest (Cont Vol D) 613, 275a.

Home Office v Dorset Yacht Co Ltd [1970] 2 All ER 294, [1970] AC 1004, [1970] 2 WLR 1140,
[1970] 1 Lloyd's Rep 453, HL, 36(1) Digest (Reissue) 27, 93.

Indian Towing Co v United States (1955) 350 US 61.

Rivtow Marine Ltd v Washington Iron Works [1973] 6 WWR 692.

g   *Robbins v Jones* (1863) 15 CBNS 221, 3 New Rep 85, [1861-73] All ER Rep 544, 33 LJCP 1,
9 LT 523, 10 Jur NS 239, 143 ER 768, 36(1) Digest (Reissue) 353, 1417.

SCM (United Kingdom) Ltd v W J Whittall & Son Ltd [1970] 3 All ER 245, [1971] 1 QB
337, [1970] 3 WLR 694, CA, 36(1) Digest (Reissue) 28, 94.

Sheppard v Glossop Corpn [1921] 3 KB 132, [1921] All ER Rep 61, 90 LJKB 994, 125 LT
520, 85 JP 205, 19 LGR 357, CA, 38 Digest (Repl) 26, 133.

h   *Sparham-Souter v Town and Country Developments (Essex) Ltd* [1976] 2 All ER 65, [1976]
1 QB 858, [1976] 2 WLR 493, CA.

Spartan Steel and Alloys Ltd v Martin & Co (Contractors) Ltd [1972] 3 All ER 557, [1973]
QB 27, [1972] 3 WLR 502, CA, 17 Digest (Reissue) 149, 403.

Voli v Inglewood Shire Council (1963) 110 CLR 74.

Weller & Co v Foot and Mouth Disease Research Institute [1965] 3 All ER 560, [1966] 1 QB
j   569, [1965] 3 WLR 1082, [1965] 2 Lloyd's Rep 414, 36(1) Digest (Reissue) 45, 143.

Appeal

On 21st February 1972 the plaintiffs, Michael Ralph Anns, Kenneth Rodney Blackwell,
Alfred Colston, Brian Thomas Davenport, Dermott O'Shea, Florence Mary O'Shea,
Anthony Charles Phillips and William Patrick Walker, issued writs against the first

defendants, Walcroft Property Co Ltd, and against the second defendants, the London
Borough of Merton, formerly Mitcham Borough Council ('the council'), claiming *a*
damages in respect of the building of a block of maisonettes known as Beaconsfield
Court, 91 Devonshire Road, London, SW 19, of which the plaintiffs were lessees. The
actions were consolidated. As against the first defendants, the builders and freehold
owners of the block, the plaintiffs claimed damages for breach of contract and also for
breach of the implied undertaking under s 6 of the Housing Act 1957. As against the
council the claims were for damages for negligence by their servants or agents in *b*
approving the foundations on which the block had been erected even though they had
not been taken down to a sufficient depth, and/or in failing to inspect the foundations.
The first defendants did not put in any defence but undertook to carry out certain
work. By their defence the council denied the alleged negligence and also pleaded
that the actions were statute-barred under the Limitation Act 1939. His Honour
Judge Fay QC, sitting as official referee, ordered that the issue whether the claims in *c*
the consolidated actions against the council were statute-barred be tried as a preliminary issue. On 24th October 1975 the judge held that the claims were statute-barred.
The plaintiff appealed to the Court of Appeal which allowed the appeals but gave
the council leave to appeal to the House of Lords. On 21st October 1976 the House
granted the council leave to contend at the hearing of the appeals that in the circumstances no legal duty of care was owed by the council to the plaintiffs. The facts are *d*
are set out in the opinion of Lord Wilberforce.

Keith Goodfellow QC and *John Tackaberry* for the council.
John K Wood QC, Michael Johnson and *P Vallance* for the plaintiffs.

Their Lordships took time for consideration.   *e*

12th May. The following opinions were delivered.

LORD WILBERFORCE. My Lords, this appeal requires a decision on two important points of principle as to the liability of local authorities for defects in dwellings *f*
constructed by builders in their area namely: (1) whether a local authority is under
any duty of care towards owners or occupiers of any such houses as regards inspection
during the building process; (2) what period of limitation applies to claims by such
owners or occupiers against the local authorities. Before these questions are discussed
it is necessary to explain at some tedious length the procedural background which
unfortunately complicates the decision-making task.   *g*

Procedural issues
    The present actions were begun on 21st February 1972. The plaintiffs are lessees
under long leases of seven flats or maisonettes in a two storey block at 91, Devonshire
Road, Wimbledon. The owners of the block and also the builders were the first
defendants, Walcroft Property Co Ltd. After its completion in 1962 they granted *h*
long leases of the maisonettes. The fifth and sixth plaintiffs (O'Shea) are original
lessees, having acquired their lease in 1962; the other plaintiffs acquired their leases by
assignment at dates in 1967 and 1968.
    The local authority at the time of construction was the Mitcham Borough Council.
On 9th February 1962 they passed building plans for the block, which were deposited
under the byelaws. Later this council was superseded by the London Borough of *j*
Merton, the second defendants ('the council'), which took over their duties and
liabilities.
    In February 1970 structural movements began to occur resulting in cracks in the
walls, sloping of floors, etc. The plaintiffs' case is that these were due to the block
being built on inadequate foundations, there being a depth of two feet six inches only

instead of three feet or deeper as shown on the deposited plans. On 21st February

a 1972 writs were issued against both defendants the separate proceedings were later consolidated. As against the first defendants (the builders) the claims were for damages for breach of contract and also for breach of the implied undertaking under s 6 of the Housing Act 1957. As against the council the claims were for damages for negligence by their servants or agents in approving the foundations on which the block was erected even though (sic) they had not been taken down to a sufficient depth

b and/or in failing to inspect the said foundations. This claim was expressed as follows:

'5. Further or in the alternative the said damage has been caused by the negligence of the [council] in allowing the first defendants to construct the said dwelling-house on foundations which were only 2 feet 6 inches deep instead of 3 feet or deeper as required by the said plans, alternatively of failing to carry out

c the necessary inspections sufficiently carefully or at all, as a result of which the said structural movement occurred.'

As particulars given under this paragraph the plaintiffs stated:

'Under the building byelaws the [council] were under a duty to ensure that the building was constructed in accordance with the plans, and the building should

d have been inspected inter alia before the foundations were covered. The plaintiff's case is that the [council] should have carried out such inspections as would have revealed the defective condition of the said foundations, that if any inspection was made then it was carried out negligently, and that if no inspection was made that in itself was negligent.'

e Both the allegations in the statement of claim and those in the particulars were to some extent misconceived as I shall show later.

The first defendants did not put in any defence but undertook to carry out certain work. They did not appear in the hearings to be mentioned or on this appeal.

The council filed a defence on 8th February 1973 and on 9th October 1974 the

f consolidated actions were transferred to an official referee. On 16th October 1975 an order was made, 'That the issue between the Plaintiffs and the [council] whether claim is statute barred be tried on 24th October 1975.' On 24th October 1975 this issue was tried by his Honour Judge Edgar Fay QC who decided that the claims were statute-barred. In a written judgment the judge held that time began to run from the date of the first conveyance of each of the properties concerned: the latest of these dates was 5th November 1965, which was more than six years before the date of the

g writ. In so deciding the judge (correctly) followed an observation (obiter) by Lord Denning MR in *Dutton v Bognor Regis United Building Co Ltd*[1].

The plaintiffs appealed to the Court of Appeal from this decision on 17th February 1976. Before the appeal came on, namely on 10th February 1976 the Court of Appeal (Lord Denning MR, Roskill and Geoffrey Lane LJJ) in *Sparham-Souter v Town and Country Developments (Essex) Ltd*[2] decided that the cause of action did not accrue before

h a person capable of suing discovered, or ought to have discovered, the damage. Lord Denning MR in his judgment expressly disavowed his earlier dictum in *Dutton's case*[1]. On this view of the matter none of the present plaintiffs' claims would be statute-barred. On the appeals in the present case coming before the Court of Appeal on 1st March 1976[3], that court, without further argument, following *Sparham-Souter's case*[2], allowed the plaintiffs' appeal and gave leave to appeal to this House. That

j appeal would, of course, have been confined to a preliminary issue of limitation.

---

1 [1972] 1 All ER 462 at 474, [1972] 1 QB 373 at 376
2 [1976] 2 All ER 65, [1976] 1 QB 858
3 [1976] 1 QB 882

However before the appeal to this House came on, the council presented a petition, asking for leave to argue the question whether the council was under any duty of *a* care to the plaintiffs at all.

This question had not been considered by Judge Fay, or by the Court of Appeal, because it was thought, rightly in my opinion, that it was concluded by *Dutton's* case[1]. Thus the council wished to challenge the correctness of the latter decision. In that case the defendant council of Bognor Regis was held liable for damages in negligence (viz negligent inspection by one of its officers), consisting of a breach of a duty at *b* common law to take reasonable care to see that the byelaws were complied with. On 21st October 1976 this House acceded to the petition. The council thus have leave to argue that in the circumstances they owed no duty of care to the plaintiffs.

This being a preliminary point of law, as was the argument on limitation, it has to be decided on the assumption that the facts are as pleaded. There is some difference between those facts and those on which *Dutton's* case[1] was based, and in the present *c* case the plaintiffs rely not only on negligent inspection but, in the alternative, on a failure to make any inspections.

In these circumstances I take the questions in this appeal to be: (1) whether the council were under: (a) a duty of care to the plaintiffs to carry out an inspection of the foundations (which did not arise in *Dutton's* case[1]); (b) a duty, if any inspection was made, to take reasonable care to see that the byelaws were complied with (as held in *Dutton's* *d* case[1]); (c) any other duty including a duty to ensure that the building was constructed in accordance with the plans, or not to allow the builder to construct the dwelling-house on foundations which were only two feet six inches deep instead of three feet or deeper (as pleaded); (2) if the council was under any such duty as alleged, and committed a breach of it, resulting in damage, at what date the cause of action of the plaintiffs arose for the purposes of the Limitation Act 1939. No question arises directly at this *e* stage as to the damages which the plaintiffs can recover and no doubt there will be issues at the trial as to causation and quantum which we cannot anticipate. But it will be necessary to give some general consideration to the kind of damages to which, if they succeed, the plaintiffs may become entitled. This matter was discussed in *Dutton's* case[1] and is closely connected with that of the duty which may be owed and with the arising of the cause of action. *f*

The duty of care

Through the trilogy of cases in this House, *Donoghue v Stevenson*[2], *Hedley Byrne & Co Ltd v Heller & Partners Ltd*[3] and *Home Office v Dorset Yacht Co Ltd*[4], the position has now been reached that in order to establish that a duty of care arises in a particular situation, it is not necessary to bring the facts of that situation within those of previous *g* situations in which a duty of care has been held to exist. Rather the question has to be approached in two stages. First one has to ask whether, as between the alleged wrongdoer and the person who has suffered damage there is a sufficient relationship of proximity or neighbourhood such that, in the reasonable contemplation of the former, carelessness on his part may be likely to cause damage to the latter, in which case a prima facie duty of care arises. Secondly, if the first question is answered *h* affirmatively, it is necessary to consider whether there are any considerations which ought to negative, or to reduce or limit the scope of the duty or the class of person to whom it is owed or the damages to which a breach of it may give rise (see the *Dorset Yacht* case[5], per Lord Reid). Examples of this are *Hedley Byrne & Co Ltd v Heller & Partners Ltd*[3] where the class of potential plaintiffs was reduced to those *j*

1 [1972] 1 All ER 462, [1972] 1 QB 373
2 [1932] AC 562, [1932] All ER Rep 1
3 [1963] 2 All ER 575, [1964] AC 465
4 [1970] 2 All ER 294, [1970] AC 1004
5 [1970] 2 All ER 294 at 297, 298, [1970] AC 1004 at 1027

shown to have relied on the correctness of statements made, and *Weller & Co v Foot*
a   *and Mouth Disease Research Institute*[1] and (I cite these merely as illustrations, without
discussion) cases about 'economic loss' where, a duty having been held to exist, the
nature of the recoverable damages was limited (*see SCM (United Kingdom) Ltd v
W J Whittall & Son Ltd*[2], *Spartan Steel and Alloys Ltd v Martin & Co (Contractors) Ltd*)[3].

   The factual relationship between the council and owners and occupiers of new
dwellings constructed in their area must be considered in the relevant statutory
b   setting, under which the council acts. That was the Public Health Act 1936. I must
refer to the relevant provisions.

   Section 1 confers the duty of carrying the Act into execution on specified authorities
which now include the appellant council. Part II of the Act is headed 'Sanitation and
Buildings' and contains provisions in the interest of the safety and health of occupiers
of dwelling-houses and other buildings such as provisions about sewage, drains and
c   sanitary conveniences. From s 53 onwards, this part of the Act is concerned with such
matters as the construction of buildings (s 53), the use of certain materials, construction
on ground filled up with offensive material (s 54), repair or removal of dilapidated
buildings (s 58) and fire escapes. The emphasis is throughout on health and safety.
The directly relevant provisions start with s 61. That section provided (sub-s (1)) that
every local authority may, and if required by the Minister, shall make byelaws[4] for
d   regulating (inter alia) the construction of buildings, and (sub-s (2)) that byelaws made
under the section may include provisions as to the giving of notices, the deposit of
plans and the inspection of work. Section 64 deals in a mandatory form with the
passing or rejection of deposited plans. The authority must pass plans unless they are
defective or show that the proposed work would contravene any byelaws and in the
contrary case must reject them. By s 65, if any work to which building byelaws are
e   applicable contravenes any byelaw, the authority may require the owner to pull
down the work, or, if he so elects, to effect such alteration as may be necessary to
make it comply with the byelaws. However, if any work though infringing the
byelaws, is in accordance with approved plans, removal or alteration may only be
ordered by a court which then has power to order the authority to compensate the
owner.

f   Building byelaws were duly made, under these powers, by the borough of Mitcham
in 1953 and confirmed by the Minister in 1957. Byelaw 2 imposes an obligation on a
person who erects any building to comply with the requirements of the byelaws. It
imposes an obligation to submit plans. Byelaw 6 requires the builder to give to the
council not less than 24 hours notice in writing: (a) of the date and time at which an
operation will be commenced, and (b) before the covering up of any drain, private
g   sewer, concrete or other material laid over a site, foundation or damp-proof course.
Byelaws 18 and 19 contain requirements as to foundations. The relevant provision
(18(1)(b)) is that the foundations of every building shall be taken down to such a
depth, or be so designed and constructed as to safeguard the building against damage
by swelling or shrinking of the subsoil.

   Acting under these byelaws, the first defendants on 30th January 1962 gave notice
h   to the Mitcham borough council of their intention to erect a new building (viz the
block of maisonettes) in accordance with accompanying plans. The plans showed the
base walls and concrete strip foundations of the block and stated, in relation to the
depth from ground level to the underside of the concrete foundations, '3 feet or deeper
to the approval of local authority'. These plans were approved on 8th February 1962.
The written notice of approval dated 9th February 1962 drew attention to the

j   1   [1965] 3 All ER 560, [1966] 1 QB 569
     2   [1970] 3 All ER 245, [1971] 1 QB 337
     3   [1972] 3 All ER 557, [1973] QB 27
     4   Since 1965 building work has been subject to building regulations made by the Minister
         under s 4 of the Public Health Act 1961 and local authorities no longer have the power to
         make building byelaws.

requirement of the byelaws that notice should be given to the surveyor at each of the following stages: before the commencement of the work and when the foundations were ready to be covered up.

The builders in fact constructed the foundations to a depth of only two feet six inches below ground level. It is not, at this stage, established when or whether any inspection was made.

To summarise the statutory position. The Public Health Act 1936, in particular Part II, was enacted in order to provide for the health and safety of owners and occupiers of buildings, including dwelling houses, by, inter alia, setting standards to be complied with in construction, and by enabling local authorities, through building byelaws, to supervise and control the operations of builders. One of the particular matters within the area of local authority supervision is the foundations of buildings, clearly a matter of vital importance, particularly because this part of the building comes to be covered up as building proceeds. Thus any weakness or inadequacy will create a hidden defect which whoever acquires the building has no means of discovering: in legal parlance there is no opportunity for intermediate inspection. So, by the byelaws, a definite standard is set for foundation work (see byelaw 18(1)(b) referred to above); the builder is under a statutory (sc byelaw) duty to notify the local authority before covering up the foundations; the local authority has at this stage the right to inspect and to insist on any correction necessary to bring the work into conformity with the byelaws. It must be in the reasonable contemplation not only of the builder but also of the local authority that failure to comply with the byelaws' requirement as to foundations may give rise to a hidden defect which in the future may cause damage to the building affecting the safety and health of owners and occupiers. And as the building is intended to last, the class of owners and occupiers likely to be affected cannot be limited to those who go in immediately after construction.

What then is the extent of the local authority's duty towards these persons? Although, as I have suggested, a situation of 'proximity' existed between the council and owners and occupiers of the houses, I do not think that a description of the council's duty can be based on the 'neighbourhood' principle alone or on merely any such factual relationship as 'control' as suggested by the Court of Appeal. So to base it would be to neglect an essential factor which is that the local authority is a public body, discharging functions under statute: its powers and duties are definable in terms of public not private law. The problem which this type of action creates, is to define the circumstances in which the law should impose, over and above, or perhaps alongside, these public law powers and duties, a duty in private law towards individuals such that they may sue for damages in a civil court. It is in this context that the distinction sought to be drawn between duties and mere powers has to be examined.

Most, indeed probably all, statutes relating to public authorities or public bodies, contain in them a large area of policy. The courts call this 'discretion', meaning that the decision is one for the authority or body to make, and not for the courts. Many statutes, also, prescribe or at least presuppose the practical execution of policy decisions: a convenient description of this is to say that in addition to the area of policy or discretion, there is an operational area. Although this distinction between the policy area and the operational area is convenient, and illuminating, it is probably a distinction of degree; many 'operational' powers or duties have in them some element of 'discretion'. It can safely be said that the more 'operational' a power or duty may be, the easier it is to superimpose on it a common law duty of care.

I do not think that it is right to limit this to a duty to avoid causing extra or additional damage beyond what must be expected to arise from the exercise of the power or duty. That may be correct when the act done under the statute inherently must adversely affect the interest of individuals. But many other acts can be done without causing any harm to anyone—indeed may be directed to preventing harm from occurring. In these cases the duty is the normal one of taking care to avoid harm to those likely to be affected.

a Let us examine the Public Health Act 1936 in the light of this. Undoubtedly it lays out a wide area of policy. It is for the local authority, a public and elected body, to decide on the scale of resources which it can make available in order to carry out its functions under Part II of the Act—how many inspectors, with what expert qualifications, it should recruit, how often inspections are to be made, what tests are to be carried out, must be for its decision. It is no accident that the Act is drafted in terms of functions and powers rather than in terms of positive duty. As was well said, public

b authorities have to strike a balance between the claims of efficiency and thrift (du Parcq LJ in *Kent and Porter v East Suffolk Rivers Catchment Board*[1]): whether they get the balance right can only be decided through the ballot box, not in the courts. It is said, there are reflections of this in the judgments in *Dutton's* case[2], that the local authority is under no duty to inspect, and this is used as the foundation for an argument, also found in some of the cases, that if it need not inspect at all, it cannot be

c liable for negligent inspection: if it were to be held so liable, so it is said, councils would simply decide against inspections. I think that this is too crude an argument. It overlooks the fact that local authorities are public bodies operating under statute with a clear responsibility for public health in their area. They must, and in fact do, make their discretionary decisions responsibly and for reasons which accord with the statutory purpose; cf *Ayr Harbour Trustees v Oswald*[3], per Lord Watson:

d
> '... the powers which [s 10] confers are discretionary ... But it is the plain import of the clause that the harbour trustees ... shall be vested with, and shall avail themselves of, these discretionary powers, whenever and as often as they may be of opinion that the public interest will be promoted by their exercise.'

e If they do not exercise their discretion in this way they can be challenged in the courts. Thus, to say that councils are under no duty to inspect, is not a sufficient statement of the position. They are under a duty to give proper consideration to the question whether they should inspect or not. Their immunity from attack, in the event of failure to inspect, in other words, though great is not absolute. And because it is not absolute, the necessary premise for the proposition 'if no duty to inspect, then no duty to take care in inspection' vanishes.

f Passing then to the duty as regards inspection, if made. On principle there must surely be a duty to exercise reasonable care. The standard of care must be related to the duty to be performed, namely to ensure compliance with the byelaws. It must be related to the fact that the person responsible for construction in accordance with the byelaws is the builder, and that the inspector's function is supervisory. It must be related to the fact that once the inspector has passed the foundations they will be

g covered up, with no subsequent opportunity for inspection. But this duty, heavily operational though it may be, is still a duty arising under the statute. There may be a discretionary element in its exercise, discretionary as to the time and manner of inspection, and the techniques to be used. A plaintiff complaining of negligence must prove, the burden being on him, that action taken was not within the limits of a discretion bona fide exercised, before he can begin to rely on a common law duty of

h care. But if he can do this, he should, in principle, be able to sue.

Is there, then, authority against the existence of any such duty or any reason to restrict it? It is said that there is an absolute distinction in the law between statutory duty and statutory power—the former giving rise to possible liability, the latter not; or at least not doing so unless the exercise of the power involves some positive act creating some fresh or additional damage.

j My Lords, I do not believe that any such absolute rule exists: or perhaps, more accurately, that such rules as exist in relation to powers and duties existing under

---

1 [1939] 4 All ER 174 at 184, [1940] 1 KB 319 at 338
2 [1972] 1 All ER 462, [1972] 1 QB 373
3 (1883) 8 App Cas 623 at 639

particular statutes, provide sufficient definition of the rights of individuals affected by
their exercise, or indeed their non-exercise, unless they take account of the possibility
that, parallel with public law duties there may coexist those duties which persons,
private or public, are under at common law to avoid causing damage to others in
sufficient proximity to them. This is, I think, the key to understanding of the main
authority relied on by the council, *East Suffolk Rivers Catchment Board v Kent*[1].

The statutory provisions in that case were contained in the Land Drainage Act 1930
and were in the form of a power to repair drainage works including walls or banks.
The facts are well known. There was a very high tide which burst the banks protecting
the respondent's land. The catchment board, requested to take action, did so with
an allocation of manpower and resources (graphically described by MacKinnon LJ)
which was hopelessly inadequate and which resulted in the respondent's land being
flooded for much longer than it need have been. There was a considerable difference
of judicial opinion. Hilbery J[2] who tried the case held the board liable for the damage
caused by the extended flooding and his decision was upheld by a majority of the
Court of Appeal[3]. This House, by majority of four to one reached the opposite
conclusion. The speeches of their Lordships contain discussion of earlier authorities,
which well illustrate the different types of statutory enactment under which these
cases may arise. There are private Acts conferring powers, necessarily, to interfere
with the rights of individuals: in such cases, an action in respect of damage caused by
the exercise of the powers generally does not lie, but it may do so 'for doing that
which the legislature has authorised, if it be done negligently' (*Geddis v Bann Reservoir
Proprietors*[4], per Lord Blackburn). Then there are cases where a statutory power is
conferred, but the scale on which it is exercised is left to a local authority, *Sheppard v
Glossop Corpn*[5]. That concerned a power to light streets and the corporation decided,
for economy reasons, to extinguish the lighting on Christmas night. Clearly this was
within the discretion of the authority but Scrutton LJ[6] in the Court of Appeal contrasted this situation with one where 'an option is given by statute to an authority to
do or not to do a thing and it elects to do the thing and does it negligently'. (Compare
Indian Towing Co v United States[7], which makes just this distinction between a discretion
to provide a lighthouse, and at operational level, a duty, if one is provided, to use due
care to keep the light in working order.) Other illustrations are given.

My Lords, a number of reasons were suggested for distinguishing the *East Suffolk*
case[1], apart from the relevant fact that it was concerned with a different Act, indeed
type of Act. It was said to be a division on causation: I think that this is true of at least
two of their Lordships (Viscount Simon LC and Lord Thankerton). It was said that the
damage was already there before the board came on the scene. So it was, but the
board's action or inaction undoubtedly prolonged it, and the action was in respect of
the prolongation. I should not think it right to put the case aside on such arguments.
To me the two significant points about the case are, first, that it is an example, and a
good one, where operational activity, at the breach in the wall, was still well within a
discretionary area, so that the plaintiff's task in contending for a duty of care was a
difficult one. This is clearly the basis on which Lord Romer, whose speech is often
quoted as a proposition of law, proceeded. Secondly, although the case was decided
in 1940, only one of their Lordships considered it in relation to a duty of care at
common law. It need cause no surprise that this was Lord Atkin. His speech starts
with this passage[8]:

1 [1940] 4 All ER 527, [1941] AC 74
2 [1939] 2 All ER 207
3 [1939] 4 All ER 174, [1940] 1 KB 319
4 (1878) 3 App Cas 430 at 455, 456
5 [1921] 3 KB 132, [1921] All ER Rep 61
6 [1921] 3 KB 132 at 145, 146, [1921] All ER Rep 61 at 68
7 (1955) 350 US 61
8 [1940] 4 All ER 527 at 533, [1941] AC 74 at 88

a   'On the first point [sc whether there was a duty owed to the plaintiffs and what was its nature], I cannot help thinking that the argument did not sufficiently distinguish between two kinds of duties—(i) a statutory duty to do or abstain from doing something, and (ii) a common law duty to conduct yourself with reasonable care so as not to injure persons liable to be affected by your conduct.'

b   And later he refers to *Donoghue v Stevenson*[1], the only one of their Lordships to do so, though I think it fair to say that Lord Thankerton (who decided the case on causation) in his formulation of the duty must have been thinking in terms of that case. My Lords, I believe that the conception of a general duty of care, not limited to particular accepted situations, but extending generally over all relations of sufficient proximity, and even pervading the sphere of statutory functions of public bodies, had not at that time become fully recognised. Indeed it may well be that full recognition of the

c   impact of *Donoghue v Stevenson*[1] in the latter sphere only came with the decision of this House in *Home Office v Dorset Yacht Co Ltd*[2].

In that case the borstal officers, for whose actions the Home Office was vicariously responsible, were acting, in their control of the boys, under statutory powers. But it was held that, nevertheless they were under a duty of care as regards persons who might suffer damage as the result of their carelessness: see per Lord Reid[3], Lord

d   Morris of Borth-y-Gest[4], Lord Pearson[5] ('The existence of the statutory duties does not exclude liability at common law for negligence in the performance of the statutory duties'.) Lord Diplock[6] in his speech gives this topic extended consideration with a view to relating the officers' responsibility under public law to their liability in damages to members of the public under private, civil law. My noble and learned friend points out that the accepted principles which are applicable to powers con-

e   ferred by a private Act of Parliament, as laid down in *Geddis v Bann Reservoir Proprietors*[7], cannot automatically be applied to public statutes which confer a large measure of discretion on public authorities. As regards the latter, for a civil action based on negligence at common law to succeed, there must be acts or omissions taken outside the limits of the delegated discretion; in such a case 'its actionability falls to be determined by the civil law principles of negligence[8]'.

f   It is for this reason that the law, as stated in some of the speeches in the *East Suffolk* case[9], but not in those of Lord Atkin or Lord Thankerton, requires at the present time to be understood and applied with the recognition that, quite apart from such consequences as may flow from an examination of the duties laid down by the particular statute, there may be room, once one is outside the area of legitimate discretion or policy, for a duty of care at common law. It is irrelevant to the existence

g   of this duty of care whether what is created by the statute is a duty or a power: the duty of care may exist in either case. The difference between the two lies in this, that, in the case of a power, liability cannot exist unless the act complained of lies outside the ambit of the power. In *Home Office v Dorset Yacht Co Ltd*[2] the officers may (on the assumed facts) have acted outside any discretion delegated to them and having disregarded their instructions as to the precautions which they should take to prevent

h   the trainees from escaping (see per Lord Diplock[10]). So in the present case, the allegations made are consistent with the council or its inspector having acted outside

j

1 [1932] AC 562, [1932] All ER Rep 1
2 [1970] 2 All ER 294, [1970] AC 1004
3 [1970] 2 All ER 294 at 300, [1970] AC 1004 at 1030
4 [1970] 2 All ER 294 at 305, [1970] AC 1004 at 1036
5 [1970] 2 All ER 294 at 322, [1970] AC 1004 at 1055
6 [1970] 2 All ER 294 at 329 et seq, [1970] AC 1004 at 1064 et seq
7 (1878) 3 App Cas 430
8 [1970] 2 All ER 294 at 332, [1970] AC 1004 at 1068
9 [1940] 4 All ER 527, [1941] AC 74
10 [1970] 2 All ER 294 at 333, [1970] AC 1004 at 1069

any delegated discretion either as to the making of an inspection, or as to the manner in which an inspection was made. Whether they did so must be determined at the trial. In the event of a positive determination, and only so, can a duty of care arise. I respectfully think that Lord Denning MR in *Dutton's* case[1] puts the duty too high. *a*

To whom the duty is owed. There is, in my opinion, no difficulty about this. A reasonable man in the position of the inspector must realise that if the foundations are covered in without adequate depth or strength as required by the byelaws, injury to safety or health may be suffered by owners or occupiers of the house. The duty is *b* owed to them, not of course to a negligent building owner, the source of his own loss. I would leave open the case of users, who might themselves have a remedy against the occupier under the Occupiers Liability Act 1957. A right of action can only be conferred on an owner or occupier, who is such when the damage occurs (see below). This disposes of the possible objection that an endless, indeterminate class of potential plaintiffs may be called into existence. *c*

The nature of the duty. This must be related closely to the purpose for which powers of inspection are granted, namely to secure compliance with the byelaws. The duty is to take reasonable care, no more, no less, to secure that the builder does not cover in foundations which do not comply with byelaw requirements. The allegations in the statements of claim, insofar as they are based on non-compliance with the plans, are misconceived. *d*

The position of the builder. I agree with the majority in the Court of Appeal in thinking that it would be unreasonable to impose liability in respect of defective foundations on the council, if the builder, whose primary fault it was, should be immune from liability. So it is necessary to consider this point, although it does not directly arise in the present appeal. If there was at one time a supposed rule that the doctrine of *Donoghue v Stevenson*[2] did not apply to realty, there is no doubt under *e* modern authority that a builder of defective premises may be liable in negligence to persons who thereby suffer injury: see *Gallagher v N McDowell Ltd*[3], per Lord Mac-Dermott CJ, a case of personal injury. Similar decisions have been given in regard to architects (*Clayton v Woodman & Son (Builders) Ltd*[4], *Clay v A J Crump & Sons Ltd*[5]. *Gallagher's* case[3] expressly leaves open the question whether the immunity against action of builder-owners, established by older authorities (e g *Bottomley v Bannister*[6]) *f* still survives.

That immunity, as I understand it, rests partly on a distinction being made between chattels and real property, partly on the principle of 'caveat emptor' or, in the case where the owner leases the property, on the proposition that (fraud apart) there is no law against letting a 'tumbledown house' (*Robbins v Jones*[7], per Erle CJ). But leaving aside such cases as arise between contracting parties, when the terms of the contract *g* have to be considered (see *Voli v Inglewood Shire Council*[8], per Windeyer J), I am unable to understand why this principle or proposition should prevent recovery in a suitable case by a person, who has subsequently acquired the house, on the principle of *Donoghue v Stevenson*[2]: the same rules should apply to all careless acts of a builder: whether he happens also to own the land or not. I agree generally with the conclusions of Lord Denning MR on this point (*Dutton's* case[9]). In the alternative, since it is the *h* duty of the builder (owner or not) to comply with the byelaws, I would be of opinion that an action could be brought against him, in effect, for breach of statutory duty by

---

1 [1972] 1 All ER 462 at 470, [1972] 1 QB 373 at 392
2 [1932] AC 562, [1932] All ER Rep 1
3 [1961] NI 26   *j*
4 [1962] 2 All ER 33, [1962] 1 WLR 585
5 [1963] 3 All ER 687, [1964] 1 QB 533
6 [1932] 1 KB 458, [1931] All ER Rep 99
7 (1863) 15 CBNS 221, [1861-73] All ER Rep 544
8 (1963) 110 CLR 74 at 85
9 [1972] 1 All ER 462 at 471, 472, [1972] 1 QB 373 at 392-394

any person for whose benefit or protection the byelaw was made. So I do not think *a* that there is any basis here for arguing from a supposed immunity of the builder to immunity of the council.

Nature of the damages recoverable and arising out of the cause of action. There are many questions here which do not directly arise at this stage and which may never arise if the actions are tried. But some conclusions are necessary if we are to deal with the issue as to limitation. The damages recoverable include all those which foreseeably *b* arise from the breach of the duty of care which, as regards the council, I have held to be a duty to take reasonable care to secure compliance with the byelaws. Subject always to adequate proof of causation, these damages may include damages for personal injury and damage to property. In my opinion they may also include damage to the dwelling-house itself; for the whole purpose of the byelaws in requiring foundations to be of certain standard is to prevent damage arising from weakness of *c* the foundations which is certain to endanger the health or safety of occupants.

To allow recovery for such damage to the house follows, in my opinion, from normal principle. If classification is required, the relevant damage is in my opinion material, physical damage, and what is recoverable is the amount of expenditure necessary to restore the dwelling to a condition in which it is no longer a danger to the health or safety of persons occupying and possibly (depending on the circumstances) expenses *d* arising from necessary displacement. On the question of damages generally I have derived much assistance from the judgment (dissenting on this point, but of strong persuasive force) of Laskin CJ in the Canadian Supreme Court case of *Rivtow Marine Ltd v Washington Iron Works*[1] and from the judgments of the New Zealand Court of Appeal (furnished by courtesy of that court) in *Bowen v Paramount Builders (Hamilton) Ltd and McKay*[2].

e *When does the cause of action arise?* We can leave aside cases of personal injury or damage to other property as presenting no difficulty. It is only the damage for the house which required consideration. In my respectful opinion the Court of Appeal was right when, in *Sparham-Souter v Town and Country Developments (Essex) Ltd*[3], it abjured the view that the cause of action arose immediately on delivery, i e conveyance of the defective house. It can only arise when the state of the building is such *f* that there is present or imminent danger to the health or safety of persons occupying it. We are not concerned at this stage with any issue relating to remedial action nor are we called on to decide on what the measure of the damages should be; such questions, possibly very difficult in some cases, will be for the court to decide. It is sufficient to say that a cause of action arises at the point I have indicated.

The Limitation Act 1939. If the fact is that defects to the maisonettes first appeared in *g* 1970, then, since the writs were issued in 1972, the consequence must be that none of the present actions are barred by the Act.

Conclusion. I would hold: (1) that *Dutton v Bognor Regis United Building Co Ltd*[4] was in the result rightly decided; the correct legal basis for the decision must be taken to be that established by your Lordships in this appeal; (2) that the question whether the council by itself or its officers came under a duty of care toward the plaintiffs must *h* be considered in relation to the powers, duties and discretions arising under the Public Health Act 1936; (3) that the council would not be guilty of a breach of duty in not carrying out inspection of the foundations of the block unless it were shown (a) not properly to have exercised its discretion as to the making of inspections, and (b) to have failed to exercise reasonable care in its acts or omissions to secure that the byelaws applicable to the foundations of the block were complied with; (4) that the council *j* would be liable to the plaintiffs for breach of duty if it were proved that its inspector,

---

1   [1973] 6 WWR 692 at 715
2   (22nd December 1976) unreported
3   [1976] 2 All ER 65, [1976] 1 QB 858
4   [1972] 1 All ER 462, [1972] 1 QB 373

having assumed the duty of inspecting the foundations, and acting otherwise than in
the bona fide exercise of any discretion under the Act, did not exercise reasonable
care to ensure that the byelaws applicable to the foundations were complied with;
(5) that on the facts as pleaded none of the actions is barred by the Limitation Act 1939.
And consequently that the appeal should be dismissed with costs.

LORD DIPLOCK. My Lords, I have had the advantage of reading in draft the
speech of my noble and learned friend, Lord Wilberforce. I agree with it and the order
that he proposes.

LORD SIMON OF GLAISDALE. My Lords, I have had the privilege of reading
in draft the speech delivered by my noble and learned friend, Lord Wilberforce.
I agree with it, and I would therefore dismiss the appeal.

LORD SALMON. My Lords, the procedural issues, the undisputed facts, the relevant statutory provisions and the byelaws made under them are fully and lucidly
expounded in the first part of the speech of my noble and learned friend, Lord Wilberforce, which I gratefully adopt and need not repeat.

The one fact which is at present unknown and which may be of vital importance at
the trial is whether or not the foundations of the block of maisonettes in question were
ever examined by the council through one of its building inspectors prior to their
being covered up.

As I understand para 5 of the statement of claim and the particulars delivered
under it, the gist of the claim is that it was the council's duty through one of its
building inspectors to inspect the foundations of the building before they were
covered; that in breach of this duty the council negligently failed to carry out any
inspection of the foundations; alternatively that if it did so, the inspection was carried
out negligently; that as a result, the inspection failed to reveal that the foundations
did not comply with byelaw 18(1)(b) nor with the deposited and approved plans in
that they were only two feet six inches deep instead of three feet or deeper as shown
on the plans; that if these defects in the foundations had been detected by the
council's inspector (as they should have been) the council would have been under a
duty to insist that the foundations should be taken down to a sufficient depth to give
the building a sound base and that if this had been done the structural movements and
their resulting damage to the building which began to occur in February 1970 would
have been avoided.

Since this appeal is being decided on preliminary points of law, all the facts in the
statement of claim, including those pleaded in the alternative, must be assumed to be
true. Accordingly, at least two different hypotheses need to be examined: (1) that no
inspections of the foundations by the council took place; (2) that such an inspection did
take place but because of the building inspector's failure to use reasonable care and
skill, the inspection failed to reveal the inadequacy of the foundations to which I have
referred.

As to (1). This hypothesis raises the question whether or not the council owed a duty
to the plaintiffs to inspect the foundations before the building was erected. Obviously
if no such duty existed, the failure to inspect could not found a cause of action.

The Public Health Act 1936 and the building byelaws made under it confer ample
powers on the council for the purpose, amongst other things, of enabling it to protect
the health and safety of the public in its locality against what is popularly known as
jerry-building. We are concerned particularly with the safeguards relating to building
foundations; these foundations are clearly of the greatest importance because the
stability of the building depends on them and they are covered up at a very early
stage.

Powers are undoubtedly conferred on the council in order to enable it to inspect the

foundations and ensure that any defects which the inspection may reveal are remedied
a before the erection of the building begins. There is, however, nothing in the 1936 Act
nor in the byelaws which explicitly provides how the council shall exercise these
powers. This, in my view, is left to the council's discretion—but I do not think that
this is an absolute discretion. It is a discretion which must be responsibly exercised.

The council could resolve to inspect the foundations of all buildings in its locality
before they are covered but certainly, in my view, it is under no obligation to do so.
b It could, e g resolve to inspect the foundations of a proportion of all buildings or of all
buildings of certain types in its locality.

During the course of argument it was suggested on behalf of the council that if it
were held to owe any duty to use reasonable care in carrying out an inspection of
foundations and could therefore be liable in damages for any such inspections carried
out negligently, it might well resolve to make no such inspections at all. I find it
c impossible to conceive that any council could be so irresponsible as to pass any such
resolution. If it did, this would, in my view, amount to an improper exercise of discretion which, I am inclined to think, might be corrected by certiorari or mandamus.
I doubt however whether this would confer a right on any individual to sue the council
for damages in respect of its failure to have carried out an inspection.

This point has however little bearing on this appeal because the correspondence
d makes it plain that the council had certainly not decided against exercising its statutory
powers of inspection. On 19th March 1971 we find the borough surveyor writing to
the plaintiffs' solicitors:

'I regret that I am unable to trace any record of statutory inspections . . . by
officers of the former Borough of Mitcham, but do not doubt for a moment,
that all the proper inspections were made.'

e

On 24th June 1971 the borough surveyor again wrote:

'I have been unable to trace details of all inspections made to the above premises
but have been assured that all statutory inspections have been carried out.'

f If there was no inspection of the foundations before they were covered up, the
plaintiffs' claims would fail because the statute imposed no obligation on the council
to inspect the foundations of these maisonettes nor of any other particular building.
It will be for the plaintiffs, with the help of interrogatories, discovery of documents
and a search for fresh witnesses to establish, on a balance of probabilities, that such an
inspection did take place. The extracts from the letters I have just read do not suggest
that this is likely to impose any insuperable difficulties on them.

g *As to* (2). I now propose to examine the second hypothesis, namely that an inspection
of the foundations before they were covered up was carried out by the council through
one of its building inspectors. This immediately raises the important question: did the
inspector, acting on behalf of the council, owe a duty to future tenants to use reasonable care and skill in order to discover whether the foundations conformed with the
approved plans and with the byelaws? Precisely the same point was raised in *Dutton v*
h *Bognor Regis United Building Co Ltd*[1] and was answered in the affirmative. I agree with
that decision.

In *Home Office v Dorset Yacht Co Ltd*[2] Lord Reid said:

'*Donoghue v Stevenson*[3] may be regarded as a milestone, and the well-known
passage in Lord Atkin's speech[4] should I think be regarded as a statement of
j principle. It is not to be treated as if it were a statutory definition. It will require

1   [1972] 1 All ER 462, [1972] 1 QB 373
2   [1970] 2 All ER 294 at 297, [1970] AC 1004 at 1027
3   [1932] AC 562, [1932] All ER Rep 1
4   [1932] AC 562 at 580, [1932] All ER Rep 1 at 11

qualification in new circumstances. But I think that the time has come when we can and should say that it ought to apply unless there is some justification or valid explanation for its exclusion.'

He then set out some of the circumstances in which such justification or explanation would exist. He added[1]:

'But where negligence is involved the tendency has been to apply principles analogous to those stated by Lord Atkin[2] (cf *Hedley Byrne & Co Ltd v Heller & Partners Ltd*[3]) . . . I can see nothing to prevent our approaching the present case with Lord Atkin's principles[2] in mind.'

I respectfully agree with and adopt that passage in Lord Reid's speech which, to my mind, is just as apt in the instant case as it was in *Home Office v Dorset Yacht Co Ltd*[4]. The seven maisonettes which comprise the building were to be let on 999 year leases at nominal rents and acquired for substantial capital sums. The building inspector and the council who sent him to inspect the foundations must have realised that the inspection was of great importance for the protection of future occupants of the maisonettes who indeed might suffer serious damage if the inspection was carried out negligently. The inspection should have revealed that this block of maisonettes was about to be erected on insecure foundations, that is to say foundations which failed to comply with the approved plans and the byelaws, and that therefore there was a real danger that within a decade the whole structure would suffer damage and might indeed collapse. Nor was there any likelihood that any survey on behalf of the original tenants or their assignees would include an inspection of the foundations since they would be concealed by the building. The whole purpose of the inspection on behalf of the council before the foundations were covered up was to discover whether the foundations were secure and to ensure that, if they were not, they should be made so for the protection of future tenants before the building was erected. It is impossible to think of anyone more closely and directly affected by the inspection than the original tenants of the maisonettes and their assignees. I have therefore come to the clear conclusion that the council acting through their building inspector when he inspected the foundations owed a duty to the plaintiffs to carry out the inspection with reasonable care and skill. There can, I think, be no doubt but that the building inspector failed to use reasonable care and skill since the underside of the concrete foundations was only two feet six inches below ground level, whereas the plans delivered to the council showed the foundations as being three feet below ground level or deeper if required. A surveyor's report set out in the record states:

'3 feet is the accepted minimum depth for foundation excavations, always provided a reasonable bottom is found at that level and in this case we have found the sub-soil beneath the concrete to be of very doubtful and variable quality, consisting of a mixture of sand and gravel with traces of soft clay. We are therefore of the opinion that the defects in this property arise from inadequate foundation depth having regard to the site conditions, and that movement has probably been accentuated by all or any of the following factors.'

These factors are then enumerated and the report continues:

'Whilst we are in some difficulty in arriving at the most likely of the above causes, all of them could have been avoided had the foundations been taken down to an adequate depth according to site conditions, and in our view this is where the fault lies.'

1　[1970] 2 All ER 294 at 297, 298, [1970] AC 1004 at 1027
2　[1932] AC 562 at 580, [1932] All ER Rep 1 at 11
3　[1963] 2 All ER 575, [1964] AC 465
4　[1970] 2 All ER 294, [1970] AC 1004

At the trial, it will be for the court to decide, having heard the evidence, whether if
a the foundations had been down to three feet instead of only two feet six inches the
damage would have been avoided, and if not whether the building inspector, had he
used reasonable care and skill, should have recognised that the soil conditions required
the foundations to have been taken down lower than three feet in order to achieve
security.

I must now refer to *East Suffolk Rivers Catchment Board v Kent*[1] on which the council
b strongly relied in an attempt to negative any duty of care on their part if and when
they inspected the foundations. The *East Suffolk* case[1], which is not very satisfactory,
is certainly a very different case from the present. Here, at the time the council
elected to inspect the foundations in the exercise of its statutory powers, no damage
had occurred nor could thereafter have occurred if the building inspector had noticed
the inadequacy of the foundations. It seems to me to be a fair inference that probably
c he must have indicated to the builder by word or gesture that he approved them.
At any rate he could have made no report to the council as to their inadequacy;
otherwise the council would or certainly should have ensured that the builders
made the foundations conform with the byelaws before the council allowed the
building to be erected on them.

Even if the inspector did not give the builders any intimation as to his view of the
d foundations, the builders would have naturally assumed from the council's silence
after the inspection that they (the builders) had the council's blessing to build on the
existing foundations.

'It is undoubtedly a well settled principle of law that when statutory powers
are conferred they must be exercised with reasonable care, so that if those who
exercise them could by reasonable precaution have prevented an injury which
has been occasioned . . . by their exercise, damage for negligence may be recovered.'
e

Great Central Railway Co v Hewlett[2], per Lord Parker of Waddington.

In my opinion a negligent inspection for which the council is vicariously liable
coupled with subsequent inaction by the council would amount to an implicit approval
of the foundations by the council and would have occasioned the damage which
f ensued.

In the *East Suffolk* case[1], the damage had already occurred before the catchment
board arrived on the scene and purported to carry out the work of repairing a river
wall under its statutory powers. The river close to its estuary had burst through a
breach it had made in the wall at high tide and swamped about 50 acres of adjoining
pasture which was below the level of the river bed. At each high tide more salt water
g came into the pasture and the longer this went on the greater was the risk of pasture
being permanently ruined. The catchment board attempted to repair the breach in
the wall with one man who had been in their employment for 18 months and was
totally inexperienced in this kind of work, four labourers from the employment
exchange and with practically no equipment. It took 178 days to close the breach
which could have been closed in 14 days had the work been carried out with reasonable
h care and skill. It would appear that there had been exceptionally high tides as well as
gales and that the catchment board had to cope with a number of similar problems
with limited funds and insufficient experienced men at their disposal.

In the instant case, as far as we know, the council was not faced, as was the catchment
board, with a task of any difficulty, nor with any damage because nothing had been
built on the foundations, nor with the lack of a reasonably competent building
j inspector well able to measure the depth of the foundations and, if necessary, assess
whether they were deep enough, having regard to the soil on which they rested.

It is, in my view, impossible to say that because in one set of circumstances a body

1   [1940] 4 All ER 527, [1941] AC 74
2   [1916] 2 AC 511 at 519

acting under statutory powers may not owe any duty to exercise reasonable care and skill, therefore another body acting under statutory powers in totally different *a* circumstances cannot owe such a duty. I confess that I am not at all sure what point of law the *East Suffolk* case[1] is said to decide. Viscount Simon LC[2] seems to have based his decision against the plaintiffs on the ground that the catchment board did not cause the damage. Lord Thankerton[3] undoubtedly based his decision on that ground alone. He also stressed the importance of the special circumstances of each case in deciding what amounts to a failure to exercise reasonable care and skill by a *b* body acting under a statutory power and added, having referred to the circumstances of the catchment board: 'I am unable to find that Hilbery, J., was not entitled to hold that the appellants committed a breach of their duty to the respondents in adopting a method of repair which no reasonable man would have adopted.'

Lord Romer and Lord Porter seem to have considered that, on the facts of the case which they were deciding, no negligence could be attributed to the catchment board. *c* Lord Romer, however, observed[4]:

'. . . it has been laid down time and again that, in exercising a power which has been conferred upon it, a statutory authority is under an obligation not thereby— i.e., by the exercise of the power—to inflict upon others any damage that may be avoided by reasonable care.'
d

Lord Porter[5] referred with approval to a passage from Scrutton LJ's judgment in *Sheppard v Glossop Corpn*[6]:

'But it is going far beyond Lord Blackburn's dictum to say that because, when an option is given by statute to an authority to do or not to do a thing and it elects to do the thing and does it negligently, it is liable, therefore it is liable if it *e* elects not to do the thing, which by the statute it is not bound to do at all.'

Lord Porter also referred to the celebrated passage in the speech of Lord Blackburn in *Geddis v Bann Reservoir Proprietors*[7], a most lucid passage which has been explained so often that I fear its true meaning is in some danger of being explained away. Lord Blackburn said:
f

'. . . it is now thoroughly well established that no action will lie for doing that which the legislature has authorized, if it be done without negligence, although it does occasion damage . . . but an action does lie for doing that which the legislature has authorized, if it be done negligently.'

If, which I doubt, Lord Romer and Lord Porter intended to lay down that because a *g* local authority or other body endowed with statutory powers, owes no one any duty to exercise those powers in a particular case, it cannot in circumstances such as exist in the instant case, owe anyone a duty when it does exercise the powers to exercise them with reasonable care and skill, then I cannot agree with them.

Personally, I respectfully agree with the dissenting decision of Lord Atkin in the *East Suffolk* case[8]. His views as to the duty of care owed by anyone exercising statu- *h* tory powers did not differ from those of Lord Thankerton nor I think from those of Viscount Simon LC and I have some doubt whether they differed from the views of

1 [1940] 4 All ER 527, [1941] AC 74
2 [1940] 4 All ER 527 at 533, [1941] AC 74 at 87, 88
3 [1940] 4 All ER 527 at 539, [1941] AC 74 at 96   *j*
4 [1940] 4 All ER 527 at 540, [1941] AC 74 at 97
5 [1940] 4 All ER 527 at 545, [1941] AC 74 at 105
6 [1921] 3 KB 132 at 145, 146, [1912] All ER Rep 61 at 68
7 (1878) 3 App Cas 430 at 455, 456
8 [1940] 4 All ER 527 at 533, [1941] AC 74 at 88

Lord Romer and Lord Porter which seem to have turned largely on the facts of that
a particular case, Lord Atkin said[1]:   *approved*

> '. . . every person, whether discharging a public duty or not, is under a common *NB*
> law obligation to some persons in some circumstances to conduct himself with
> reasonable care so as not to injure those persons likely to be affected by his want
> of care. This duty exists whether a person is performing a public duty, *or merely*
b > *exercising a power which he possesses* either *under statutory authority* or in pursuance
> of his ordinary rights as a citizen.' (The italics are mine.)

For the reasons I have already indicated, I am convinced that if an inspection of the
foundations did take place, the council, through its building inspectors, owed a duty
to the future tenants and occupiers of the maisonettes to exercise reasonable care and
skill in carrying out that examination. The failure to exercise such care and skill may
c be shown to have caused the damage which the plaintiffs have suffered. The fact that
the inspection was being carried out under a statutory power does not exclude the
common law duty of those carrying it out to use reasonable care and skill—for it
cannot in any way diminish the obvious proximity between the inspectors and the
prospective tenants and their assignees.

d It has, however, been argued on the council's behalf that, since they were under no
obligation to inspect the foundations, had it failed to do so, it could not be liable for
the damage caused by the inadequacy of the foundations. Accordingly, so the argument runs, if the council decided to inspect the foundations in the exercise of their
statutory powers, they owed the prospective tenants and their assignees no duty to
inspect carefully because, even if the inspection was carried out negligently, the
prospective tenants and their assignees would be no worse off than if there had been
e no inspection. I reject this argument and confess that I cannot detect that it has even
any superficial attraction. The council are given these statutory powers to inspect the
foundations and furnished with public funds to enable the powers to be used for the
protection of (amongst others) prospective purchasers of the buildings which are to be
built on them. If, when the council exercise these powers, they do so negligently, it
must be obvious that those members of the public in the position of the present
f plaintiffs are likely to suffer serious damage. The exercise of power without responsibility is not encouraged by the law. I recognise that, it may not be practical to inspect
the foundations of every new building. This, however, is no excuse for a negligent
inspection of such foundations as are inspected. When a council negligently exercises
its powers of inspection, it should be and I believe are responsible in law to those who
suffer damage as a result of that negligence.
g I do not think that there is any danger that the responsibility which, in my view,
lies on the council is likely to lead to any flood of litigation. It is not a common
occurrence for foundations to give way, nor for their inspection to be negligently
carried out. If the foundations do give way, there is no warranty by the council which
has inspected them that they are sound. The council is responsible only if it has
exercised its powers to inspect and the defects in the foundations should have been
h detected by reasonable care and skill. It seems to me to be manifestly fair that any
damage caused by negligence should be borne by those responsible for the negligence
rather than by the innocents who suffer from it.
I recognise that it would be unjust if, in the circumstances of this case, the whole
burden should fall on the council whilst the contractor who negligently put in the
faulty foundations remained free from liability. It has, however, been decided in
j *Gallagher v N McDowell Ltd*[2] that a building contractor owes a duty of care to the lawful
user of a house and that accordingly the contractor is liable for any damage caused to

1 [1940] 4 All ER 527 at 534, [1941] AC 74 at 89
2 [1961] NI 26

a lawful user by the contractor's negligence in constructing the house. I agree with that decision for the reasons given by Lord MacDermott CJ in delivering the leading judgment in the Northern Ireland Court of Appeal. I also adopt what Lord Denning MR said on this topic in *Dutton's* case[1]:

'The distinction between chattels and real property is quite unsustainable [in relation to the principles laid down in *Donoghue v Stevenson*[2]]. If the manufacturer of an article is liable to a person injured by his negligence, so should the builder of a house be liable.'

The contrary view seems to me to be entirely irreconcilable with logic or common sense.

The instant case differs from *Gallagher's* case[3] in that the contractors were also the owners of the land on which they built the block of maisonettes. In *Bottomley v Bannister*[4] (decided just before *Donoghue v Stevenson*[2]) Scrutton LJ said:

'Now it is at present well established English law that, in the absence of express contract, a landlord of an unfurnished house is not liable to his tenant, or a vendor of real estate to his purchaser, for defects in the house or land rendering it dangerous or unfit for occupation, even if he has constructed the defects himself or is aware of their existence.'

I certainly do not agree with the words in that passage 'even if he has constructed the defects himself'. The immunity of a landlord who sells or lets his house which is dangerous or unfit for habitation is deeply entrenched in our law. I cannot, however, accept the proposition that a contractor who has negligently built a dangerous house can escape liability to pay damages for negligence to anyone who, e g falls through a shoddily constructed floor and is seriously injured, just because the contractor happens to have been the owner of the land on which the house stands. If a similar accident had happened next door in a house which the contractor had also negligently built on someone else's land, he would not be immune from liability. This does not make any sense. In each case the contractor would be sued for his negligence as a contractor and not in his capacity as a landowner: the fact that he had owned one plot of land and not the other would be wholly irrelevant. I would hold that in each case he would be liable to pay damages for negligence. To the extent that *Bottomley v Bannister*[5] differs from this proposition it should, in my view, be overruled. *Cavalier v Pope*[6] is so far away from the present case that I express no opinion about it.

It was also contended on behalf of the council that the plaintiffs do not even allege that they relied on the inspection of the foundations by the council. Nor they did, and I daresay they never even knew about it. This, however, is irrelevant. I think that the noble Lords who decided *Hedley Byrne & Co Ltd v Heller & Partners Ltd*[7] would have been very surprised that what they said about reliance in that case would one day be cited as relevant to a case such as the present. There are a wide variety of instances in which a statement is negligently made by a professional man which he knows will be relied on by many people besides his client, e g a well-known firm of accountants certifies in a prospectus the annual profits of the company issuing it and unfortunately, due to negligence on the part of the accountants, the profits are seriously overstated. Those persons who invested in the company in reliance on the accuracy of the accountants' certificate would have a claim for damages against the accountants

---

1 [1972] 1 All ER 462 at 471, 472 [1972] 1 QB 373 at 393
2 [1932] AC 562, [1932] All ER Rep 1
3 [1961] NI 26
4 [1932] 1 KB 458 at 468, [1931] All ER Rep 99 at 102
5 [1932] 1 KB 458, [1931] All ER Rep 99
6 [1906] AC 428
7 [1963] 2 All ER 575, [1964] AC 465

for any money they might have lost as a result of the accountants' negligence: see the
a *Hedley Byrne* case[1].

In the present case, however, the loss is caused not by any *reliance* placed by the
plaintiffs on the council or the building inspector but by the fact that if the inspection
had been carefully made, the defects in the foundations would have been rectified
before the erection of the building was begun. The categories of negligence, as Lord
Macmillan said, are never closed and there are now a great many of them. In a few,
b 'reliance' is of importance. In the present case reliance is not even remotely relevant.

The remaining question is whether this action is statute-barred, as found by the
learned judge. In my view he had no real option except to find as he did. In *Dutton's*
case[2] Lord Denning MR said, obiter, that 'The damage was done when the foundations
were badly constructed. The period of limitation (six years) then began to run.' In *Bagot
v Stevens Scanlan & Co*[3] Diplock LJ said, obiter, that if the drains were not properly
c designed and built—

'the damage from any breach of that duty must have occurred at the time
when the drains were improperly built, because the plaintiff at that time was
landed with property which had bad drains when he ought to have been provided
with property which had good drains, and the damage accordingly, occurred on
d   that date.'

There may be a difference between the effect of badly constructed foundations and
improperly built drains, since badly constructed foundations may not for some years
cause any damage to the building or its occupiers; on the other hand, improperly
built drains may cause some damage to the amenities and health of the occupier from
the moment he occupies the building. In *Higgins v Arfon Borough Council*[4] Mars-Jones
e J, founding his judgment on the two obiter dicta to which I have referred, held that
the erection of a defective building without proper foundations was caused by the
local authority's negligence, but the action against the authority was statute-barred
because the damage occurred during the construction of the building and time therefore began to run from 22nd March 1966 when the property was purchased. In the
light of these authorities I think that it would have been very difficult, if not
f impossible, for the learned judge to have held that the instant action was not statute-
barred since the foundations were badly constructed and all the original conveyances
were executed more than six years before the writ was issued.

In *Sparham-Souter v Town and Country Developments (Essex) Ltd*[5], Lord Denning MR
reconsidered and handsomely withdrew his obiter dictum in *Dutton's* case[6] to the
effect that the period of limitation began to run from that date when the foundations
g were badly constructed. He acknowledged that the true view was that the cause of
action in negligence accrued at the time when damage was sustained as a result of
negligence, i e when the building began to sink and the cracks appeared. He therefore
concluded that in *Higgins v Arfon Borough Council*[4] and in the instant case, it had been
wrongly decided that the action was statute-barred, and as I read their judgments
Roskill and Geoffrey Lane LJJ agreed with that view; and I certainly do.

h All the plaintiffs, other than Mrs O'Shea, acquired their maisonettes substantially
less than six years before their writs were issued. Accordingly their claims cannot be
affected by the Limitation Act 1939 since clearly they could suffer no damage before
they became the purchasers of the maisonettes. The duty of care if and when the
inspection of the foundations was carried out was owed to all future tenants or assignees who might suffer damage as a result of the negligent inspection. At the time of

j
1   [1963] 2 All ER 575, [1964] AC 465
2   [1972] 1 All ER 462 at 474, [1972] 1 QB 373 at 396
3   [1964] 3 All ER 577 at 579, [1966] 1 QB 197 at 203
4   [1975] 2 All ER 589, [1975] 1 WLR 524
5   [1976] 2 All ER 65, [1976] 1 QB 858
6   [1972] 1 All ER 462 at 474, [1972] 1 QB 373 at 376

the inspection it was, of course, readily foreseeable that if the inspection was carelessly carried out future tenants or assignees would suffer damage but their identity was, of *a* course, then unknown, just as the identity of the plaintiff in *Davie v New Merton Board Mills Ltd*[1] was unknown to the defendants at the time when they negligently manufactured a defective tool seven years before a part of it broke off and flew into the plaintiff's eye. The plaintiff, Mrs O'Shea, however acquired her maisonette on 12th December 1962. The writ was issued on 22nd February 1972. If it could be proved that the building suffered damage prior to 22nd February 1966 which en- *b* dangered the safety of its occupants or visitors Mrs O'Shea's claim would be statute-barred. It seems to me, however, that since in fact no damage manifested itself until February 1970 it may be very difficult to prove that damage had in fact occurred four years previously. In the unlikely event of the defendants overcoming this difficulty, the fact that the damage went undetected for four years would not prevent the statute running from the date when the damage first occurred: see *Cartledge v E Jopling &* *c* *Sons Ltd*[2]. In such circumstances Mrs O'Shea could not have recovered damages because her cause of action would have accrued more than six years before the issue of her writ. Section 2(1) of the Limitation Act 1939 bars any action in tort after the expiration of the six years (amended by the Law Reform (Limitation of Actions, etc) Act 1954 to three years in actions for damages for personal injuries) from the date when the cause of action accrued. Every member of this House in *Cartledge v E* *d* *Jopling & Sons Ltd*[2] expressed the view that it was unreasonable and unjust that a cause of action should be held to accrue before it is possible to discover any injury, and therefore before it is possible to raise any action. A strong recommendation was made for the legislature to remedy this injustice and that recommendation was accepted and carried into effect by the Limitation Act 1963; but that Act was confined to actions for damages for personal injury. I do not think that if and when this action comes to *e* be tried, the defendants should be prevented from attempting to prove that the claim by Mrs O'Shea is statute-barred. A building may be able to stand undamaged on defective foundations for years and then perhaps eight years or so later damage may occur. Whether it is possible to prove that damage to the building had occurred four years before it manifested itself is another matter, but it can only be decided by evidence. *f*

I should perhaps add a word about the damages to which the plaintiffs would in my view be entitled should they succeed in the action. Clearly the damage to the building constitutes a potential danger to the plaintiffs' safety and the cost of under-pinning the building and making it stable and safe would be recoverable from the defendants. So would the costs of rectifying any damage to the individual maisonettes and the reasonable expense incurred by any of the plaintiffs should it be necessary *g* for them to find alternative accommodation whilst any of the structural repairs were being carried out. I express no opinion as to what the measure of damages should be, if it proved impossible to make the structure safe.

My Lords, for the reasons I have explained (1) I would dismiss the council's appeal from the order of the Court of Appeal setting aside the judgment of his Honour Judge Fay. (2) I would hold that the council was under no obligation to exercise its *h* power to inspect the foundations before or after the building now occupied by the plaintiffs was constructed, but that if it did exercise such powers of inspection before the building was constructed, it was under a legal duty to the plaintiffs to use reasonable care and skill in making the inspection. (3) I would order the council to pay the costs of and incidental to this appeal.

LORD RUSSELL OF KILLOWEN. My Lords, I was at one time attracted by the *j* simple proposition that *East Suffolk Rivers Catchment Board v Kent*[3] afforded a sufficient

1 [1959] 1 All ER 346, [1959] AC 604
2 [1963] 1 All ER 341, [1963] AC 758
3 [1940] 4 All ER 427, [1941] AC 74

shield for the council, even on the assumption that there was an inspection of the foundations which was so carelessly conducted that it failed to reveal that the proposed depth was only two feet six inches below ground level (which we are to assume was and should have been known to be inadequate to cope with swelling or shrinkage of the sub-soil) and not three feet (which we are to assume would have been adequate for that purpose). On reflection I do not adhere to that view.

I have, my Lords, had an opportunity to consider closely in draft the speech delivered by my noble and learned friend, Lord Wilberforce. I am in agreement with it on all points and am content to add nothing of my own. Accordingly I also would dismiss this appeal.

Appeal dismissed.

Solicitors: *Barlow Lyde & Gilbert* (for the council); *W H Matthews & Co* (for the plaintiffs).

Mary Rose Plummer   Barrister.